IMAGES
of America

FORT FISHER

On the Cover: The Civil War–era photographer Timothy O'Sullivan took this self-portrait observing the destruction inside the fort, including the heavy 32-pounder upon which he is standing, after the Second Battle of Fort Fisher in January 1865. (Library of Congress.)

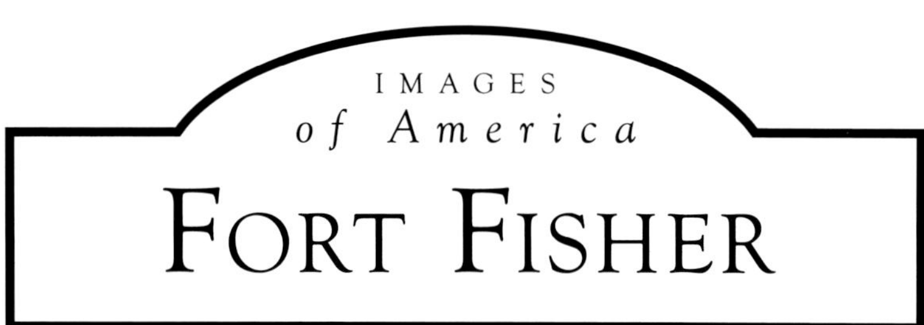

John Hairr

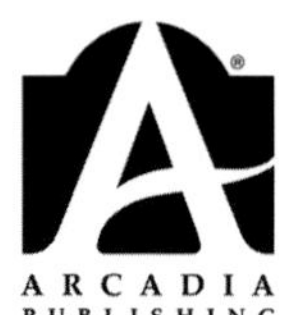

ISBN 978-1-4671-6165-7

Published by Arcadia Publishing
Charleston, South Carolina

Printed in the United States of America

Library of Congress Control Number: 2024942381

For all general information, please contact Arcadia Publishing:
Telephone 843-853-2070
Fax 843-853-0044
E-mail sales@arcadiapublishing.com

Visit us on the Internet at www.arcadiapublishing.com

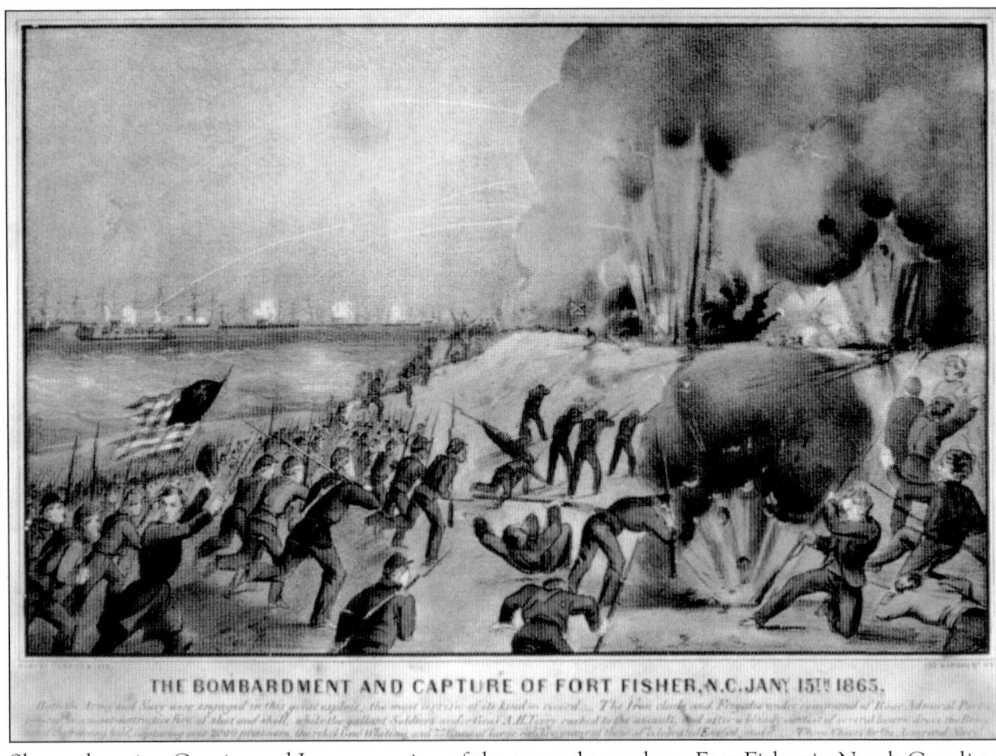

Shown here is a Currier and Ives engraving of the second assault on Fort Fisher in North Carolina on January 15, 1865. (Library of Congress.)

Contents

ACKNOWLEDGMENTS

Fort Fisher is one of the best remembered of the coastal forts that protected North Carolina shores during the War between the States. Some defensive works like Fort Hatteras or Fort Ocracoke proved to be easy prizes picked off early in the war by the Federal forces. Even the imposing masonry walls of Fort Macon, which had been built shortly after the end of the War of 1812 to protect the strategically important port at Beaufort and later Morehead City, were no match to the heavy siege guns that evolved during the 19th century and following a brief siege was surrendered on April 26, 1862. The Confederates needed to find a better way to defend the much more strategically important mouth of the Cape Fear River and thus was born the sandy earthworks known as Fort Fisher.

The activities of the blockade runners as well as the fighting that took place at the fort were well documented by participants from both sides. We are fortunate that there is such a plethora of visual materials chronicling what went on describing not only the design work behind the sandy fort but also the people who lived and fought here. Since it was such an important part of the defenses of the Southern coast, there are several repositories where people took time to set aside items such as books, maps, charts, paintings, drawings, and ephemera. Several people and institutions have helped over the years to document what went on here. Within the body of my present work, all photographs are part of the author's collection except as noted in the captions. Many of the images are from the National Archives and Library of Congress (cited as LOC in the book) in Washington, DC.

Another valuable source in Washington are the collections of the US Navy Department Library, especially the photographic collections of the US Naval History and Heritage Command, which holds a great deal of material pertaining to both Union and Confederate naval personnel and ships. Matt Proietta and the staff of the Navy Department Library were especially helpful tracking down a good copy of the diagram of the Butler's powder ship.

Outside Washington, the collections of the North Carolina Department of Natural and Cultural Resources were important, both those at Fort Fisher as well as those in Raleigh. In Wilmington, Shannon Vaughn of the New Hanover County Public Library's Local History Room helped pin down some elusive details about the defenders of the fort, especially Maj. James Reilly. Up in Virginia, Anne Johnson of the Earl Gregg Swem Library at William & Mary University was especially helpful running down items in that institution's Special Collections Research Center, while out in Tennessee, Kevin Cason of the Tennessee State Library & Archives helped track down elusive images from its collection.

Finally, I am grateful to the folks at Arcadia Publishing for giving me the opportunity to once again work with them chronicling this important aspect of the history of the Old North State.

To all who helped, a hearty "Thank you!"

INTRODUCTION

Few people today realize that the idyllic shores where millions come each year to bask in the sun were once the scenes of some of the most intense fighting of the War Between the States in North Carolina, as Federal forces went to great lengths to close the Cape Fear and the Port of Wilmington. Southerners invested much time and energy here defending their home and over a three-year period constructed some of the most intricate defenses built anywhere during the war. Though only a small remnant of these defenses remains today, in its heyday this place was known as the "Confederate Gibraltar." Fort Fisher drew the attention of the Union government, which set about wiping it from the face of the earth, including setting off a great explosion just offshore that rocked the beach back on Christmas Eve 1864, a blast meant to literally vaporize Fort Fisher and its defenders.

By late 1864, Fort Fisher and the other works protecting the entrance to the Cape Fear River were the last remaining Confederate strongholds along the coast. As the blockade runners were sneaking through the screen of Federal ships and into the city of Wilmington with much needed supplies for the Confederacy, the Northerners were desirous to close off this last remaining lifeline to Gen. Robert E. Lee's army pinned down in Virginia. Trouble was, how to take such a formidable stronghold without risking a major loss? After all, some of the most skilled military engineers in the Confederacy, especially Gen. W.H.C. Whiting, had been hard at work for four years improving the defenses guarding New Inlet.

Gen. Ben Butler, infamous for his heavy-handed occupation of New Orleans earlier in the war, came up with a creative idea—blow the fort to smithereens with a ship full of gunpowder. This idea sounded simple enough to some (outlandish to others), so a team of experts was convened to study the practicability of the plan.

The experts gathered in Washington on November 23, 1864, and their findings showed the group to be cautiously optimistic. After deciding all the technical aspects, such as type of fuses, amount of powder, and distance from the fort, the group listed the objectives they hoped to attain, including "that the explosion would injure the earthworks to a very great extent, render the guns unserviceable for a time, and probably affect the garrison to such a degree as to deprive them of power to resist the passage of naval vessels by the forts and the carrying of these works by immediate assault."

To carry out this scheme, Adm. David Porter, commander of the North Atlantic Blockading Squadron, chose the ship USS *Louisiana*, a 150-foot gunboat that had once been engaged in the cotton trade. The ship was chosen mainly because of its flat bottom, which would allow the vessel to get quite close to the beach at Fort Fisher.

The workmen up at Norfolk stripped the *Louisiana* clean of all nonessential equipment and made some modifications of the ship's layout in order to allow more space and weight for the powder. The experts agreed that for maximum effect, the explosives must be stowed above the waterline, so 185 tons of powder were placed in the berth deck, coal bunker, and aft hold. The plans called for 300 tons in all, so room was left for powder that was to be received in the Union-occupied port of Beaufort, North Carolina.

The ignition of this floating bomb was to be accomplished by a number of backup systems. Electronic clocks were the primary method, followed by slow-burning fuses, which were in turn backed up by a fire of fat lighter that was to be left burning on the ship and would eventually spread and ignite the powder. Regardless of the method, it was hoped that, for maximum effect, the powder would be ignited at separate points simultaneously to prevent any powder being dispersed due to the concussion of the initial blast.

On December 13, 1864, the USS *Sassacus* set out from Hampton Roads to Beaufort, with the floating bomb in tow. On this leg of the trip, the ship was commanded by Master Whitman Chase, who was to see the vessel through to Beaufort where the attack crew was to take over. His orders included one very important directive: "You will permit no fire to be lighted on the *Louisiana*, no cigars to be smoked in any part of the vessel."

The person chosen to lead the attack was Comdr. Alexander Rhind of the USS *Agawam*. He and a crew of 13 handpicked men were to guide the *Louisiana* as near to the fort as possible, then row an open boat back to the USS *Wilderness*, which would be waiting nearby to carry the crew to safety. Following the war, Rhind made the following observations about having been chosen to lead the attack: "Had I been aware that the proposition to employ the powder vessel as a preliminary to the attack on Fort Fisher was originated by General Butler, or that he expected such remarkable results from it, I should have required, as a condition on undertaking so hazardous a service (unsought by me), that General Butler or some of his then attachés should have accompanied the party."

The *Sassacus* and her tow arrived in Beaufort without incident, and the remaining powder was brought on board, which brought the total amount to 235 tons. Rhind and his crew then boarded their vessel, as per orders. The original plans were that the ship would be in position for attack on December 18, but due to heavy seas, the first attempt to land the craft was aborted.

The seas subsided by December 23, and Admiral Porter was restless. "Have everything ready for the powder boat to-night, for go in she must," he stated. He then gave Commander Rhind the following orders: "The moon shines at 3:25. I would like the explosion to take place at 2 am or as near to that as possible, but if there is likely to be anything to prevent the explosion at the above time let her go in when it suits you. Don't forget to build a good fire, for that is certain, and will prevent the rebels boarding her."

Around 10:30 p.m. the mission began as the *Louisiana* started its run toward the beach towed behind the USS *Wilderness*. It was deemed prudent to tow the floating bomb in as close to the beach as possible to reduce the risk of a premature explosion. The *Wilderness* was to stand by after the powder ship was cut loose, wait for her crew members, and then make the getaway to the fleet, which stood 12 miles offshore.

Within 500 yards of the beach, the *Louisiana* broke free and began the last leg of the trip under its own power. Rhind planned to get within 100 yards of the fort, but he soon passed a blockade runner headed for New Inlet so decided to follow, hoping that if they were spotted by any Confederate sentinels, the *Louisiana* would also be considered a blockade runner making a run for the Cape Fear River with a valuable cargo and allowed to pass unmolested.

When the ship reached what was estimated to be the 300-yard mark, Rhind figured he had tempted fate long enough. He ordered the engines cut, anchors aweigh, and preparations for detonation to begin. The crew set about the task of setting clocks, lighting fuses, and preparing the escape boat.

When all the others were in the launch, Rhind and Lt. S.W. Preston lit the fire of fat lighter as their final act before joining their companions, who waited in the boat. None of these preparations caught the attention of the Confederate lookouts in the fort, nor the individuals camping on the beach near an old hut, which included several Confederate naval personnel detached to help bolster the fort's garrison, including sailors from the CSS *Chickamauga* camped on the beach.

The group rowed the boat back to the awaiting *Wilderness*, which picked them up and began the dash to sea. Master Henry Arcy of the *Wilderness* ordered six rockets be fired to alert the fleet that the powder ship was in place, and they were returning to rejoin the fleet.

When the *Wilderness* came back in line with the squadron, it was only a matter of waiting. At 1:20 a.m., the time set for the clocks to detonate, all was silent. It soon became evident to the Federal attackers that those fancy electronic gadgets must have failed. The more conventional slow-burning fuses, scheduled as a backup plan, were supposed to go off five minutes later. But all was silent on the ocean in front of Fort Fisher except for the normal sounds of a North Carolina beach in winter.

Finally, the fire from the fat lighter, which Rhind and Preston had left burning, spread through the ship and ignited the powder, which created what one eyewitness described as "a huge column of fire." A loud report was heard, then the scene returned to darkness and the noises of the sea.

The explosion was quite loud. Accounts later showed that the noise was heard in Wilmington and Beaufort, but the ramparts of Fort Fisher remained undamaged. True, units from the North Carolina Junior Reserves who had just arrived and were encamped on the beach near the aforementioned hut reported that they were thrown around "like popcorn," but the great explosion made little impression upon the garrison. "A blockader got aground near the fort, set fire to herself and blew up." This is all that Col. William Lamb, commander of the fort, had to record about the incident. The sandy ramparts of this bastion absorbed most of the energy released from the blast as the shockwaves passed through the fort.

As the sun rose, the Federals moved in to inspect the damage, and the reports were quite disappointing. The guns were still in place, the sandy ramparts were intact, and the Confederate flag was flying saucily in the breeze. Butler's powder ship *Louisiana* had proven ineffective.

Admiral Porter then fell back on a more traditional plan. Using the heavy artillery of his armada, he would pound the sandy fort into submission, then clean out any life that remained, if there was any left, from the hellish torrent of fire and iron with the 8,000 troops at his disposal. Thus ensued the First Battle of Fort Fisher, in which the greatly outnumbered Confederate garrison held out against everything the combined forces of the Union army and navy could throw against them during the battle, which dragged into Christmas Day.

The resilience of their sandy defenses was a pleasant surprise to the Confederate defenders, who hunkered down inside their large sand dunes, which must have seemed a woefully inadequate place to wait out the Union bombardment. After all, the guns of the Union navy hurled over a million pounds of ordnance at them, but only a few of the defenders were harmed by the bombardment, most attributing their survival in large part to divine protection. Even General Whiting was surprised at how well the works he designed held up, pointing out in his official report, "That a great and irreparable disaster did not overtake us we owe to God."

As the battle was winding down and before making their hasty retreat from the beach to the safety of their ships waiting offshore, Union skirmishers did manage to catch some Southern prisoners. According to noted Cape Fear historian James Sprunt, one of these captives was interrogated by the Federals to ascertain the effects of their powder ship. "You say you were inside the fort?" began the questioning.

"Yes, I was thar."

"What was the effect of the explosion?"

"Mighty bad, sir—powerful bad."

"Well, what was it? Did it kill any rebels or throw down any of the works?"

"No, sir; hit didn't do that."

"Well, what did it do? Speak out."

The Southerner quipped back, "Why, stranger, hit waked up pretty nigh every man in the fort!" This was not quite what the Union military high command had in mind when designing its great floating bomb to destroy the Confederate Gibraltar along the Cape Fear. Though it failed to live up to expectations, Butler's powder ship marked the beginning of a brutal campaign that stretched into the new year, eventually sealing the fate of the Confederacy.

Union forces scampered back up the coast to regroup after their initial efforts failed and returned to resume their operations to take Fort Fisher, climaxing with the Union assault and capture of the fort during January 1865 in what is commonly known as the Second Battle of Fort Fisher. After fierce hand-to-hand combat defending the sandy ramparts of their fort, the garrison was eventually rooted out by wave after wave of enemy attackers the Union command with its almost limitless supply of cannon fodder was able to throw against them. Fort Fisher fell on January 15, 1865, sealing the fate of the young nation.

Even in the face of such overwhelming odds, Fort Fisher would have no doubt proved as impossible to take in January as it had been back in December had reinforcements waiting nearby been sent down the beach from the north to sweep the Federal attackers back into the sea. However, Gen. Braxton Bragg refused to give the orders to put the troops in motion. There have been many theories as to why he did what he did, some saying strong drink, others just pure incompetence. Had the Confederacy survived a bit longer, Bragg no doubt would have appeared before a court martial in Richmond for his actions. Even if he did avoid justice, the lives of the brave men he abandoned there at Fort Fisher no doubt weighed heavily on his conscience to the end of his days. The Confederates fought savagely while they could. After Whiting and Lamb were severely wounded, command of the garrison devolved upon Maj. James Reilly, the Irishmen who had won distinction for his skills as an artilleryman during the fighting in Northern Virginia earlier in the war. During the Second Battle of Fort Fisher, he initially commanded roughly 600 men along the fort's northwest face, whose main role was to do whatever was needed to hold the weakest link of the defenses against the 8,000 strong columns of Federal infantrymen from Adelbert Ames's division. Fighting bravely against this mass of humanity, they gave ground stubbornly as they were forced back within the ramparts of the fort, exacting a bloody toll from the Union attackers.

After taking over command from Lamb, Reilly held his post as long as he could against such overwhelming odds. As it became apparent that there was no strike coming down the beach from the north catching the enemy from behind and driving them into the sea, Reilly went about evacuating the fort, beginning with the wounded in the hospital in the Pulpit Battery, taking those well enough to survive the move to Battery Buchanan.

Gathering about him roughly 32 men to act as a sort of rear guard with what must have seemed a woefully inadequate force to hold off the thousands of enemy soldiers and sailors swarming his fort, they moved out. They gave ground slowly, often fighting hand-to-hand, maintaining order and cohesion as best they could. As they withdrew to the south, defenders from the ramparts of defenses from the Northeast Bastion all the way to the Mound Battery pulled out with them.

Reilly was hoping to regroup with the naval forces under Capt. Robert Chapman at Battery Buchanan, but the sailors had already left, fleeing across the river and taking their boats with them. Even though he still had approximately 500 men gathered about him from the fort, many were out of ammunition, wounded, or physically exhausted. Thus, abandoned for a second time that day, Reilly had no choice but to stop the fighting and put an end to further bloodshed. Years later, he pointed out that he and his brave defenders never surrendered the fort but were driven from Fort Fisher after having held out as long as humanly possible.

The pages that follow are meant to give folks a look into the story behind this unique place, which to the untrained eye may not look like much but was the scene of countless acts of bravery from the soldiers, sailors, and marines of both countries. We are fortunate that the events surrounding the fighting here drew the attention of artists and mapmakers who chronicled the activities for a variety of publications. The action of the second battle and its aftermath was documented extensively thanks to the photographs of Timothy H. O'Sullivan, whom the Union high command dispatched at the request of Bvt. Brig. Gen. Cyrus Comstock, the chief Union engineer at Fort Fisher, who wanted to document as best he could just how intricate these defenses really were and figure out the secret behind the modest-looking fort whose sandy walls had taken the best the Union navy could dish out.

We are fortunate that a photographer of O'Sullivan's caliber was so conscientious in carrying out his work, as most of the sandy ramparts of the fort, including the sea face defenses and the famous Mound Battery, have long since washed into the sea. Only a small part of the northern walls of the fort survives today, protected as well as one can protect such a structure made of sand from the effects of Mother Nature.

One

Protecting the Lifeline of the Confederacy

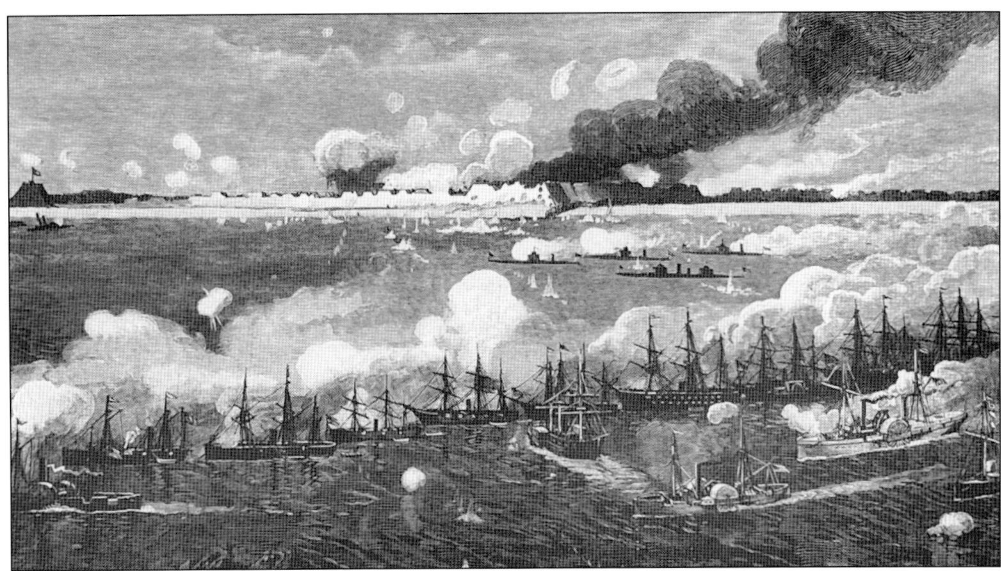

Walter Clark included this illustration called "Bombardment of Ft. Fisher, January 15, 1865, from Lithographs" in his multivolume work *Several Regiments and Battalions from North Carolina in the Civil War*, published in Raleigh in 1901, herein cited as Clark's *Regiments*. Rear Adm. David Porter and other members of the leadership team of the joint operation task force assigned to capture Fort Fisher developed a sneaky admiration for the sandy fort.

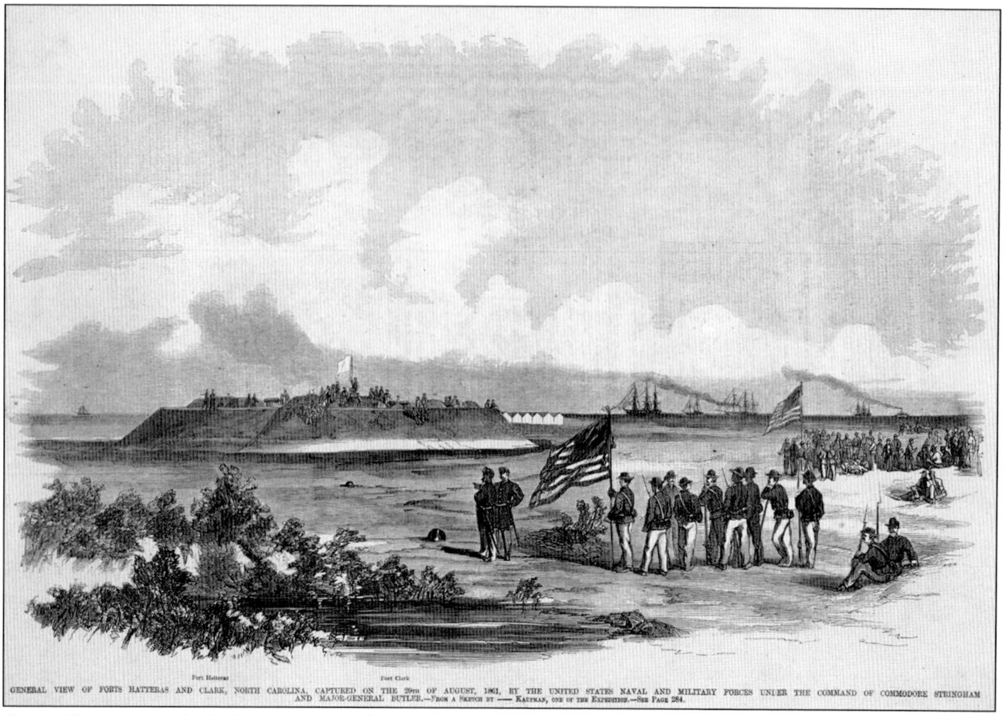

Fort Hatteras Fort Clark

GENERAL VIEW OF FORTS HATTERAS AND CLARK, NORTH CAROLINA, CAPTURED ON THE 29TH OF AUGUST, 1861, BY THE UNITED STATES NAVAL AND MILITARY FORCES UNDER THE COMMAND OF COMMODORE STRINGHAM AND MAJOR-GENERAL BUTLER.—FROM A SKETCH BY —— KAUFMAN, ONE OF THE EXPEDITION.—SEE PAGE 284.

Forts Hatteras and Clark, shown in this image from the September 14, 1861, edition of *Frank Leslie's Illustrated Newspaper*, fell to Union forces in August 1861. (North Carolina Collection Photographic Archives, Wilson Special Collections Library, University of North Carolina at Chapel Hill.)

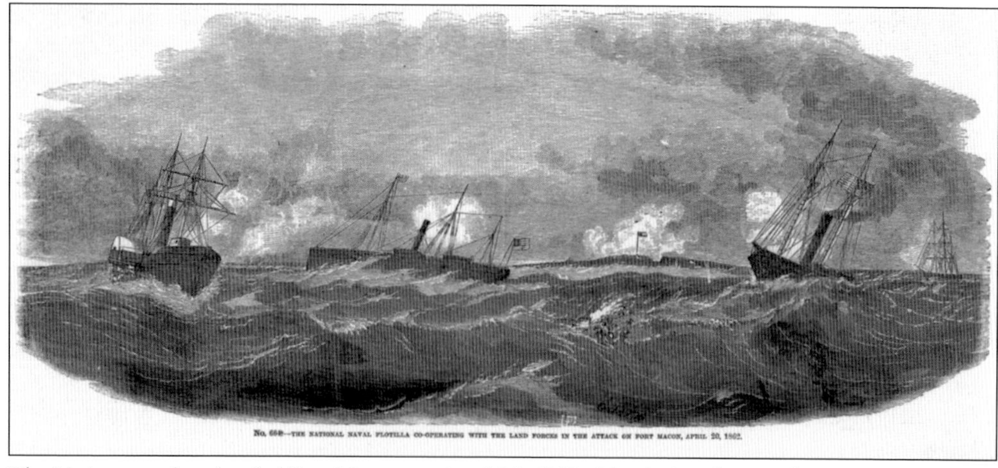

The Union navy bombarded Fort Macon on April 20, 1862. (North Carolina Collection Photographic Archives, Wilson Special Collections Library, University of North Carolina at Chapel Hill.)

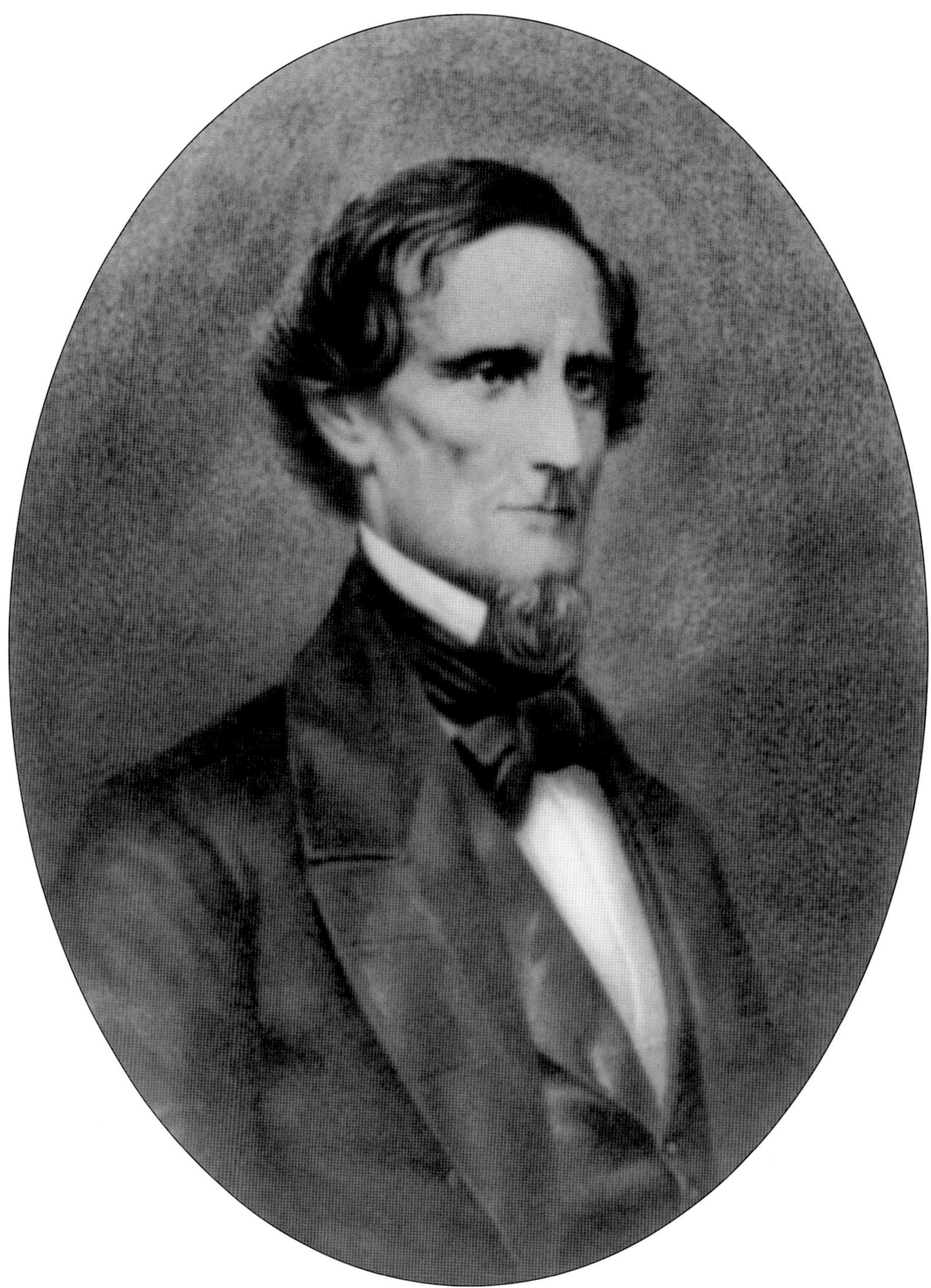

Wilmington was such an important link in the lifeline of the Confederacy that Pres. Jefferson Davis, pictured above, visited the port city, even inspecting the works at Fort Fisher. (LOC.)

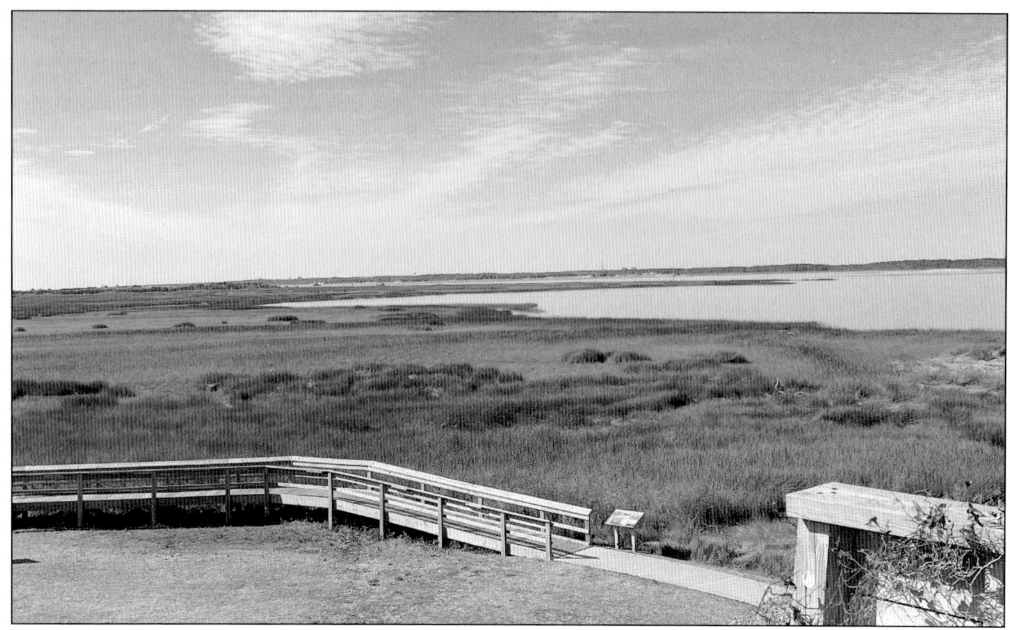

This view is looking southwest towards Battery Buchanan and the mouth of the Cape Fear River. Realizing the commercial importance of the Cape Fear River to the state, the Confederates got to work bolstering the defenses of the waterway. There were two entrances to the river in those days, one at the river's mouth and another at New Inlet, which formed during a hurricane in 1761. Fort Fisher and Battery Buchanan protected New Inlet.

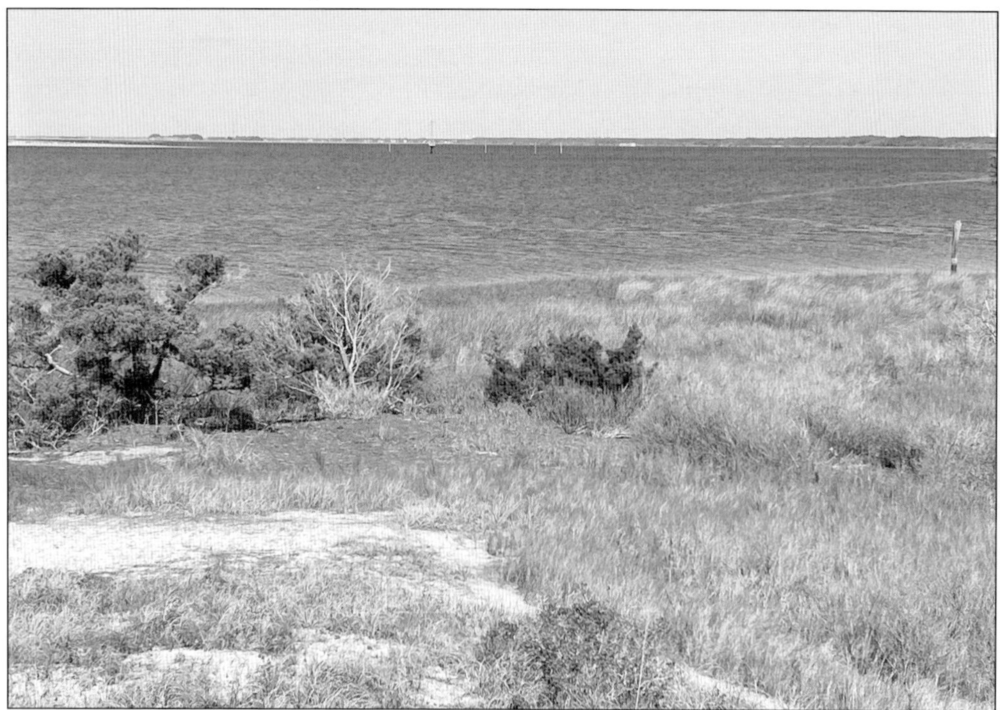

This view is looking west across the Cape Fear River from atop Battery Buchanan. The defensive network that grew into Fort Fisher and Battery Buchanan protected New Inlet.

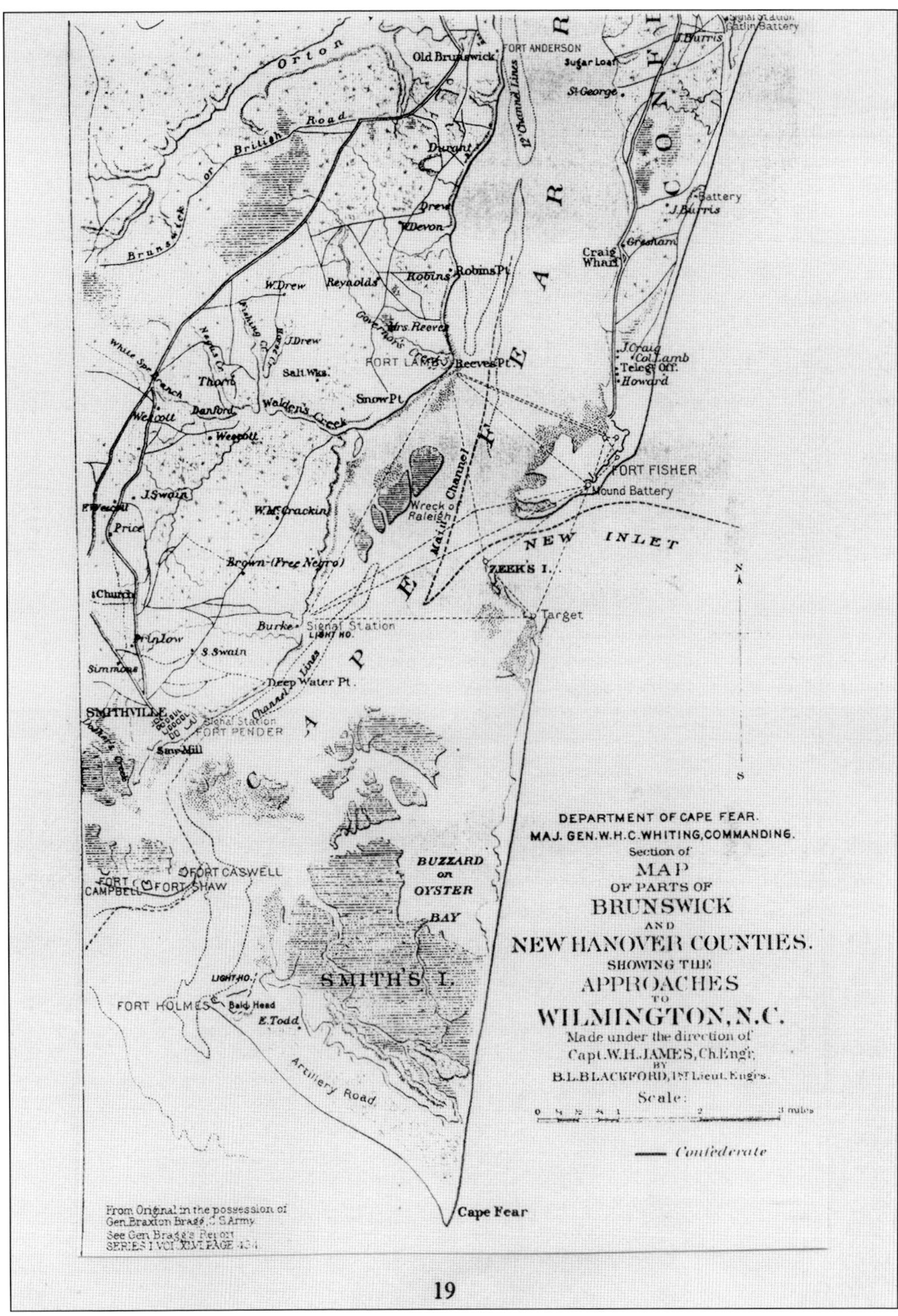

This map, prepared in 1863 by Lt. B.L. Blackford under direction of the chief engineer, Capt. W.H. James, shows the intricate network of defenses of the Cape Fear River, including Fort Fisher. (LOC.)

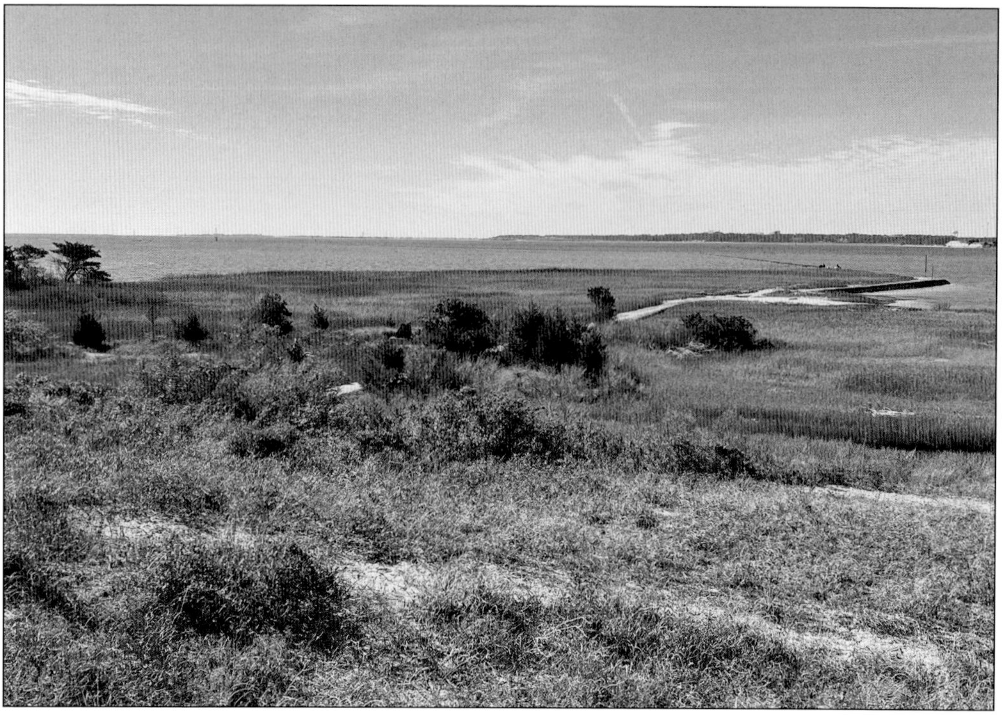

This view is looking southwest from Battery Buchanan toward the mouth of the river. New Inlet is obstructed today by vegetation, but this was not an issue during the war years.

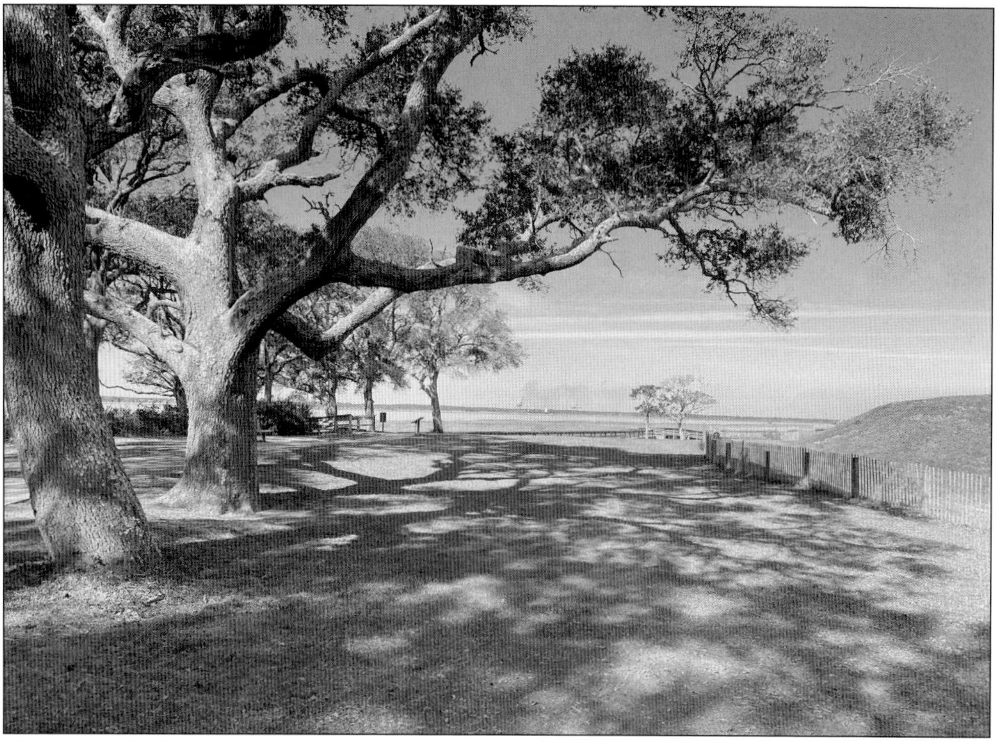

This view is looking west towards the river just outside the fort.

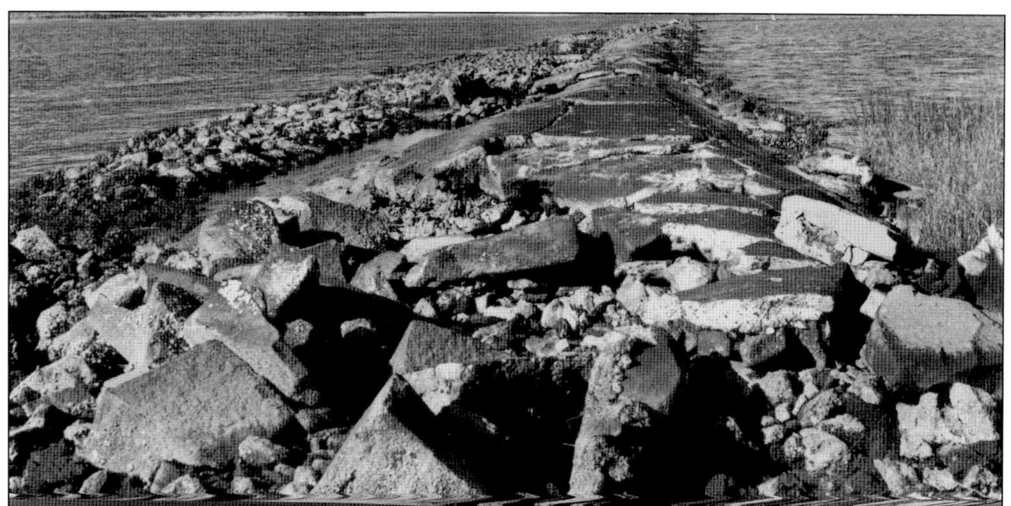

The US Army Corps of Engineers closed New Inlet in the 1880s with the New Inlet Swash Defense Dam. "The Rocks" remain a popular spot for anglers wishing to try their luck.

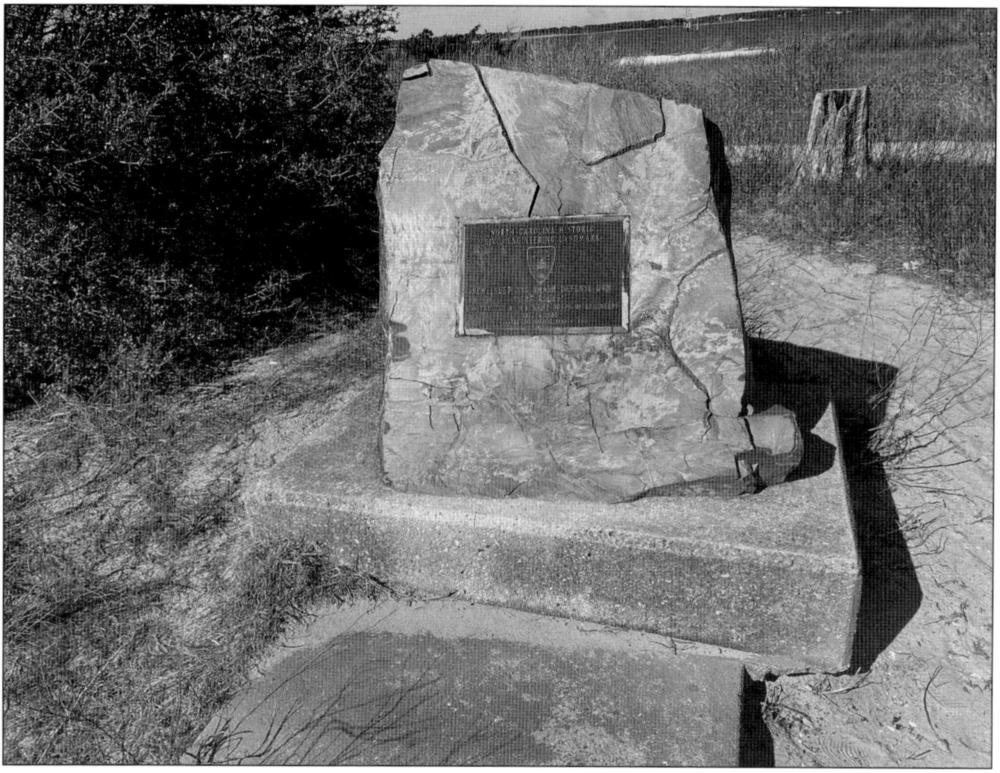

This monument erected by the American Society of Civil Engineers in 1992 commemorates completion of the New Inlet Swash Defense Dam, commonly known as "The Rocks."

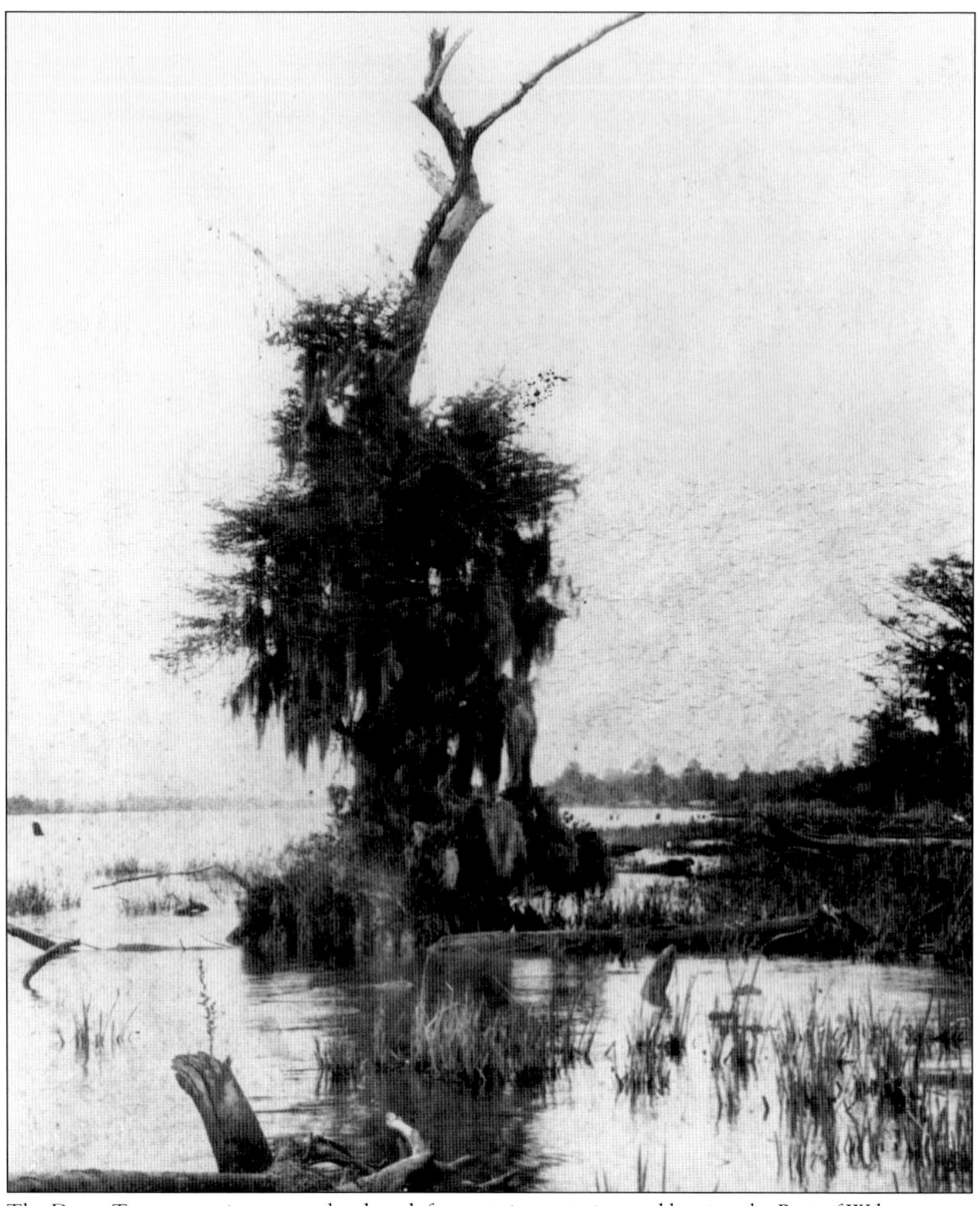

The Dram Tree was an important landmark for captains entering and leaving the Port of Wilmington. (North Carolina Archives and History.)

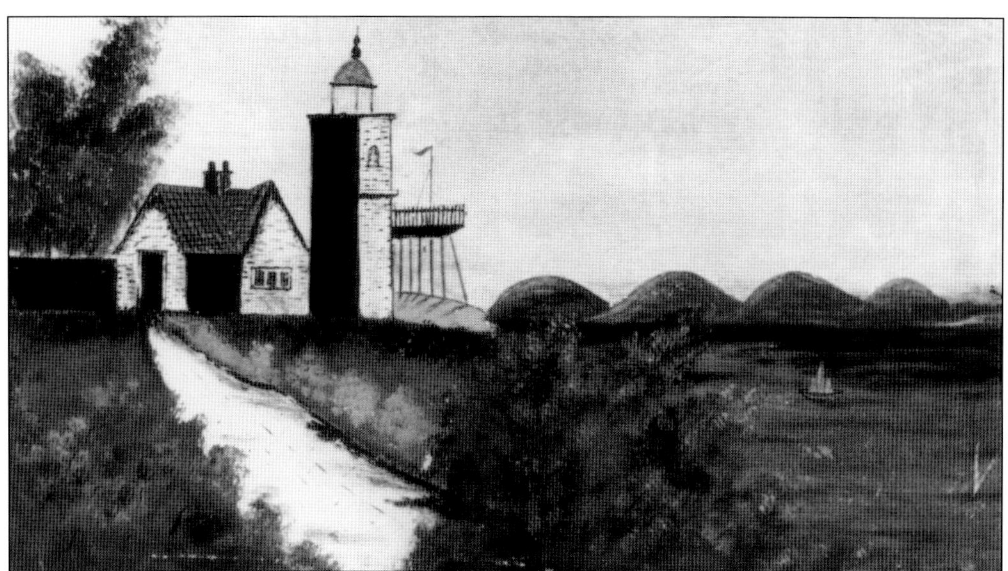

Capt. George Tait of the 40th North Carolina Regiment drew this image of the second Federal Point Lighthouse shortly before it was destroyed by Confederate troops constructing Fort Fisher in January 1863. Although Colonel Lamb used the keeper's quarters as a headquarters, the lighthouse proved to be a tempting target for Union gunners since it was accurately marked on their nautical charts, and he found it necessary to have it torn down. Unfortunately, one of Tait's men, 19-year-old Pvt. Aldred Campain of Company B, was killed by falling debris from the lighthouse as they were tearing the brick structure down. (North Carolina Archives and History.)

George Tait of Bladen County rose to be a lieutenant colonel of the 40th North Carolina Regiment. (Clark's *Regiments.*)

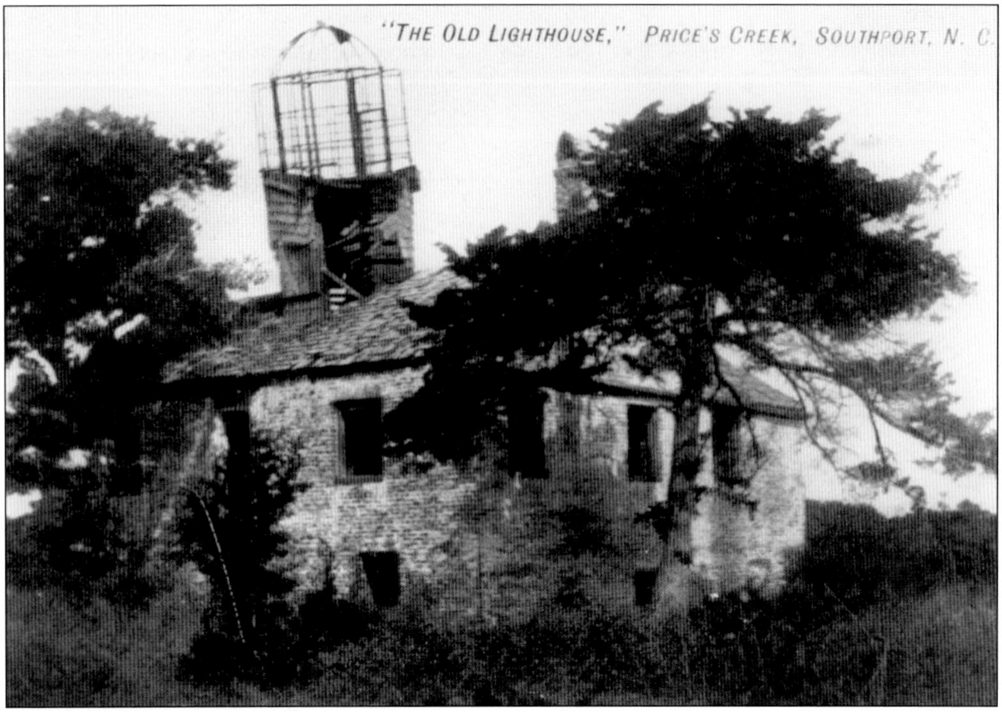

"THE OLD LIGHTHOUSE," PRICE'S CREEK, SOUTHPORT, N. C.

An early-20th-century photograph shows the remains of the original Price's Creek lightkeeper's quarters. The light at Price's Creek served as a range light for mariners coming through New Inlet. (North Carolina Archives and History.)

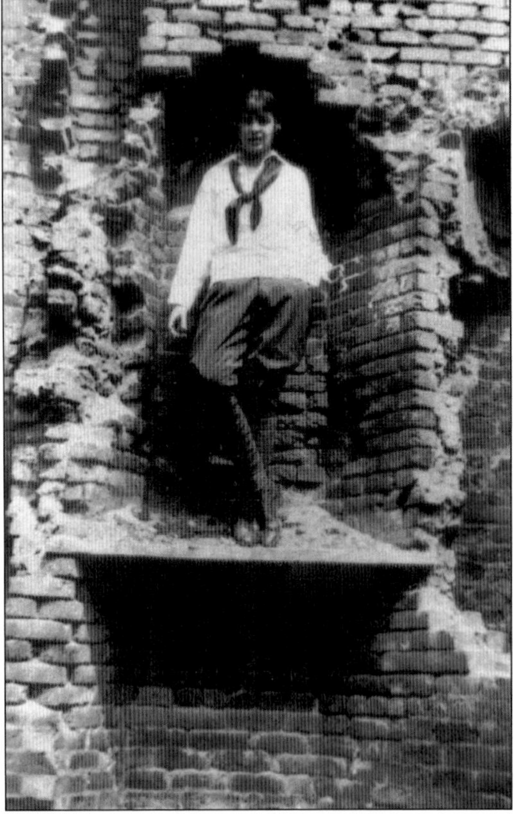

This photograph shows an unidentified young lady standing in the remains of the original Price's Creek lightkeeper's quarters. (North Carolina Archives and History.)

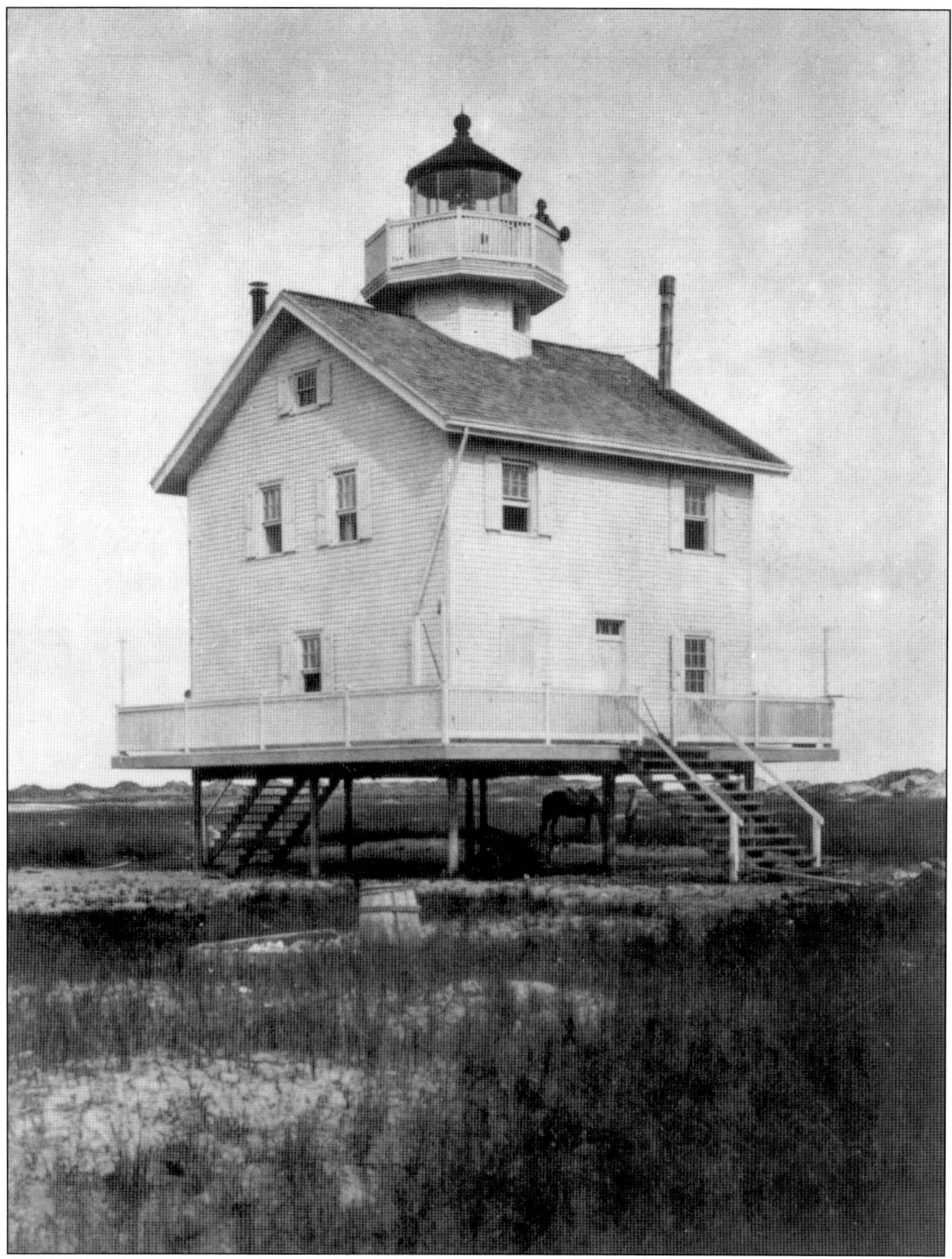

A third Federal Point Lighthouse began operations at this important spot along the Cape Fear River in April 1866. It stood near the present location of the North Carolina Aquarium at Fort Fisher. (North Carolina Archives and History.)

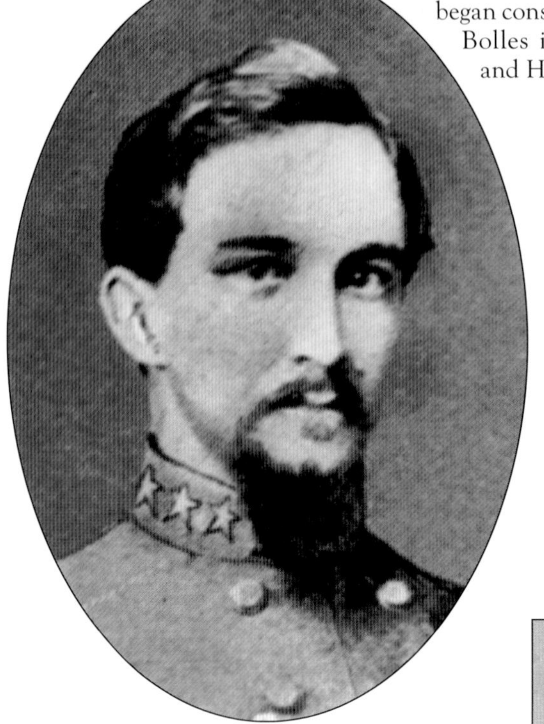

Maj. Charles Bolles was the engineer who designed and began construction of the earthworks known as Battery Bolles in April 1861. (North Carolina Archives and History.)

Capt. William DeRosset of the Wilmington Light Infantry is pictured here. He and his comrades took over construction of the defensive works Maj. Charles Bolles had begun, hastily building the sandy defenses at Federal Point in the spring 1861, which DeRosset and his men rechristened Confederate Point. (North Carolina Archives and History.)

Col. Charles F. Fisher of the 6th North Carolina Infantry Regiment was killed leading a charge during the Battle of First Manassas in Virginia on July 21, 1861. The fort was named in his honor by his friend, Col. Sewall Fremont, chief engineer of the Southern Department Coast Defences. (Clark's *Regiments.*)

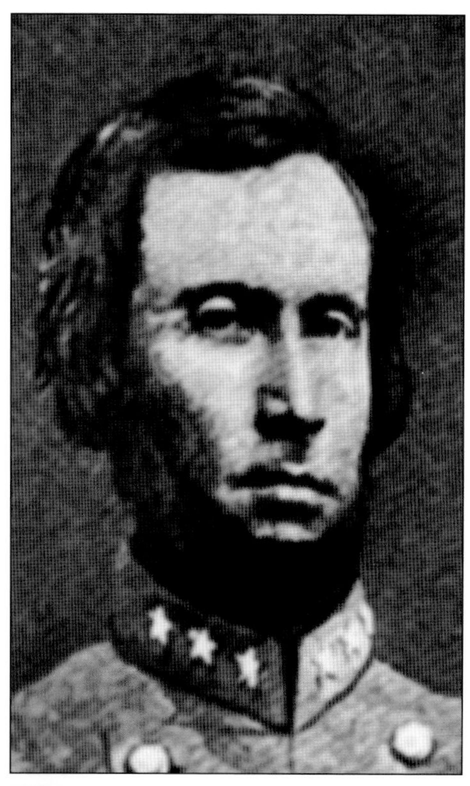

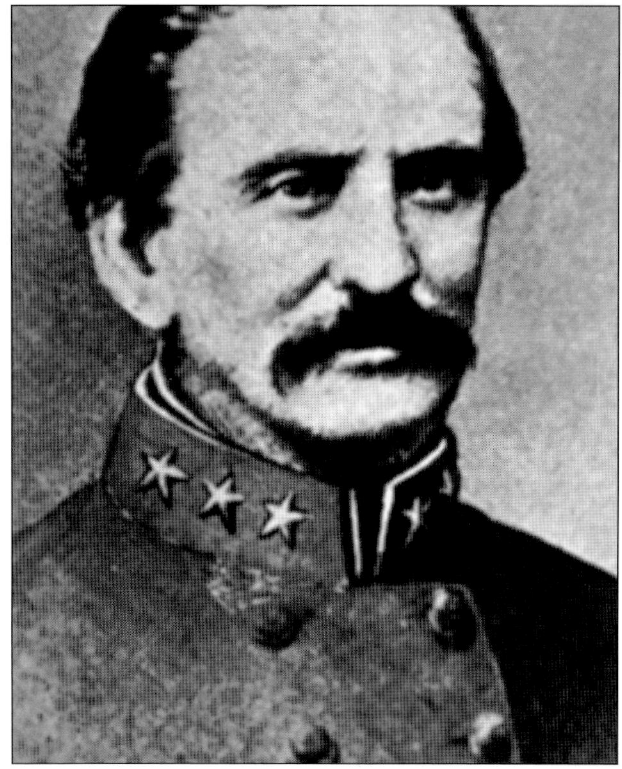

Capt. John Hedrick, later a colonel, was an early commander of the defenses at Confederate Point. The 40th North Carolina Regiment, also designated as the 3rd North Carolina Artillery, played a key role in the defenses at the mouth of the Cape Fear River. (North Carolina Archives and History.)

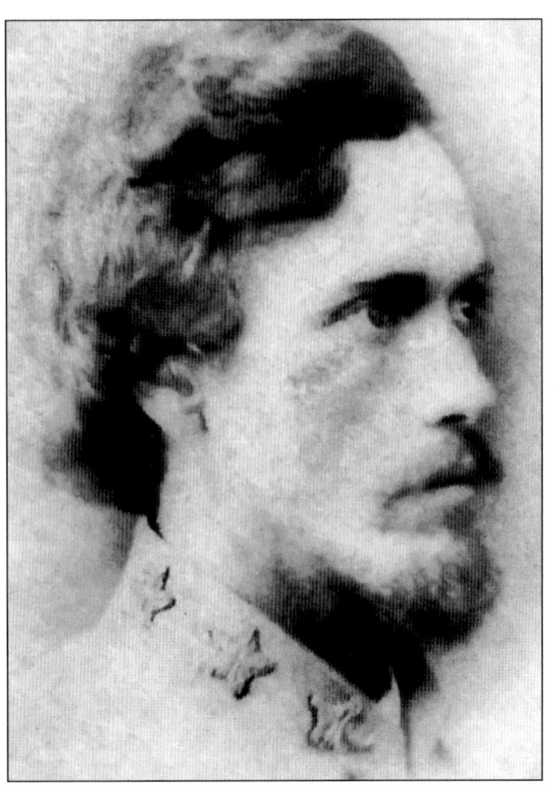

Col. William Lamb of the 36th North Carolina Regiment took over command at Fort Fisher in July 1862. He was the fort's commander through most of the war, working in close coordination with General Whiting. (North Carolina Archives and History.)

According to Cape Fear historian James Sprunt, this rustic house served as living quarters for Colonel Lamb and his wife, Daisy, during the latter half of the war. It stood roughly half a mile north of the fort. Sprunt included the image in his book *Tales and Traditions of the Lower Cape Fear.*

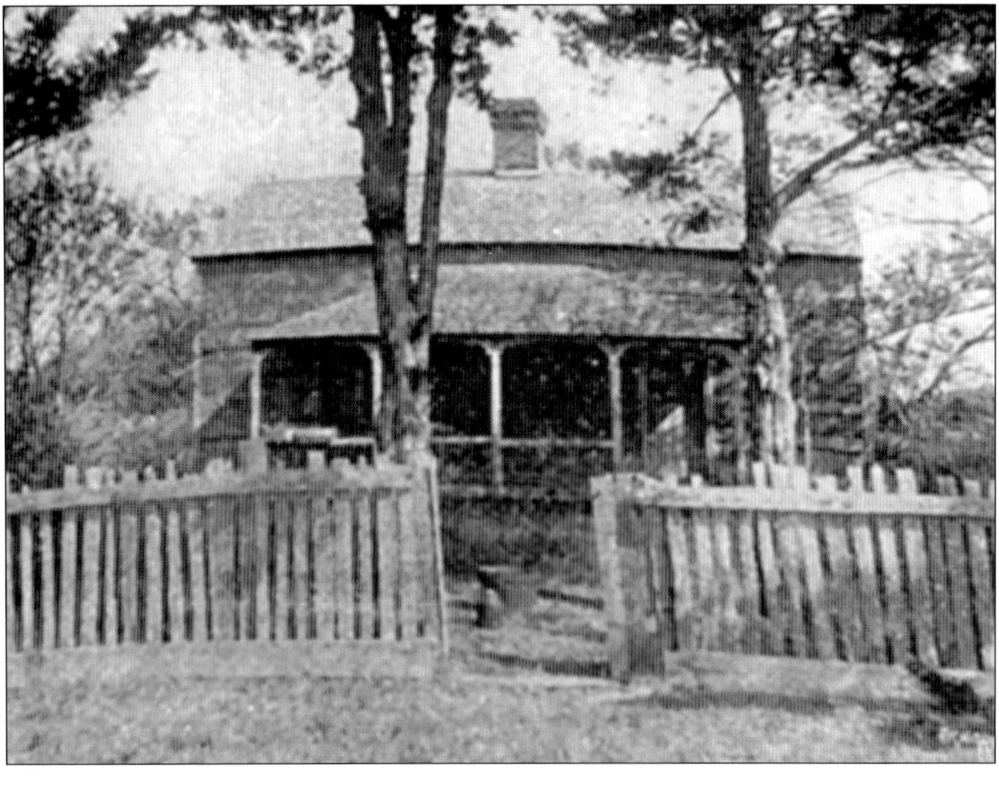

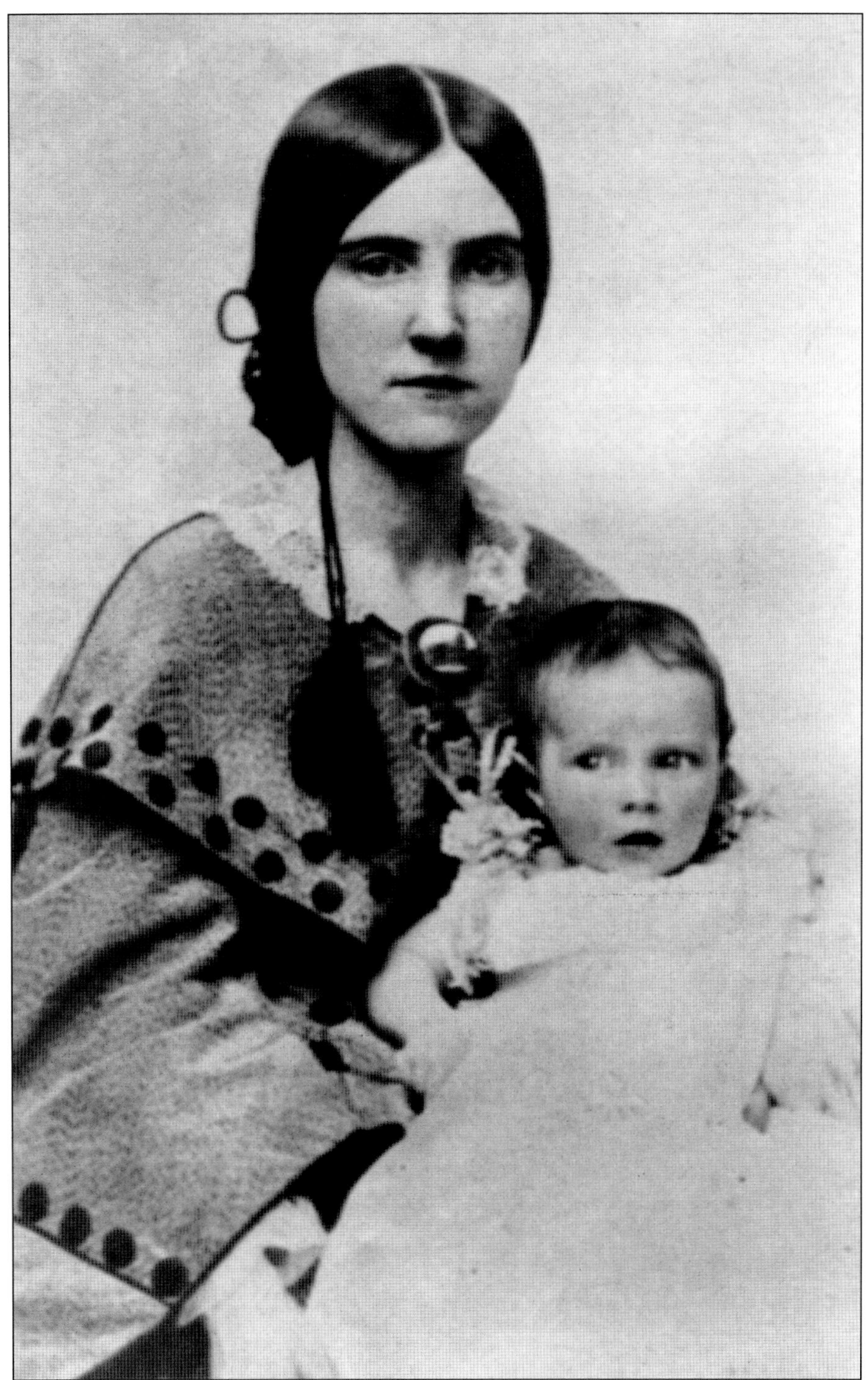

Sarah "Daisy" Lamb, Col. William Lamb's wife, is pictured with their daughter Sally on her lap. A notation on this photograph taken in 1864 points out that it was "from original found in Col. William Lamb's copy of *Running the Blockade* owned by Larry Walker." (Earl Gregg Swem Library, William & Mary University.)

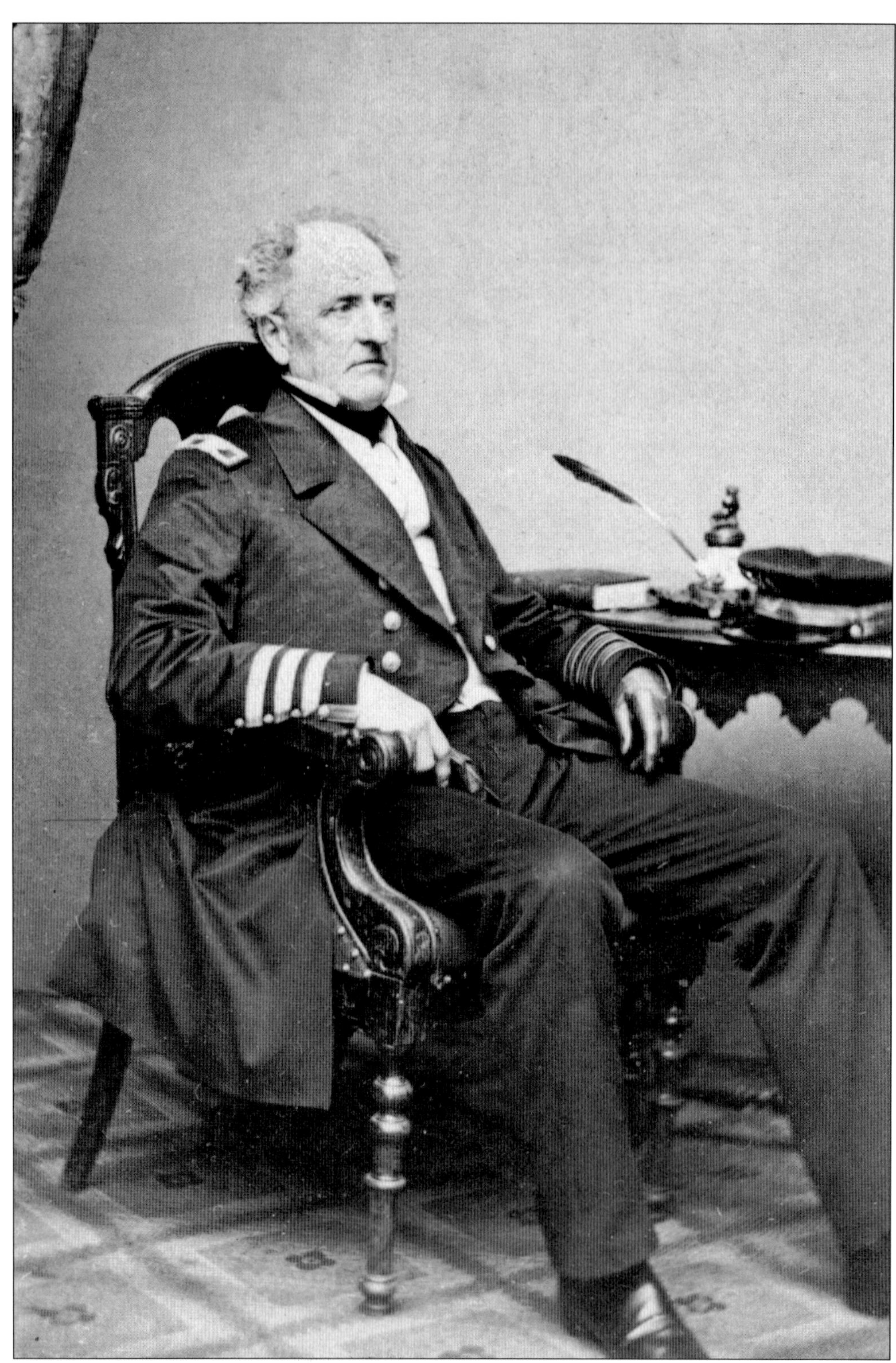

Adm. Franklin Buchanan, the namesake of Battery Buchanan, is pictured here. (LOC.)

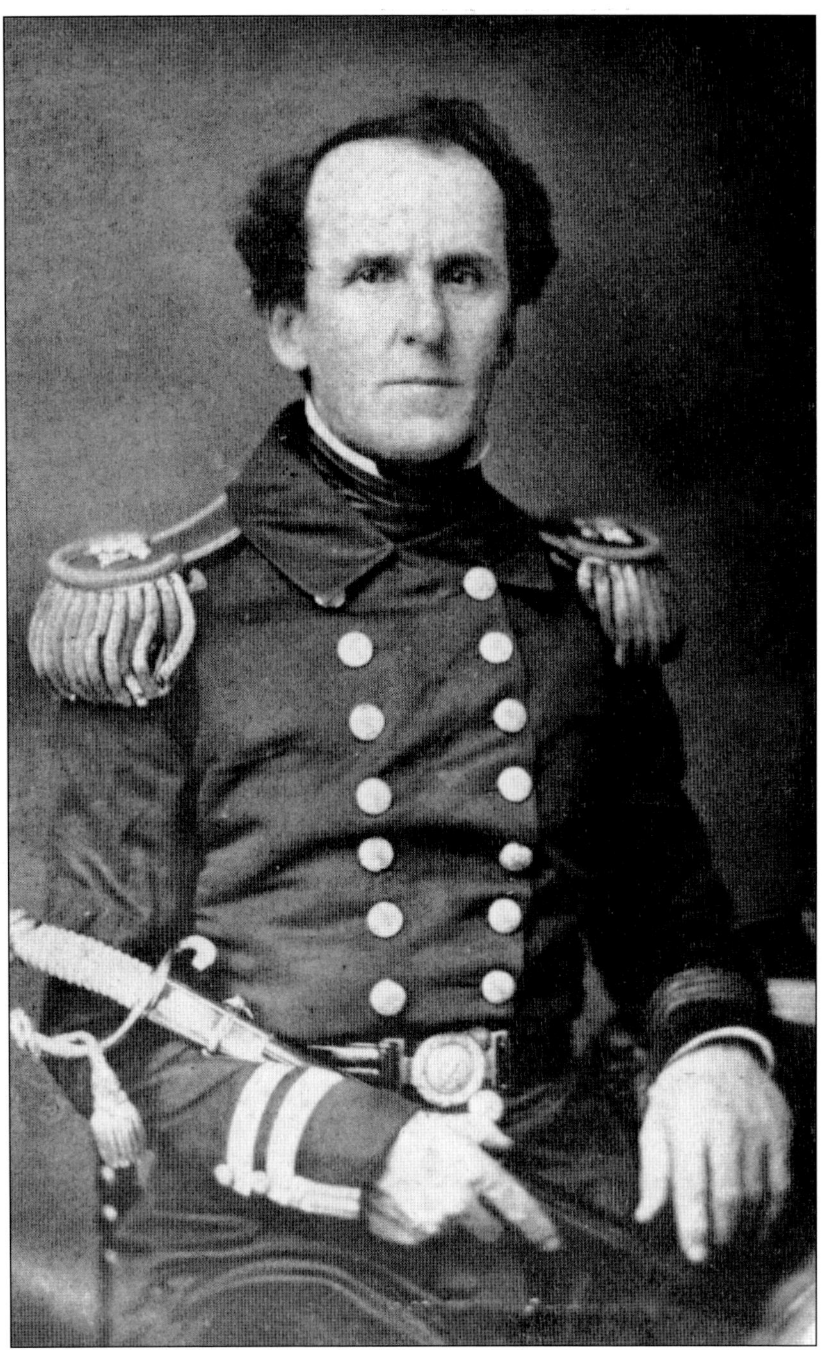

Commodore William Lynch was the flag officer in charge of Confederate naval operations at Wilmington. A native of Virginia, Lynch had a successful career in the US Navy, most notably as an explorer and author. But perhaps his most challenging task was the assignment given him by his new country of trying to figure out ways to defend the strategically important Cape Fear River. He overcame many obstacles, mainly relating to finding adequate raw materials such as wood, iron, and copper for the construction of the vessels to fend off ships of the Union navy. (US Naval History and Heritage Command.)

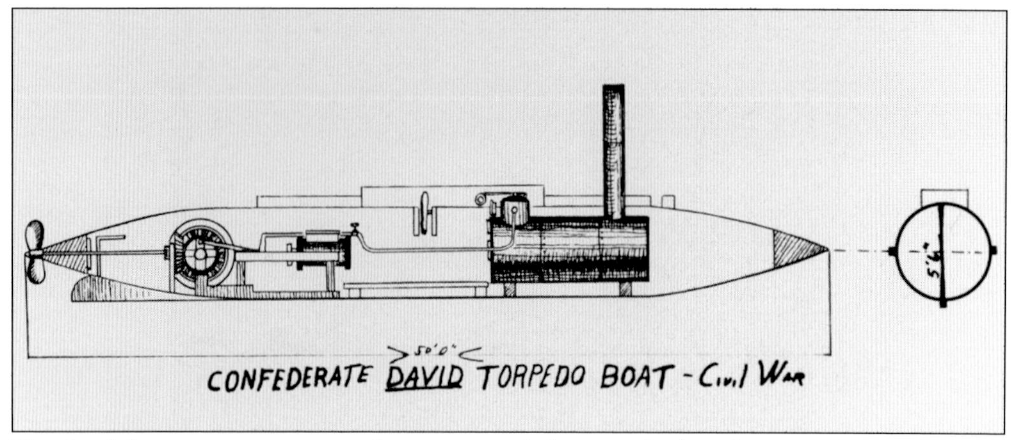

The Confederate navy was rumored to test torpedo boats and other electronic devices along the Deep River near Gulf, where a ready supply of materials, including iron, copper, and coal, were found in close proximity. The waters of the Deep River were a much safer place to test initial designs of both manned and unmanned implements, especially those susceptible to the ill effects of salt water. (US Naval History and Heritage Command.)

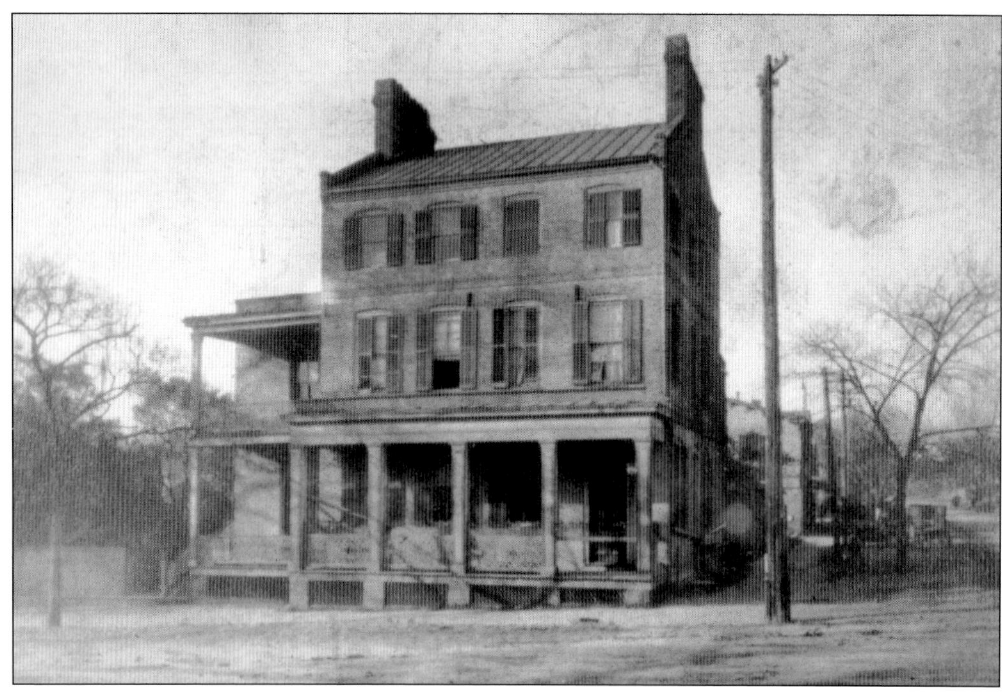

Gen. William Henry Chase Whiting used the Allen House as his headquarters in Wilmington. The house no longer stands. (New Hanover County Public Library's Local History Room.)

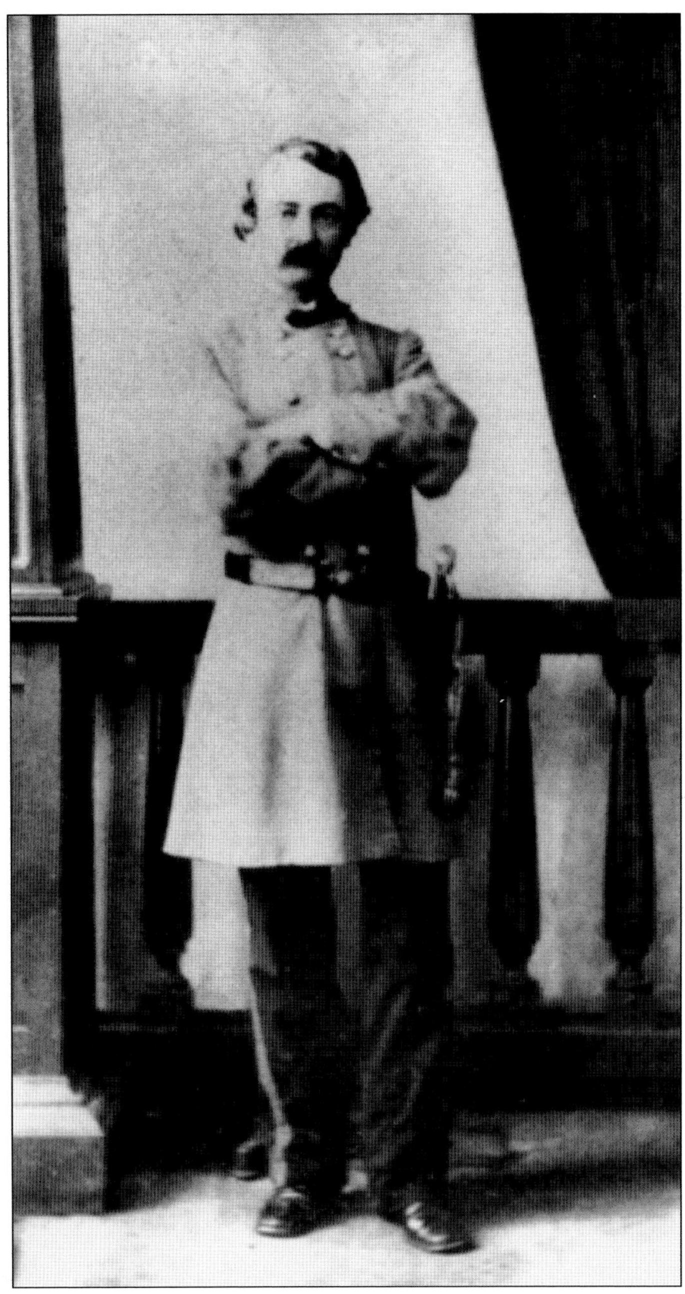

Maj. Gen. William Henry Chase Whiting was a gifted military engineer who graduated first in his class at West Point in 1845. A native of Mississippi, Whiting married Katherine Davis Walker of Wilmington in 1857, so he had ties to the area thanks to his in-laws as well as friends made during tours of duty along the Carolina coast. He resigned his commission in 1861, offering his talents to the Confederacy. Thanks to his intricate knowledge of the area, Whiting oversaw construction of the strategically important defenses at the mouth of the Cape Fear River, including Fort Fisher, where he and Colonel Lamb had great rapport in designing and implementing construction of the sandy defensive works. He was known affectionately to his men as "Little Billy," and he proved to be a tenacious fighter. (South Carolina Historical Society.)

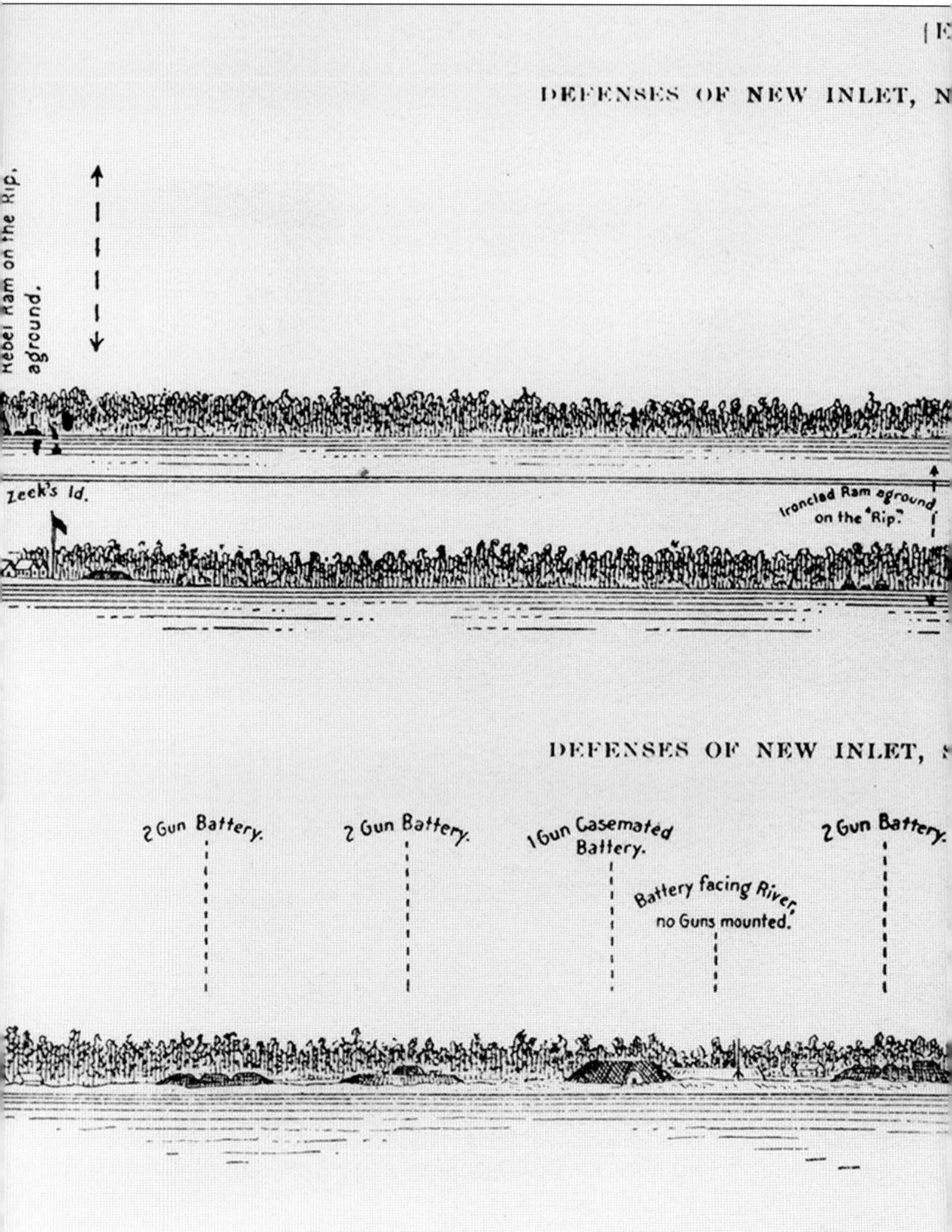

This diagram shows the ever-growing defenses at New Inlet as seen from the sea. (*Official Records,*

ro.]

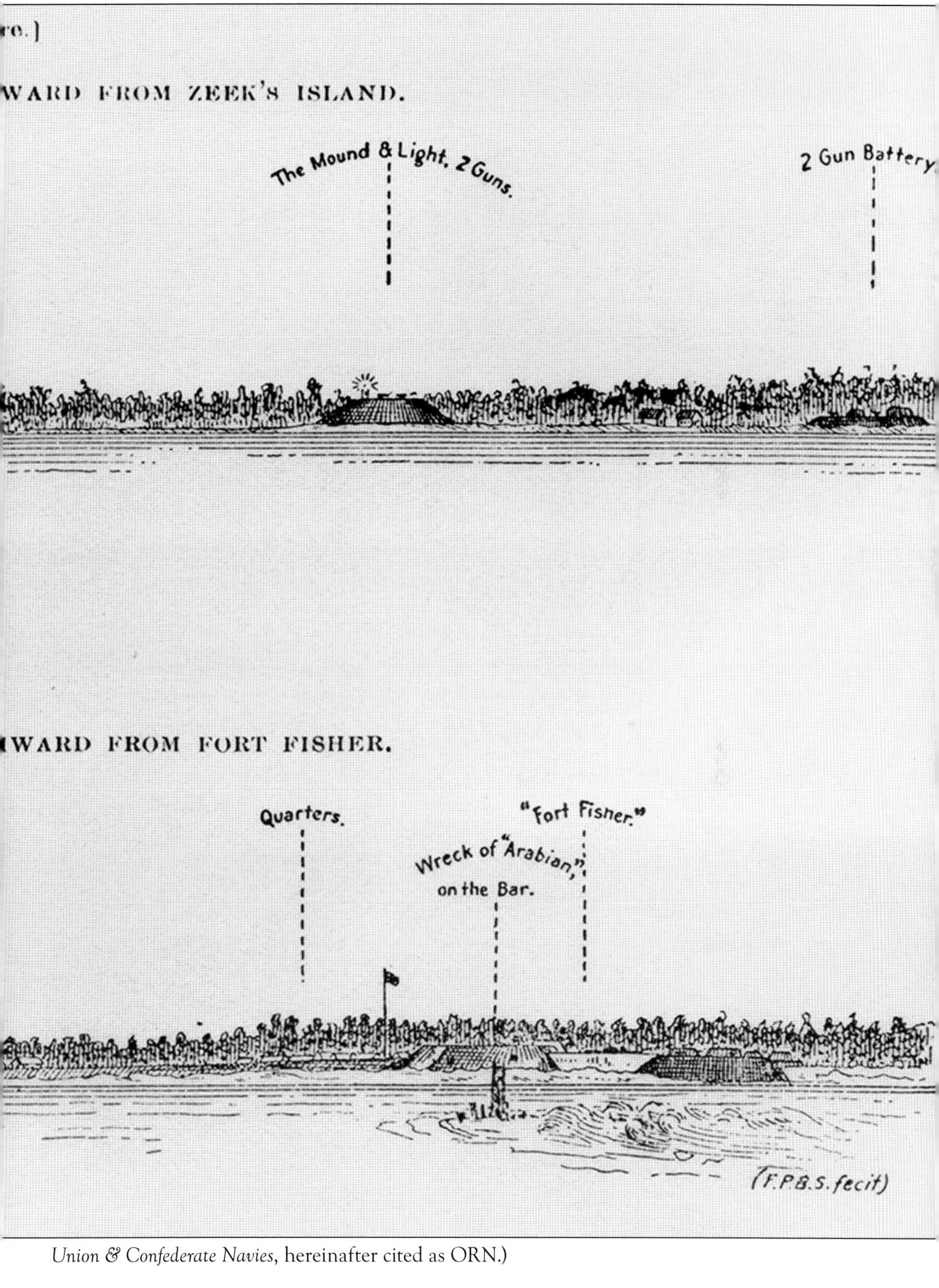

WARD FROM ZEEK'S ISLAND.

The Mound & Light, 2 Guns.

2 Gun Battery.

WARD FROM FORT FISHER.

Quarters.

"Fort Fisher."

Wreck of "Arabian," on the Bar.

(F.P.B.S. fecit)

Union & Confederate Navies, hereinafter cited as ORN.)

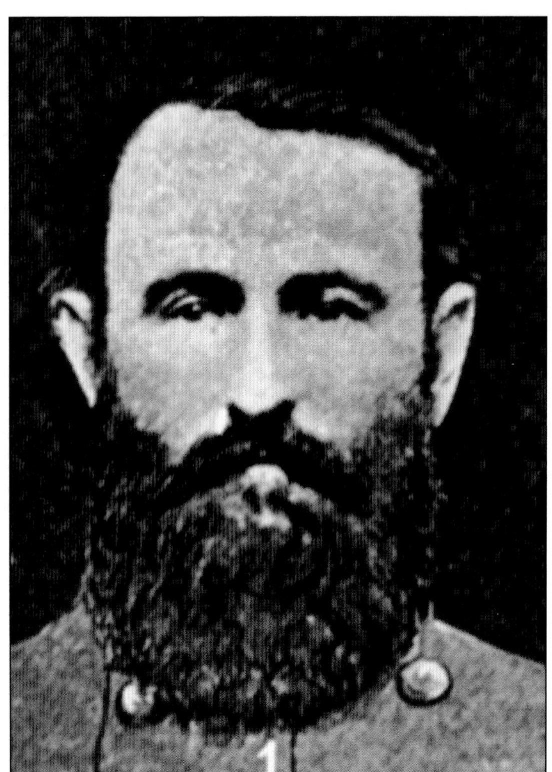

Maj. J.M. Stevenson of 36th North Carolina Regiment is pictured here. (Clark's *Regiments.*)

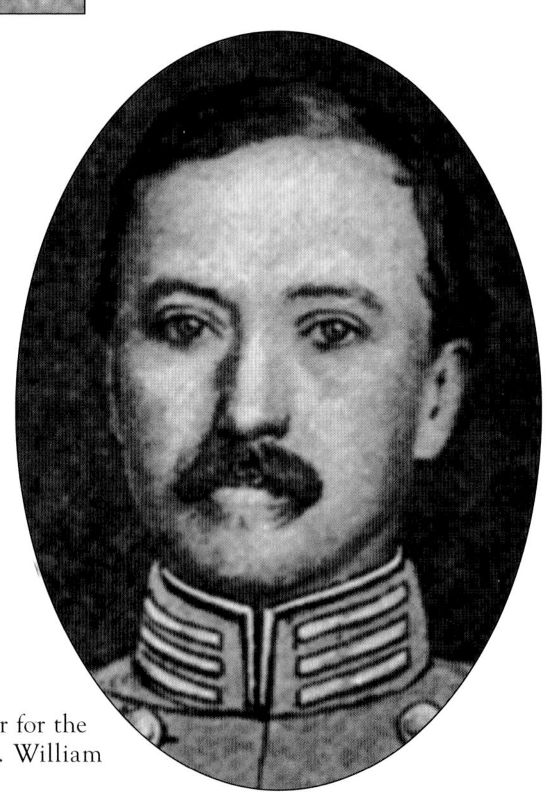

Capt. Robert Lamb, assistant quartermaster for the 36th North Carolina Regiment, was Col. William Lamb's younger brother. (Clark's *Regiments.*)

Col. William Lamb of the 36th North Carolina Regiment was named commander of Fort Fisher on July 4, 1862. (Clark's *Regiments.*)

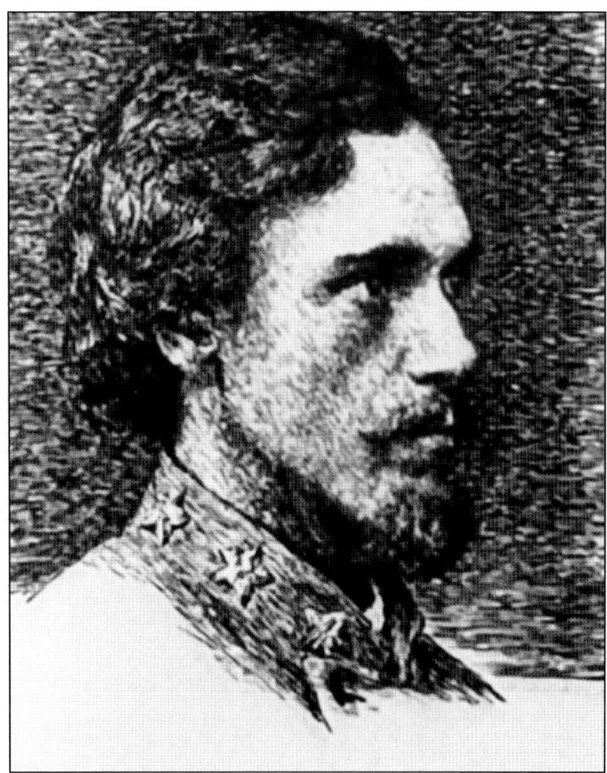

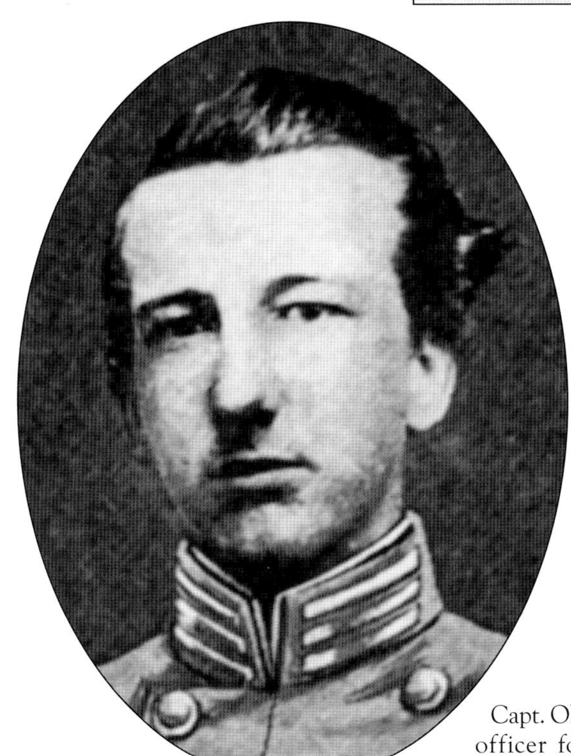

Capt. Oliver H. Blocker was the assistant commissary officer for the 36th North Carolina Regiment. (Clark's *Regiments.*)

Capt. Daniel Perry, Company B, 36th North Carolina Regiment is pictured here. (Clark's *Regiments.*)

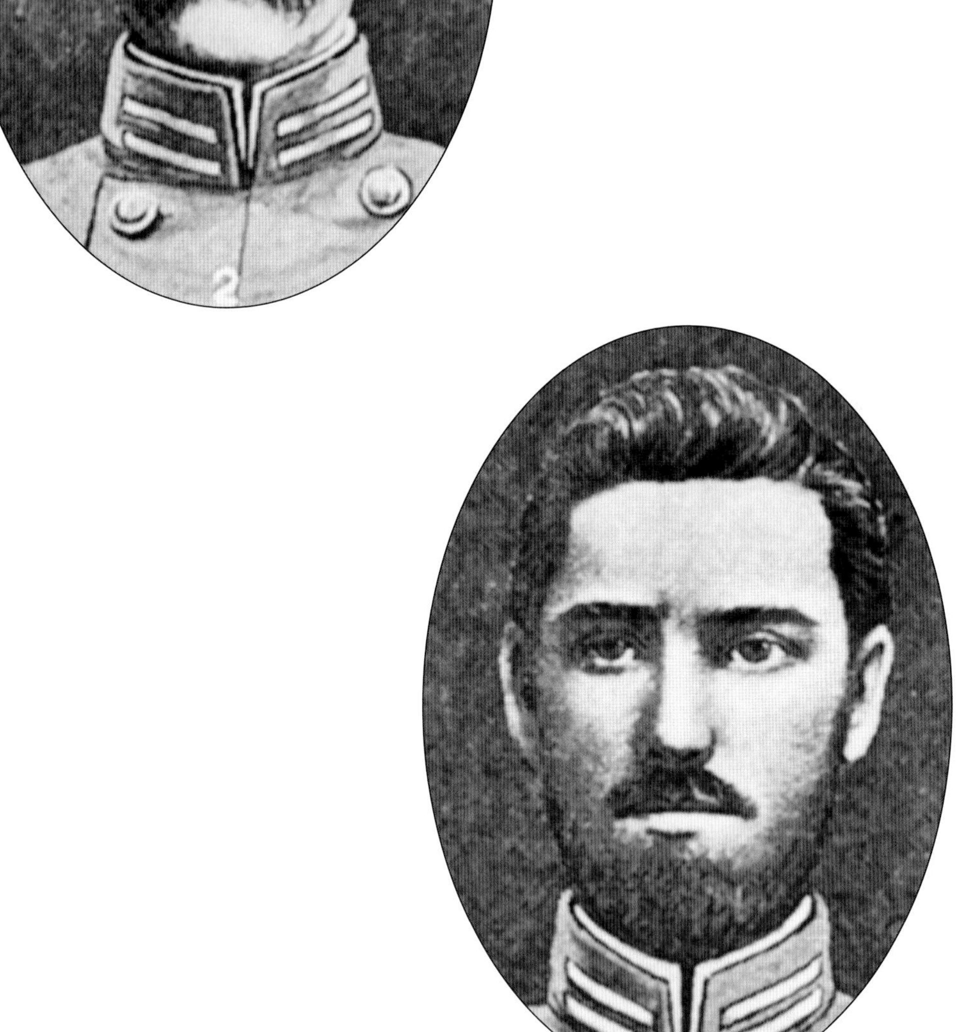

Seen here is Lt. H.D Williamson, Company E, 36th North Carolina Regiment. (Clark's *Regiments.*)

Capt. Robert J. Murphy was a soldier in 2nd Company A, 36th North Carolina Regiment. The regiment was sometimes referred to as the "King's Artillery." (Clark's *Regiments.*)

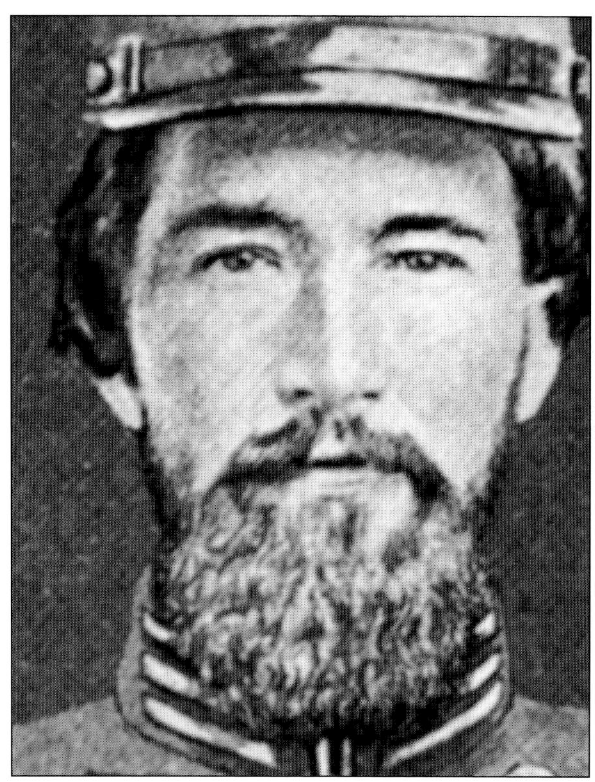

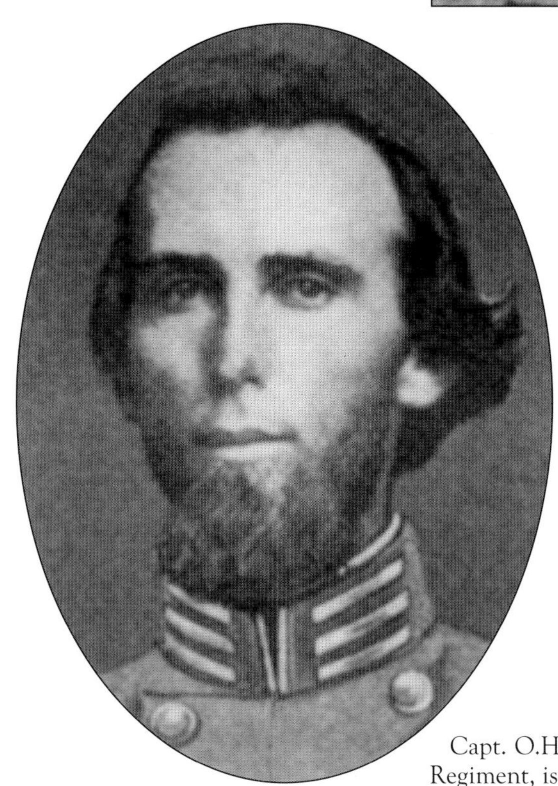

Capt. O.H. Powell, Company E, 36th North Carolina Regiment, is shown here. (Clark's *Regiments.*)

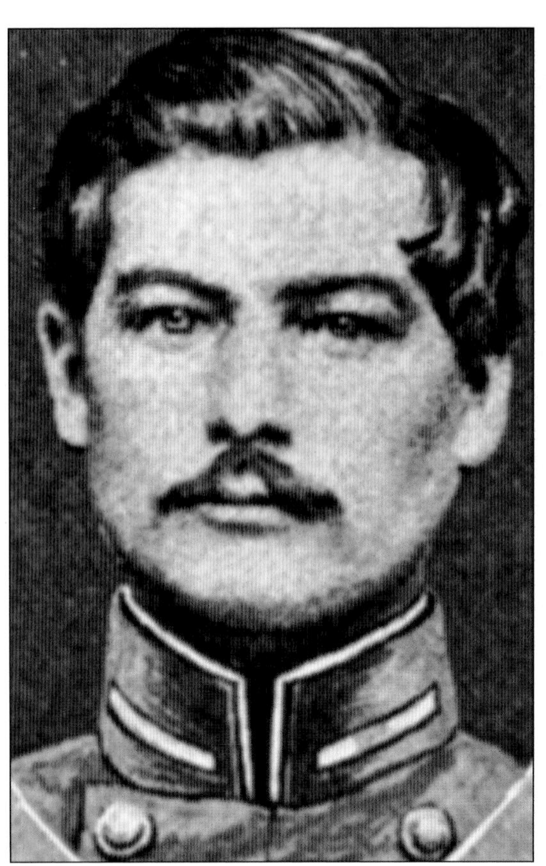

Pictured here is 2nd Lt. W.C. Daniel of the 36th North Carolina Regiment. (Clark's *Regiments.*)

Enslaved laborers were sometimes requisitioned from local farms to help with the hard labor of constructing the sandy ramparts of the fort. However, owners were hesitant to lend their valuable property to the war effort to work in the swampy lowlands of the Cape Fear River, whose swamps and morasses were known as being unhealthy locations where many people of all races died over the years from diseases, especially mosquito-borne illnesses. Thus, most of the hard labor was performed by the enlisted members of the garrison. (North Carolina Archives and History.)

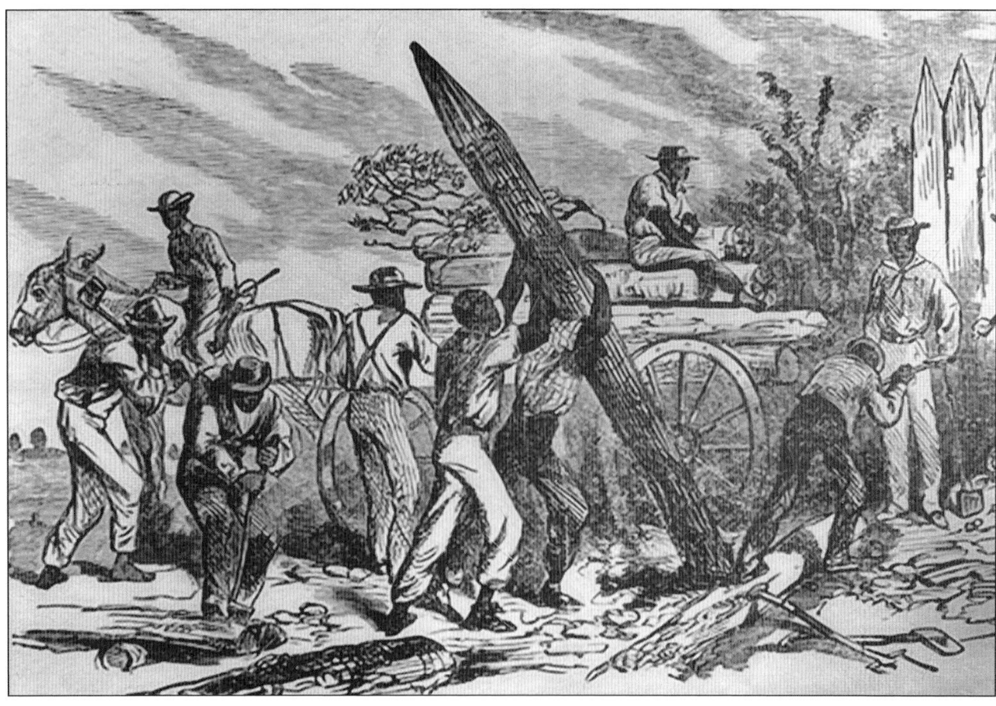

Capt. Henry Barnes, Company B, 10th Battalion, North Carolina Heavy Artillery, is pictured here. His company was also known as the "Black River Tigers." The 10th Battalion spent most of the war garrisoned at Fort Fisher but were dispatched in the fall of 1864 to help fight against Gen. William T. Sherman's army advancing through Georgia and were not on hand during the battles at Fort Fisher. (Clark's *Regiments.*)

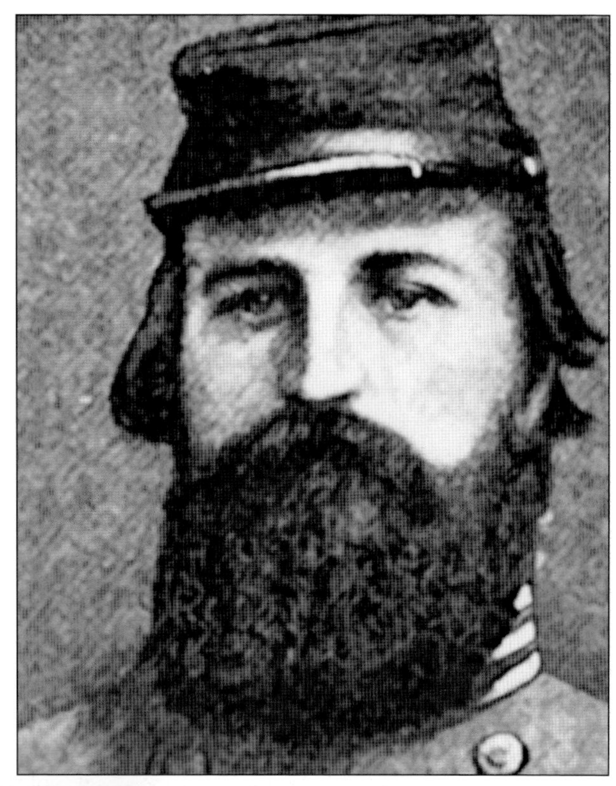

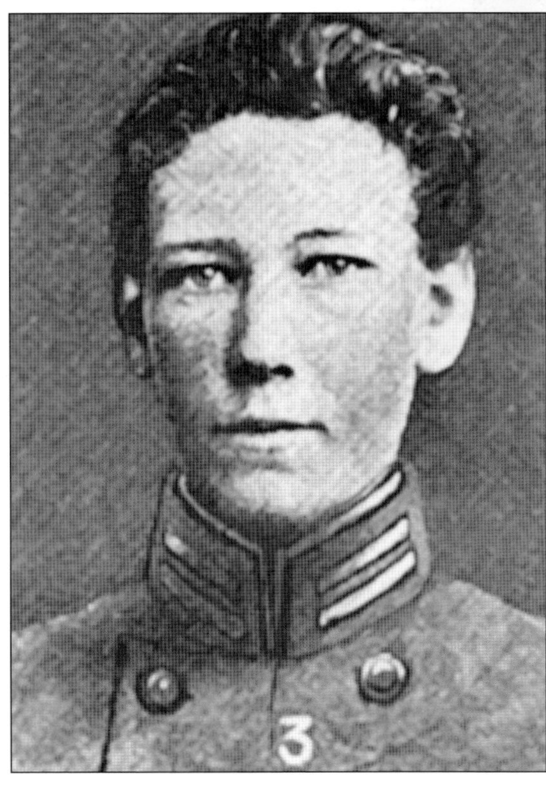

Lt. C.S. Powell from Johnston County served as adjutant for the 10th Battalion, North Carolina Heavy Artillery. (Clark's *Regiments.*)

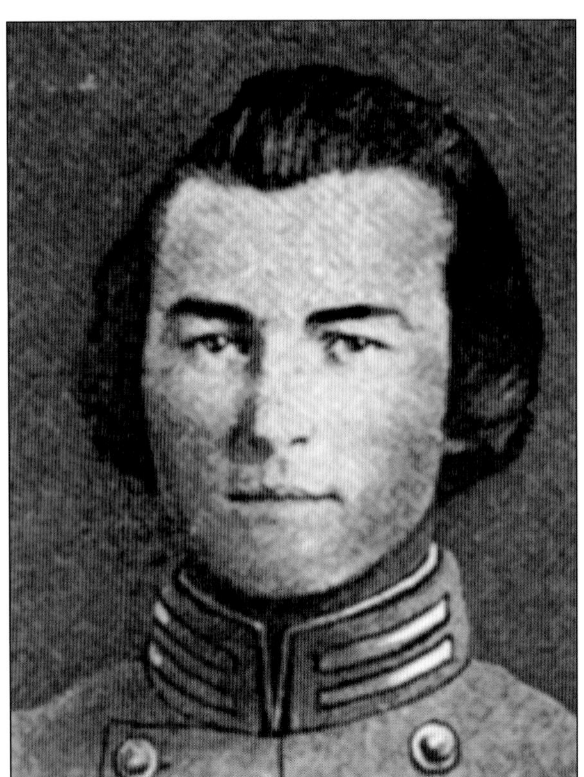

Pictured here is Capt. F.C. Frazier, Company A, 10th Battalion, North Carolina Heavy Artillery. (Clark's *Regiments.*)

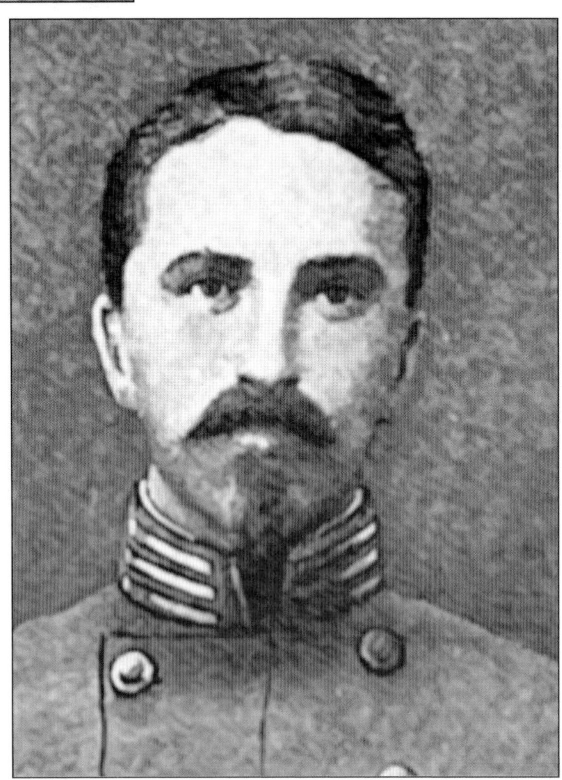

Capt. Woodbine Wheeler, Company D, 10th Battalion, North Carolina Heavy Artillery, is pictured here. (Clark's *Regiments.*)

William Rodman, shown here, was a captain with Company C, 40th North Carolina Regiment. (Clark's *Regiments.*)

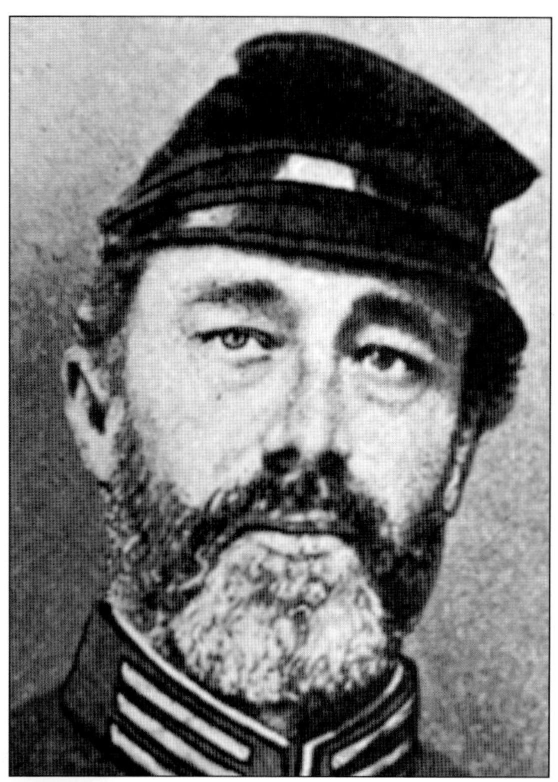

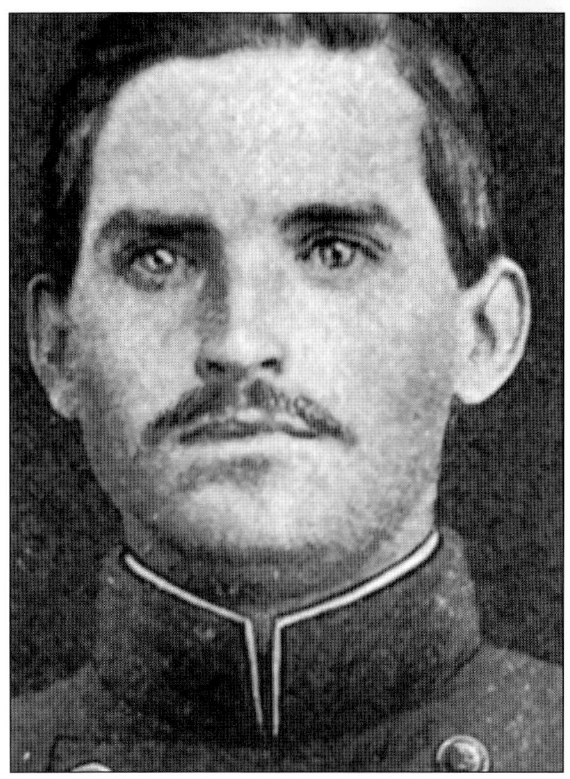

Sgt. T.C. Davis was a soldier with Company G, 40th North Carolina Regiment. (Clark's *Regiments.*)

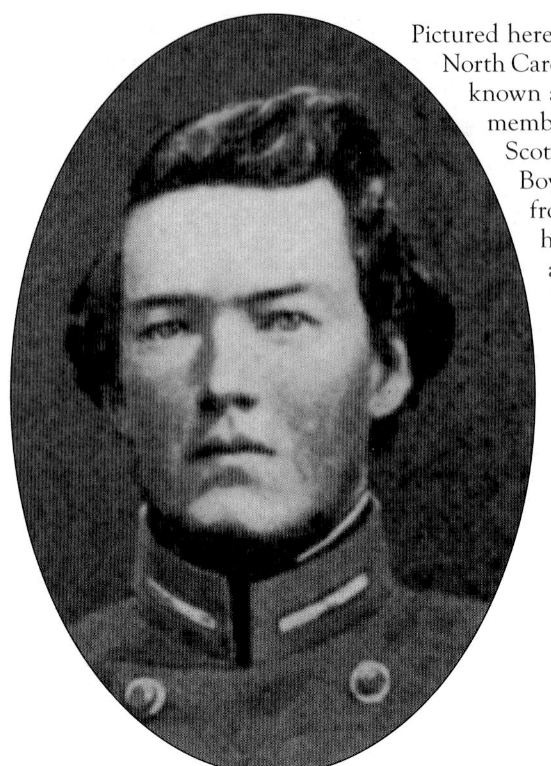

Pictured here is Lt. John W. Stewart of Company F, 8th North Carolina Regiment. The regiment was sometimes known as the "Scotch Boys" due to the fact that its members were recruited from among the former Scottish settlements in the Sandhills. The Scotch Boys were reputed to be the tallest unit to serve from either side during the war, with an average height a shade over six feet, one inch. The average height for Civil War–era soldiers was five feet, eight inches. (Clark's *Regiments.*)

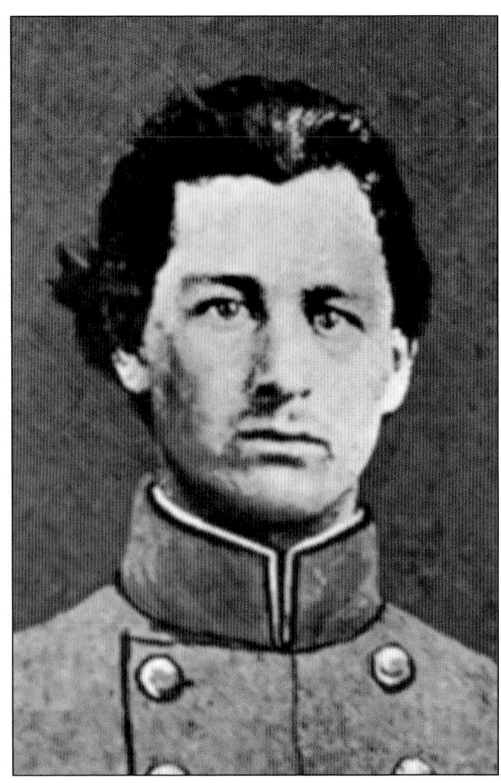

Pvt. J.L. McGimpsey was a member of Company B, 72nd North Carolina Regiment, 3rd Junior Reserves. (Clark's *Regiments.*)

This image shows Col. John Hinsdale, commander of the 72nd North Carolina Regiment, 3rd Junior Reserves. The 72nd played a key role in both battles at Fort Fisher. (Clark's *Regiments.*)

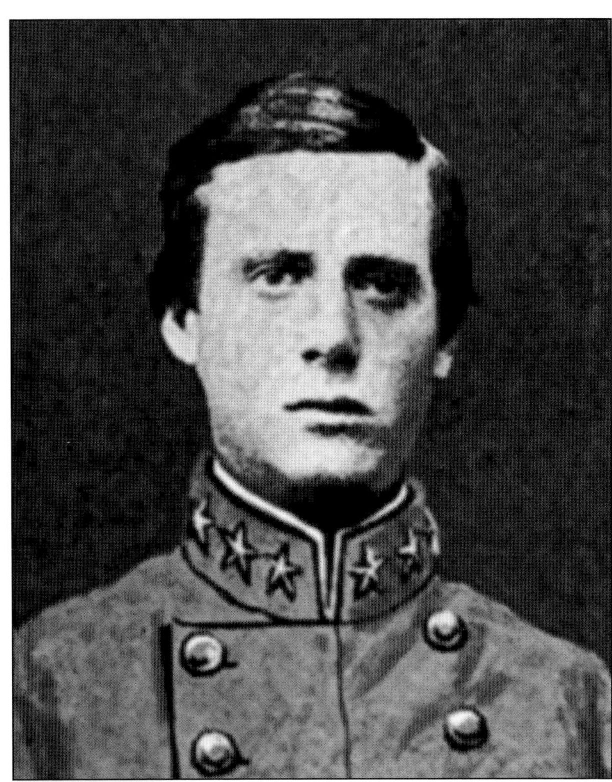

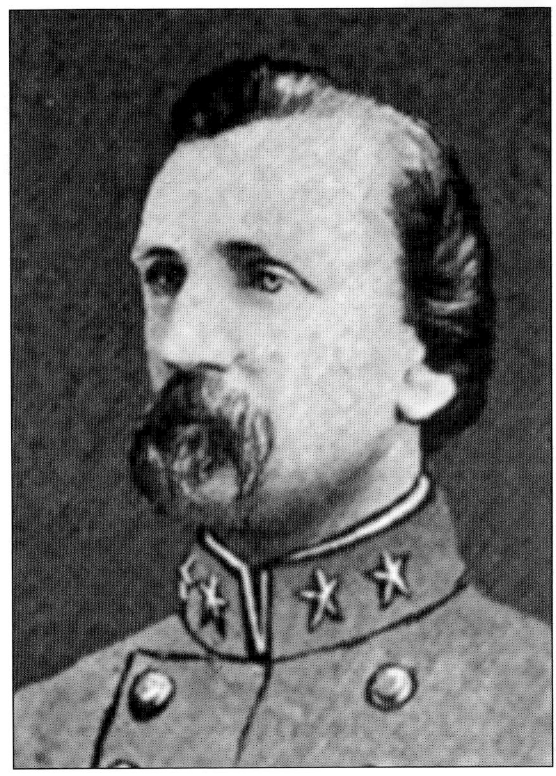

Lt. Col. W. Foster French served as second in command of the 72nd North Carolina Regiment, 3rd Junior Reserves. (Clark's *Regiments.*)

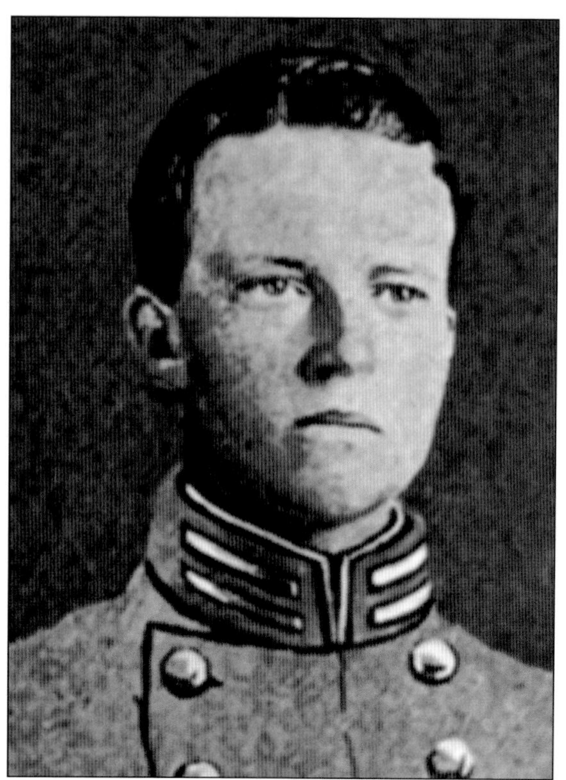

This image shows 1st Lt. W.W. King of Company A, 72nd North Carolina Regiment, 3rd Junior Reserves. (Clark's *Regiments.*)

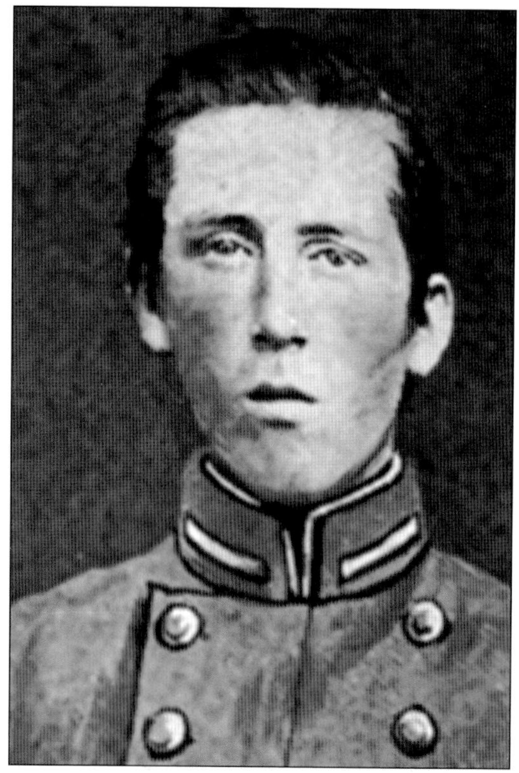

Pictured here is 2nd Lt. John W. Harper, Company C, 72nd North Carolina Regiment, 3rd Junior Reserves. (Clark's *Regiments.*)

This photograph shows 2nd Lt. H.W. Connelly, a member of Company C, 72nd North Carolina Regiment, 3rd Junior Reserves. (Clark's *Regiments.*)

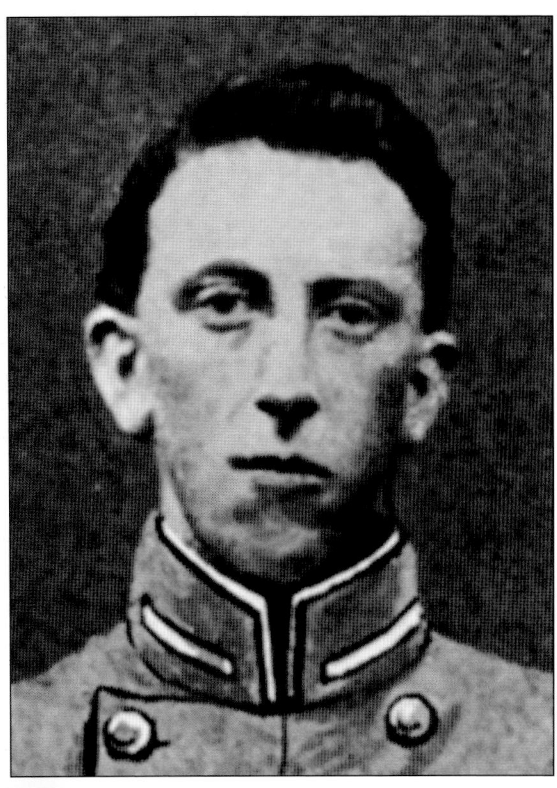

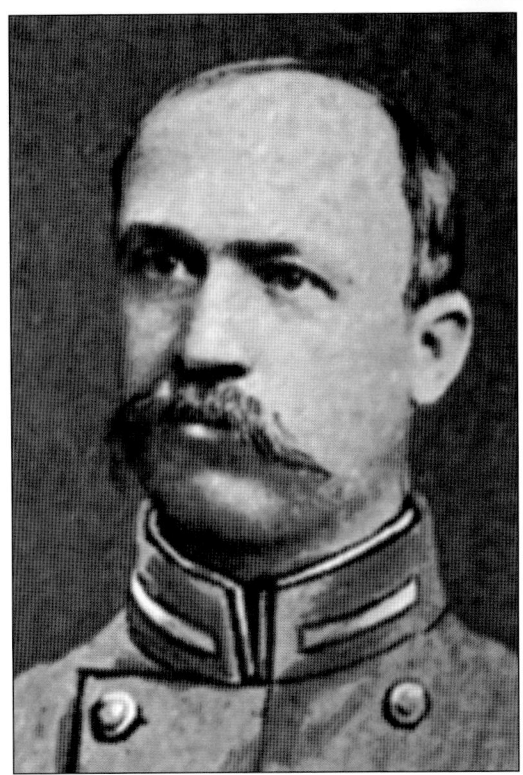

Pictured here is 2nd Lt. J.M. Bandy of Company E, 72nd North Carolina Regiment, 3rd Junior Reserves. (Clark's *Regiments.*)

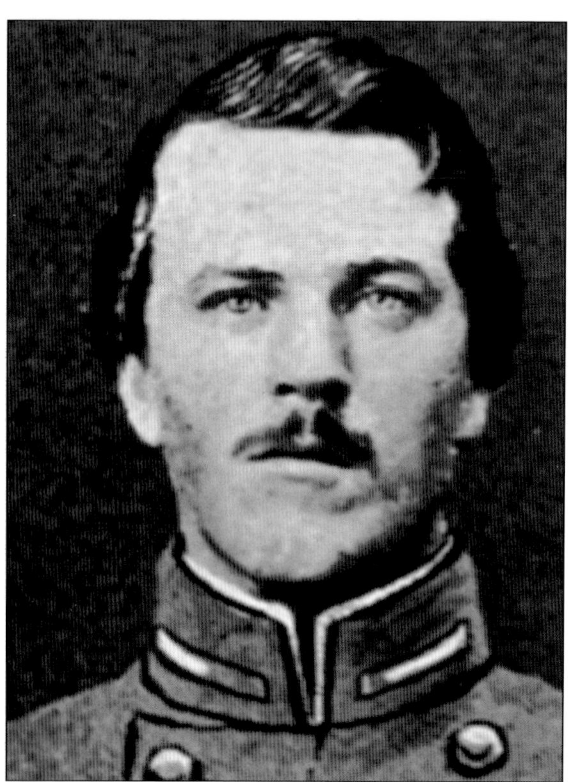

Pictured is 2nd Lt. D. S. Reid of Company K, 72nd North Carolina Regiment, 3rd Junior Reserves. (Clark's *Regiments.*)

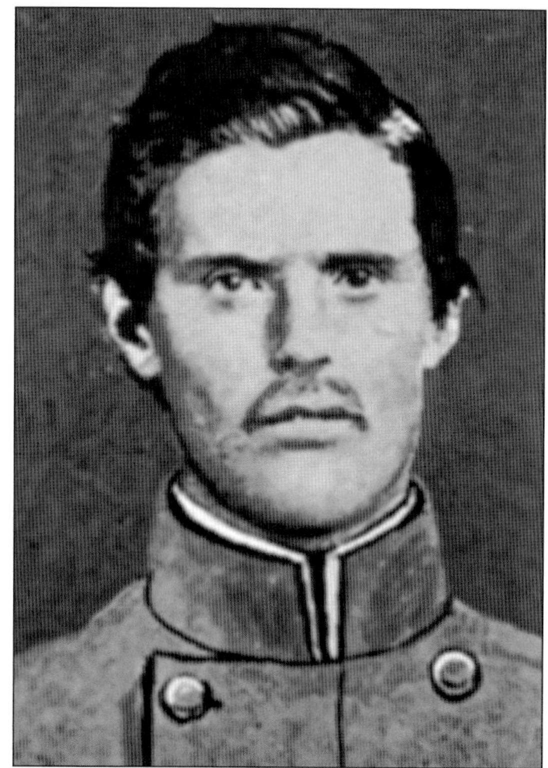

Orderly Sgt. C.W. Taylor, Company C, 72nd North Carolina Regiment, 3rd Junior Reserves, is pictured here. (Clark's *Regiments.*)

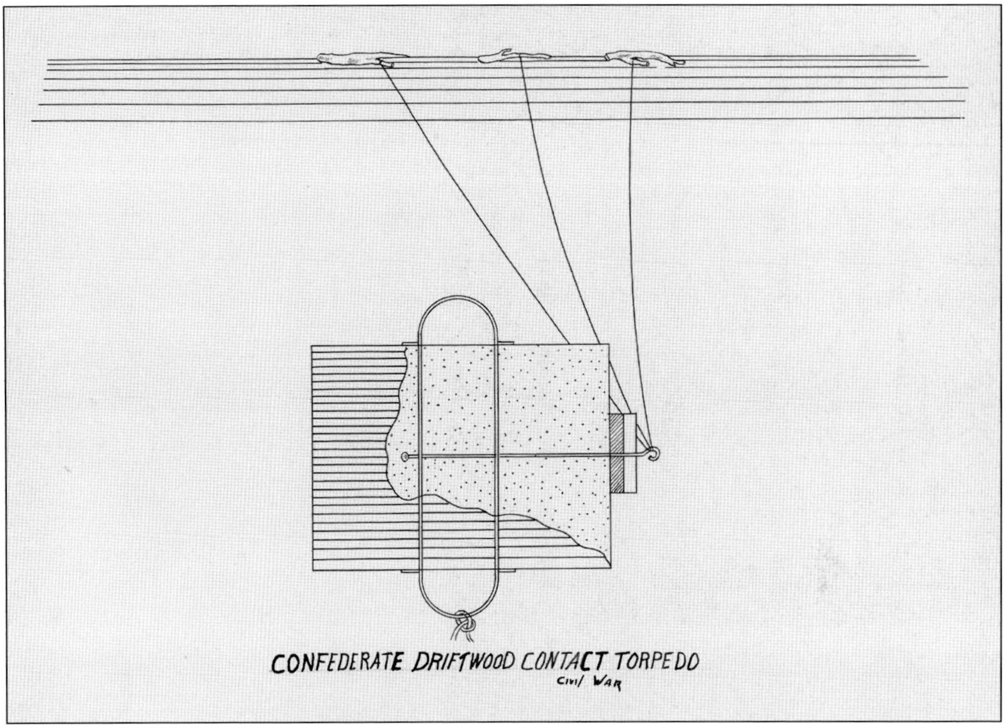

The Confederates were renowned for being pioneers in adapting electricity in the use of warfare and, by necessity, became experts at laying what is known today as antipersonnel land mines. They also used such technological marvels on water, like the "driftwood torpedo" pictured here. (US Naval History and Heritage Command.)

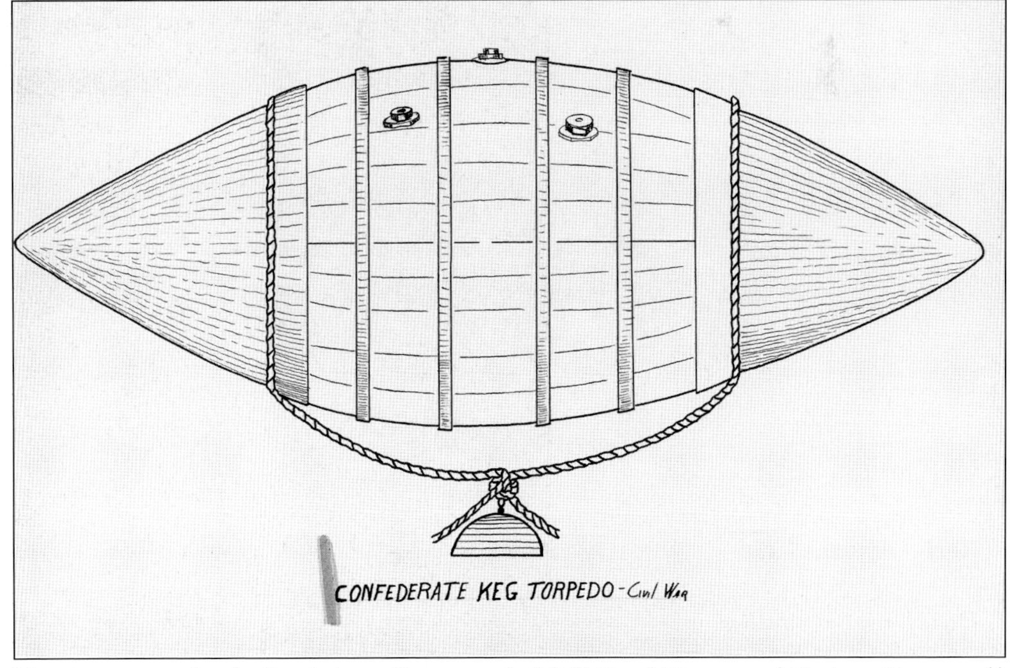

Here is an example of a Confederate "keg torpedo." (US Naval History and Heritage Command.)

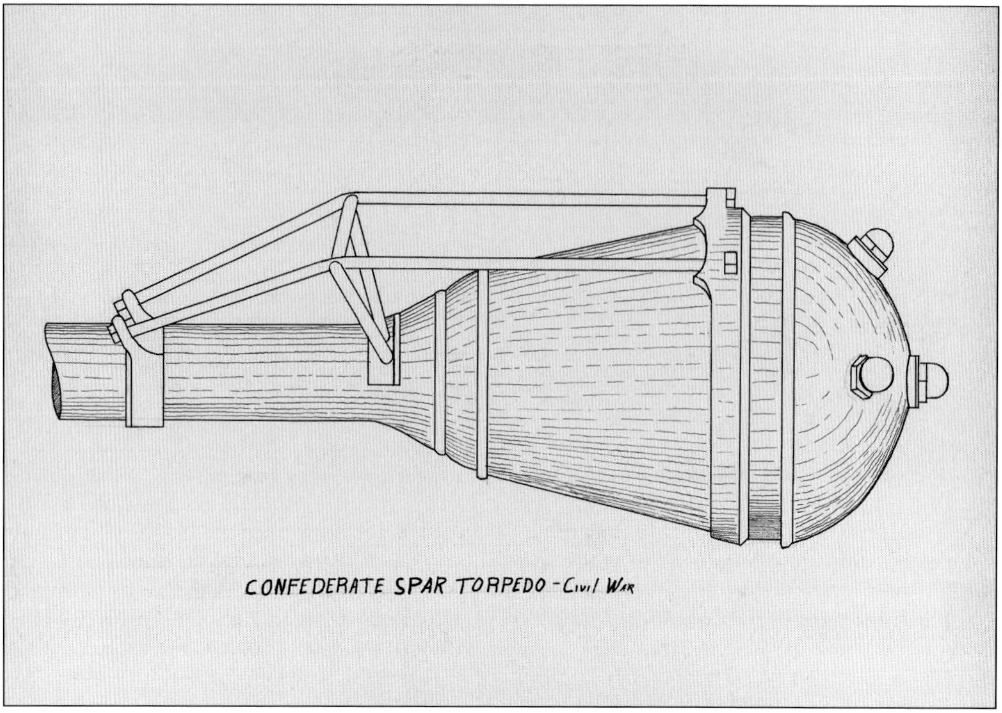

CONFEDERATE SPAR TORPEDO - Civil War

Confederate "spar torpedoes" were used by a small boat's crew and affixed manually to enemy vessels. (US Naval History and Heritage Command.)

CONFEDERATE ELECTRIC TORPEDO
Civil War

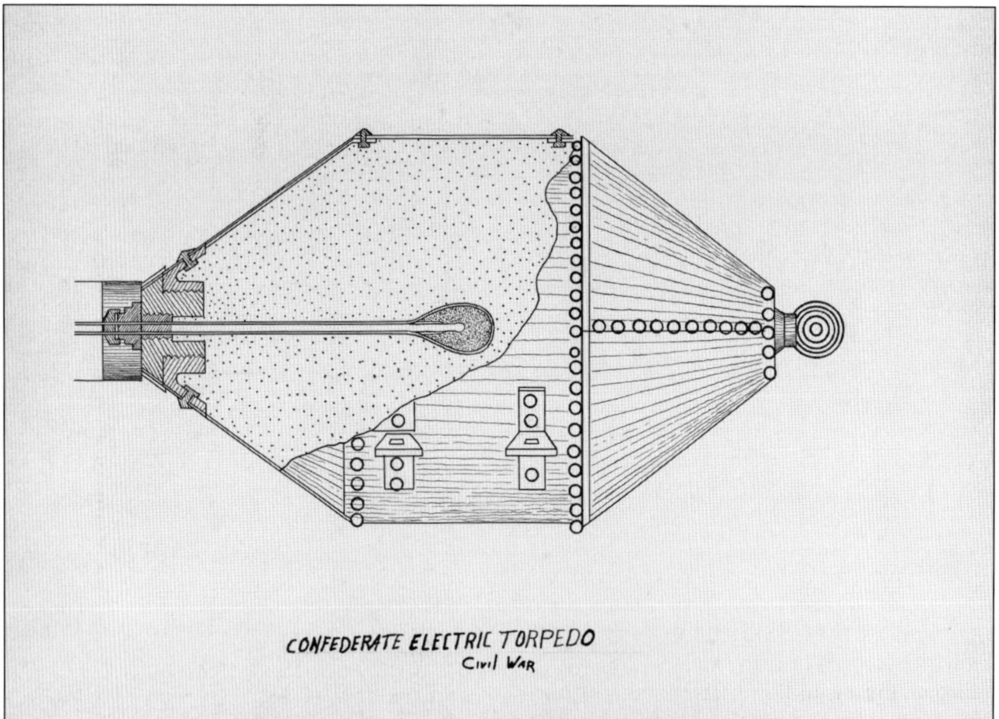

Here is an example of a Confederate "electronic torpedo." (US Naval History and Heritage Command.)

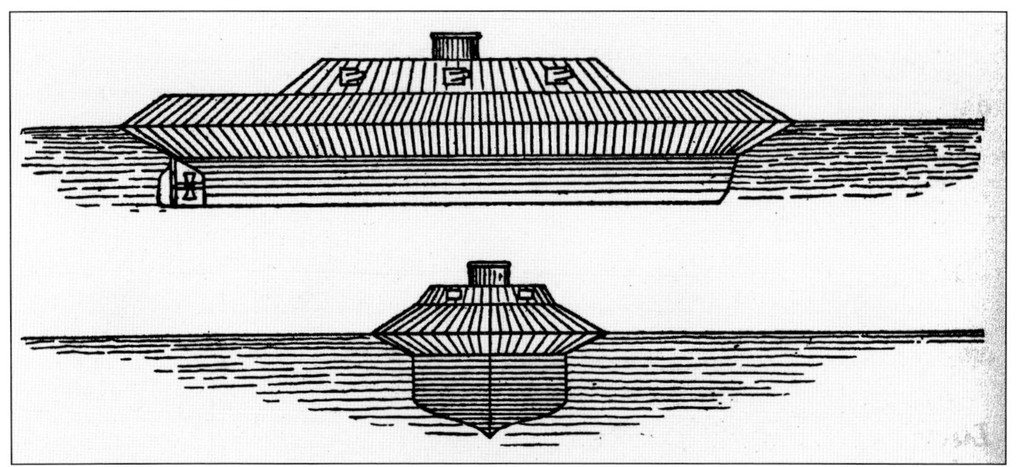

Another technological innovation employed by the Confederate high command to help defend the Port of Wilmington were ironclads, of which they met with limited success. The ironclad CSS *North Carolina* is shown above drawn by Union scouts reconnoitring the river. Though there were great plans for this ironclad to break up the blockade offshore, her designers made her draft deeper than either of the entrances to the Cape Fear River, so she was never able to make it to sea. She spent most of the war moored downstream near Battery Island, opposite Fort Pender and Southport. The ship's wooden framework became infested with teredo worms and sank just a few months before the first attack on Fort Fisher. Remains of the ill-fated ironclad still lie in the river opposite Southport. (ORN.)

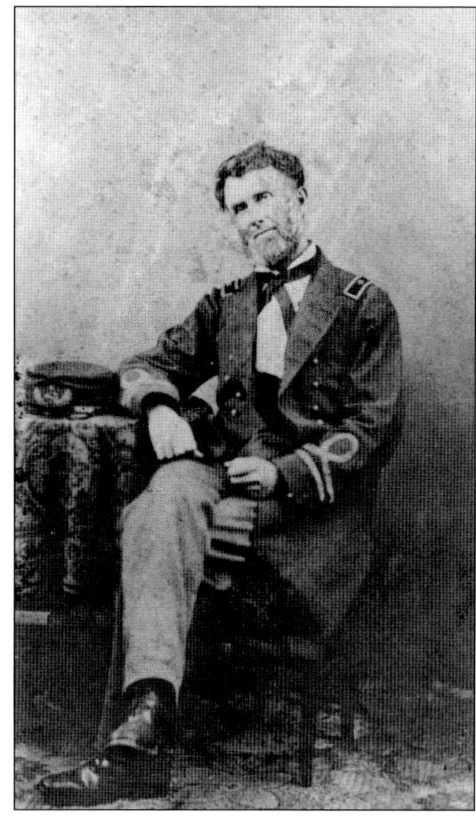

Comdr. William L. Maury is shown here in Cherbourg, France, in late 1863 while he was commanding the CSS *Georgia*. Maury served briefly as captain of the ironclad CSS *North Carolina*, but his military career was cut short after he was forced to retire due to rheumatism. (US Naval History and Heritage Command.)

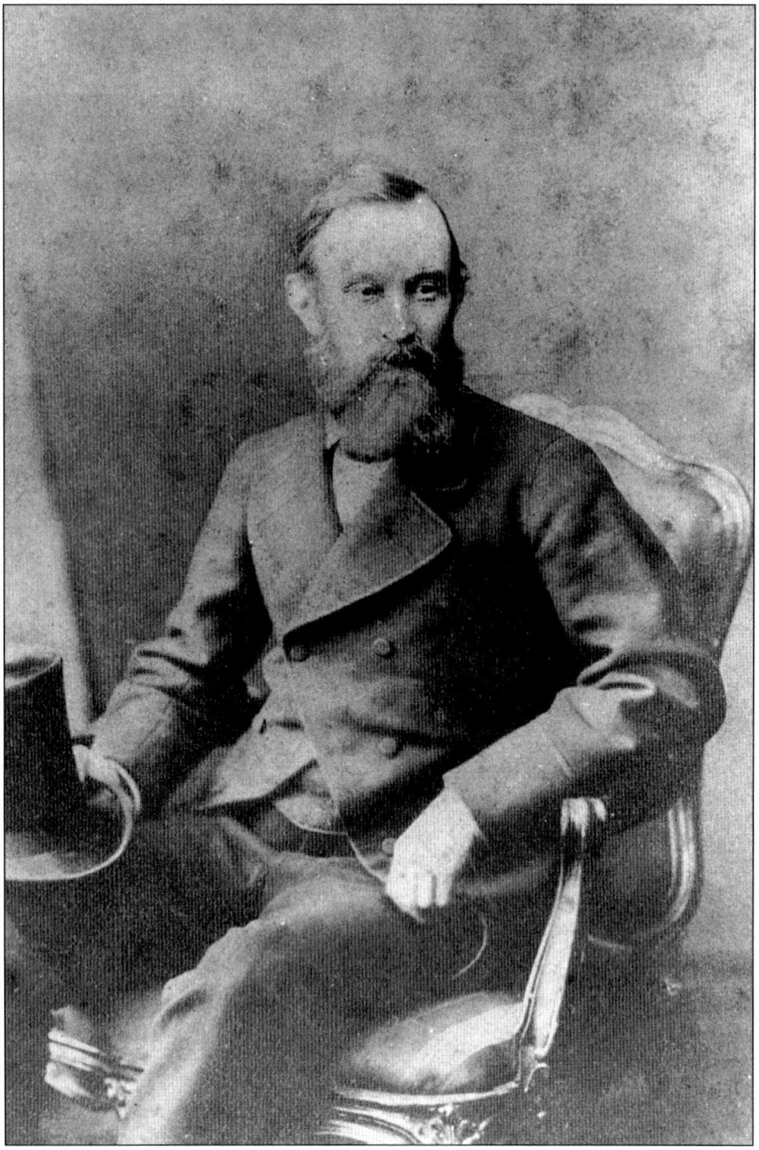

Capt. John Pembroke Jones has the distinction of losing two ironclads in the Cape Fear River. He initially served as captain of the ironclad CSS *Raleigh*, which wrecked on a sandbar in New Inlet returning from a foray against the blockading squadron in May 1864. After losing the *Raleigh*, Jones was placed in command of the CSS *North Carolina*, which sank from teredo worms four months later. (US Naval History and Heritage Command.)

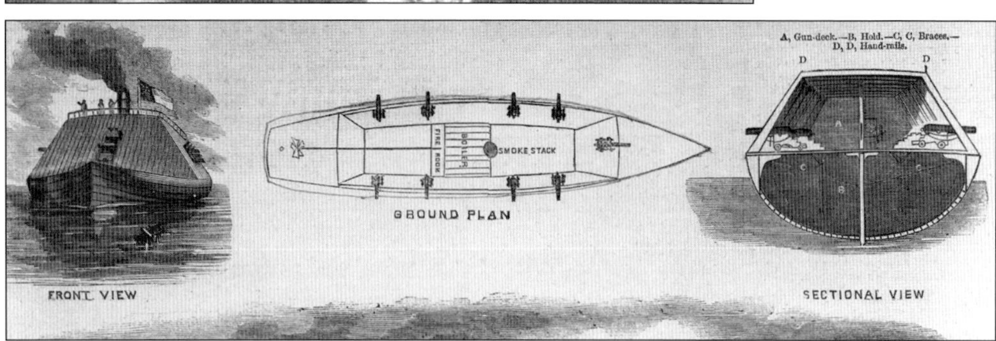

Both the CSS *North Carolina* and CSS *Raleigh* were considered Richmond-class ironclads whose designs were based on the CSS *Richmond*. (US Naval History and Heritage Command.)

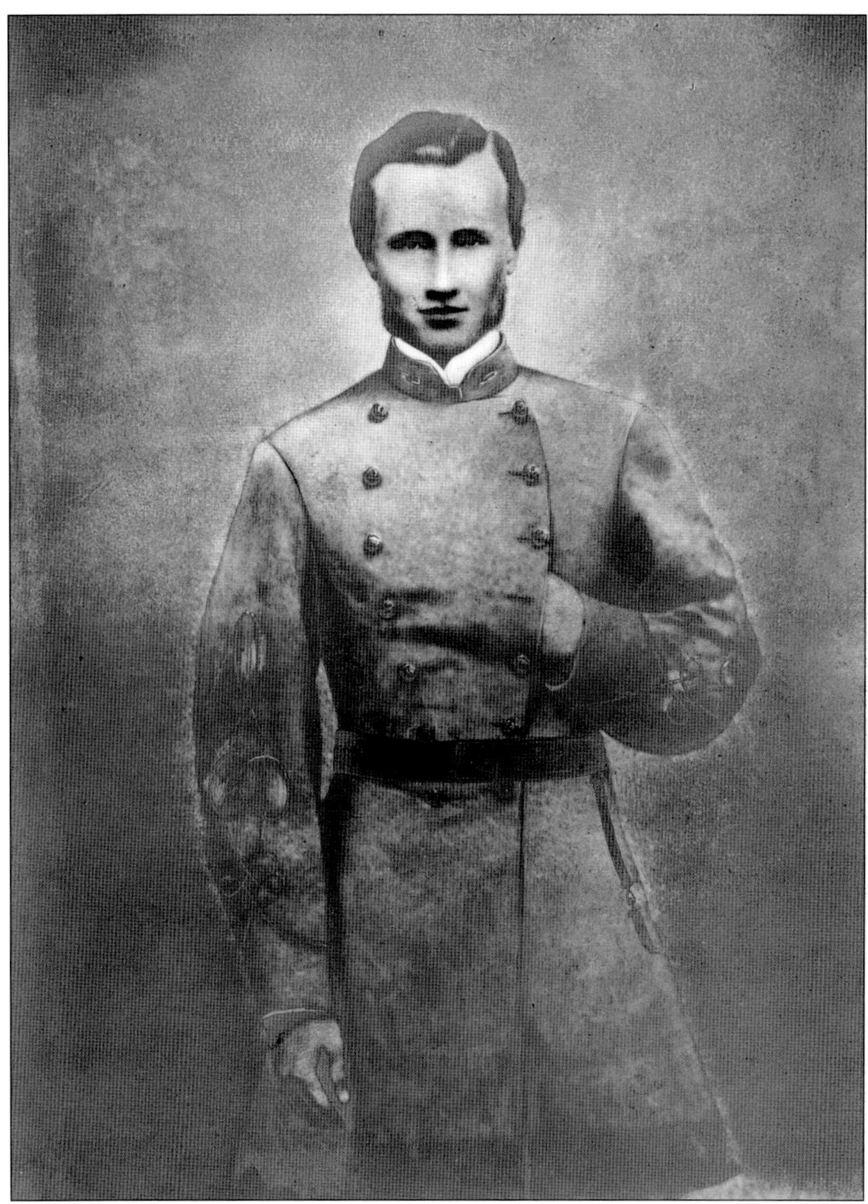

Lt. Henry Melville Doak was part of the contingent of Confederate States Marines assigned to help the naval forces operating out of Wilmington and was assigned to the CSS *Raleigh* when she made her attack off New Inlet in May 1864. While still getting used to conditions on the ironclad in the predawn darkness, the crew became disoriented, and the guns of the starboard battery inadvertently fired a shot, which landed inside Fort Fisher. Doak later wrote, "Receiving an order for my starboard gun to stand by for the next light, I threw a shell into Fort Fisher and was promptly ordered below under arrest by Admiral Lynch. Capt. Pembroke Jones, commanding the *Raleigh* convinced the Flag officer that the next light had gone by, leaving Ft. Fisher showing the next light by the time I received the order. I was promptly restored to duty." The Tennessean went on to serve with distinction during both battles of Fort Fisher, but he was often teased by his former comrades because he had the dubious distinction of discharging the only Confederate shots fired in combat at Fort Fisher. (Tennessee State Library & Archives.)

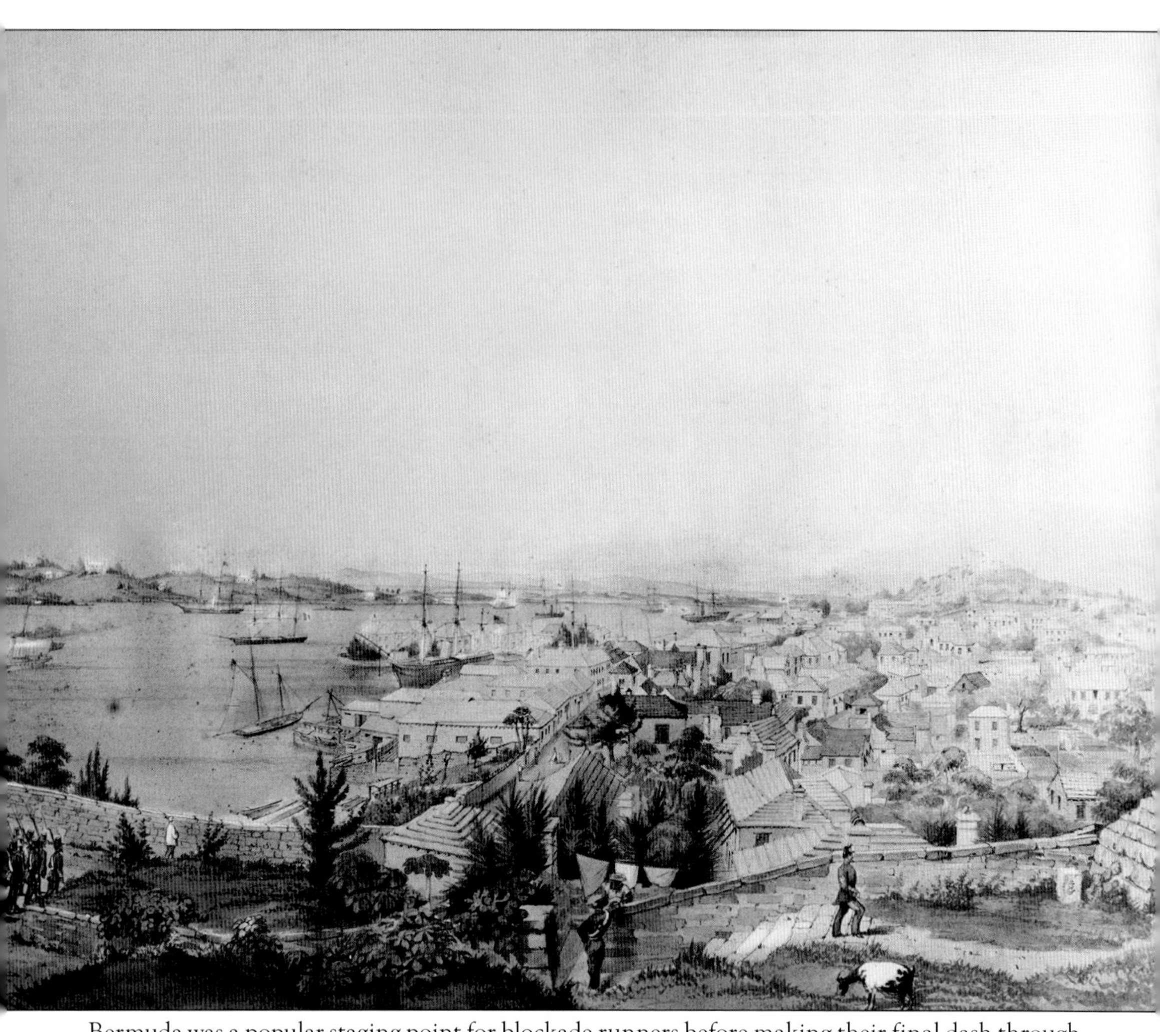

Bermuda was a popular staging point for blockade runners before making their final dash through the Union blockade. The defensive works at the mouth of the Cape Fear River, especially Fort Fisher, were a vital link in a water and rail network connecting the interior regions of not just North Carolina, but the entire Confederacy, especially the Confederate capital in Richmond. Valuable supplies originating mainly from factories in Europe came through the Port of Wilmington. This was not just war materiel, but included other items that made the war a bit more bearable for the civilians who were suffering the effects of the Federal blockade of the Southern coast. Many of the captains of these blockade runners became famous for their daring runs between staging grounds like Bermuda and the Bahamas through the blockade into Wilmington. Though they were sometimes controversial, without their services the South could not have held out against their numerically superior adversaries as well as they did. (US Naval History and Heritage Command.)

Two

Some Blockade Runners

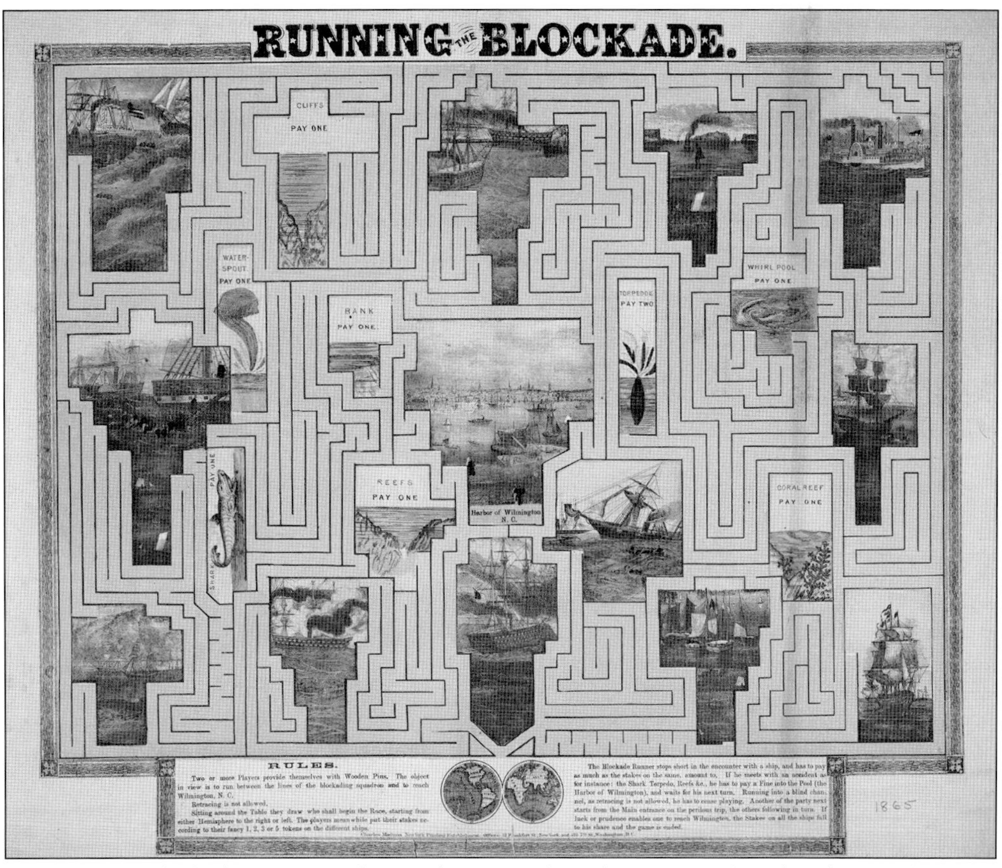

Running the Blockade was a popular Civil War–era board game. Developed and printed in New York City by Charles Magnus Printing in 1864, this game demonstrates how the daring exploits of the blockade runners captured the popular imagination, even in the North. (North Carolina Collection Photographic Archives, Wilson Special Collections Library, University of North Carolina at Chapel Hill.)

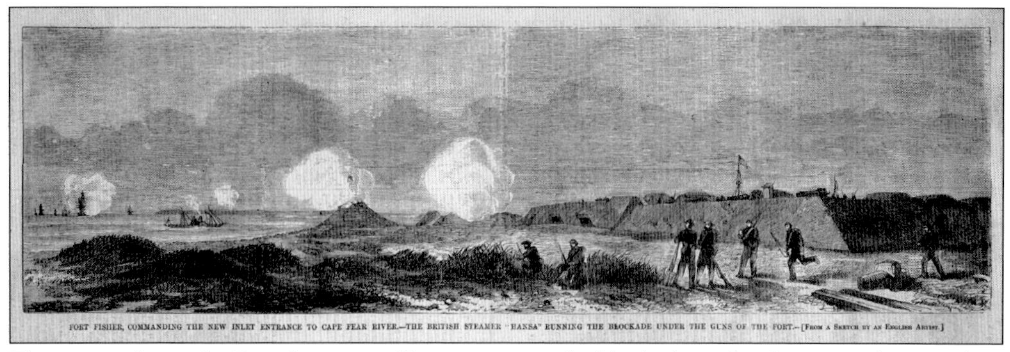

FORT FISHER, COMMANDING THE NEW INLET ENTRANCE TO CAPE FEAR RIVER.—THE BRITISH STEAMER "HANSA" RUNNING THE BLOCKADE UNDER THE GUNS OF THE FORT.—[FROM A SKETCH BY AN ENGLISH ARTIST.]

This image shows the British steamer *Hansa* running the blockade under the guns of Fort Fisher. (North Carolina Archives and History.)

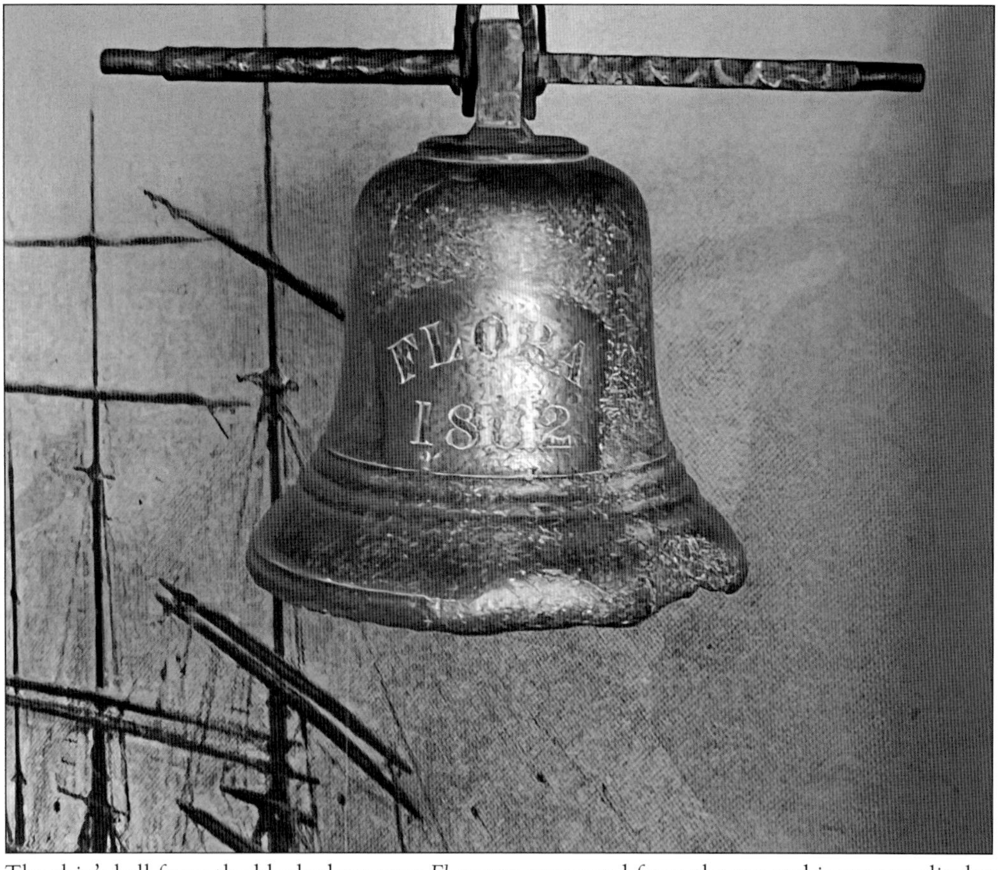

The ship's bell from the blockade runner *Flora* was recovered from the sea and is now on display at the Cape Fear Museum in Wilmington.

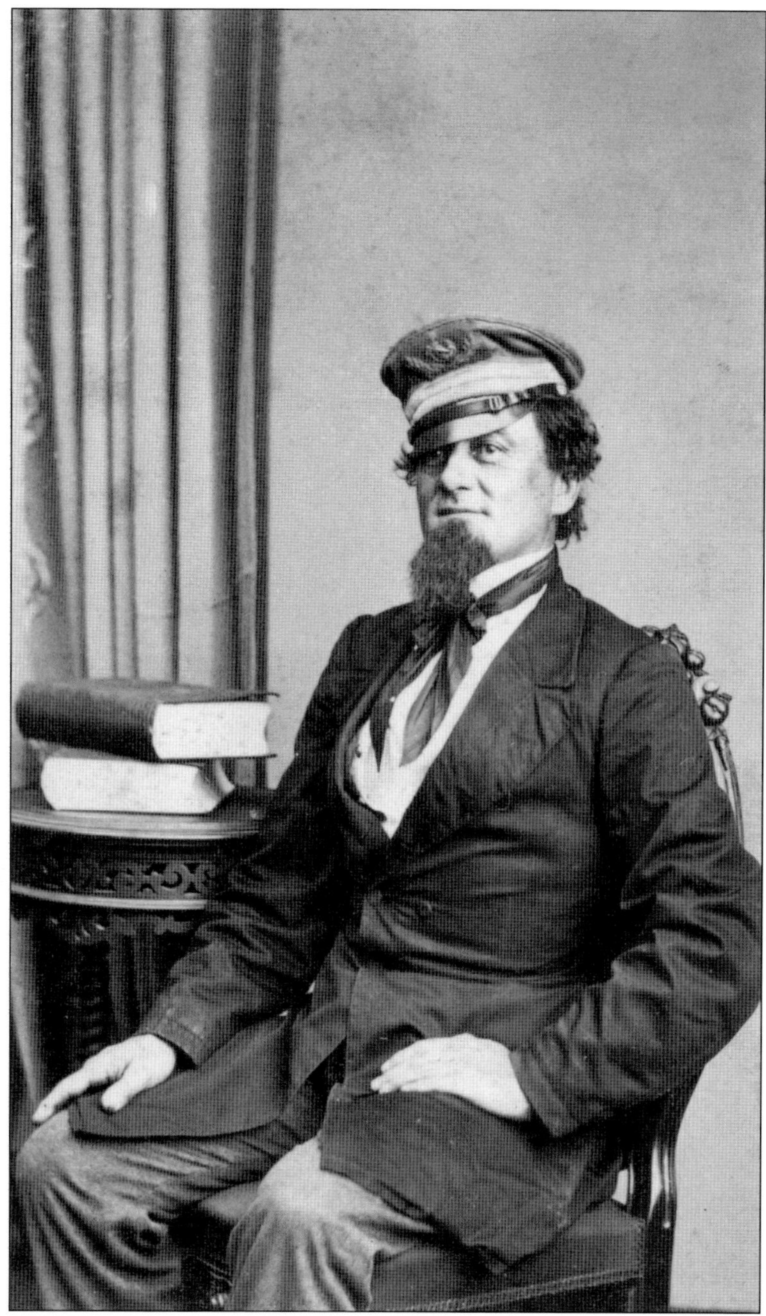

Capt. John Newland Maffitt was an expert mariner who was literally born at sea while his parents were emigrating from Ireland in 1819. He was adopted by his uncle, Dr. William Maffitt, and grew up in Cumberland County near Fayetteville, North Carolina. The younger Maffitt became a midshipman in the US Navy and gained intricate knowledge of the local waters, including the Cape Fear, thanks to his assignment with the US Coast Survey before the war. Though he is best remembered as the captain of warships such as the CSS *Florida* and the CSS *Albemarle*, Maffitt skippered many ships, including the *Owl*, the *Florrie*, and the *Lillian*, through the blockade with much-needed supplies for the Confederate government. (LOC.)

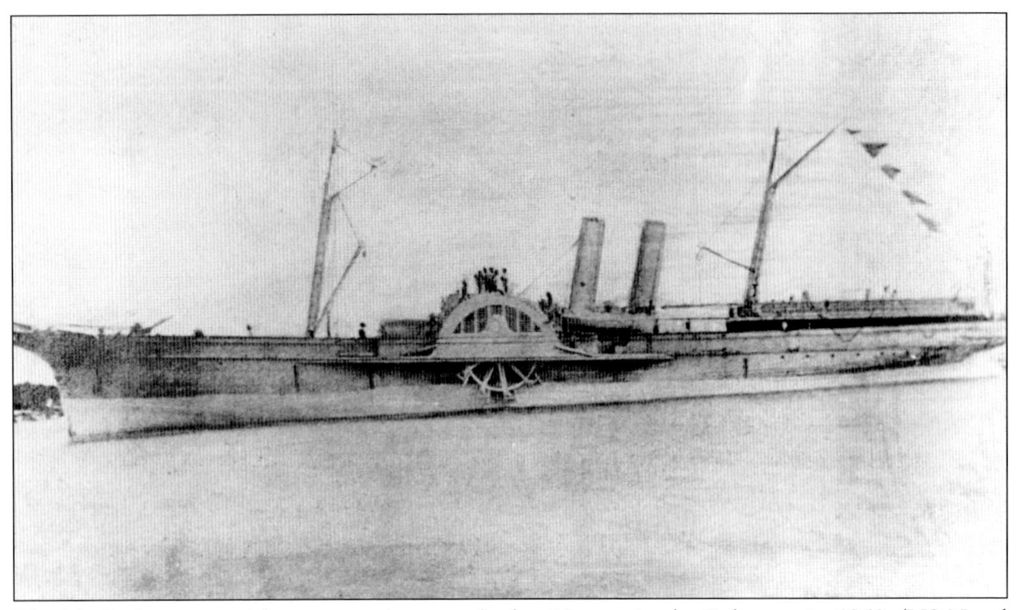

The blockade runner *Advance* was photographed at Nassau in the Bahamas in 1863. (US Naval History and Heritage Command.)

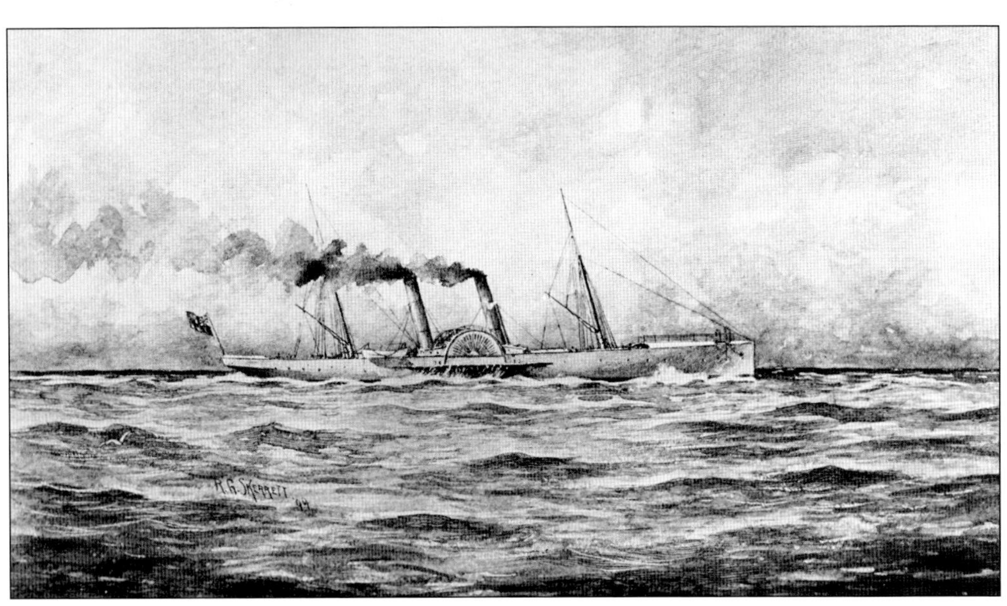

The blockade runner *Banshee* is pictured here. (US Naval History and Heritage Command.)

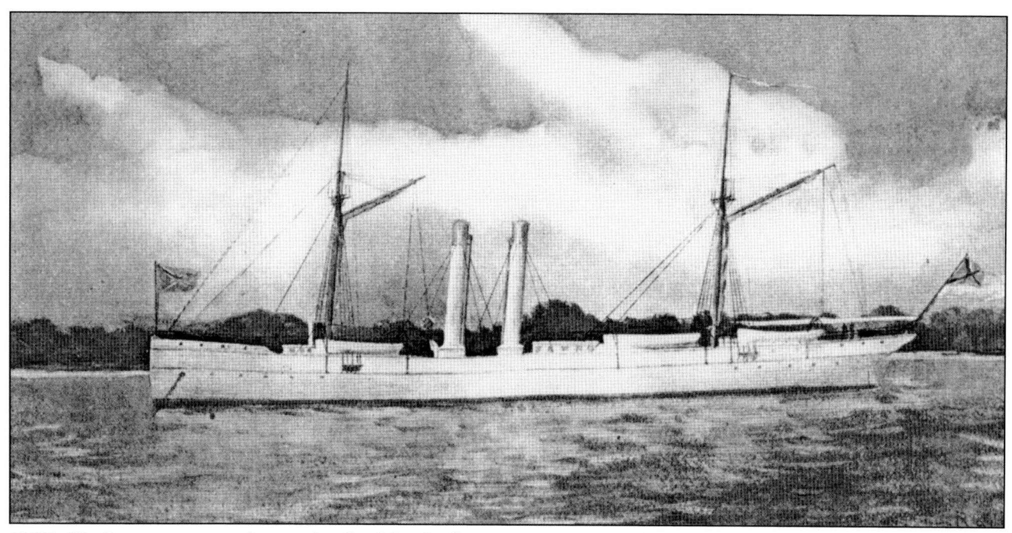

CSS *Chickamauga* was formerly the blockade runner *Edith*. The crew from the cruiser saw much action during the first battle at Fort Fisher. The ship was also used extensively during the second battle. Trapped in the river, unable to escape to the high seas to carry on the fight another day, she headed upstream, making it as far as the Indian Wells in Bladen County. (US Naval History and Heritage Command.)

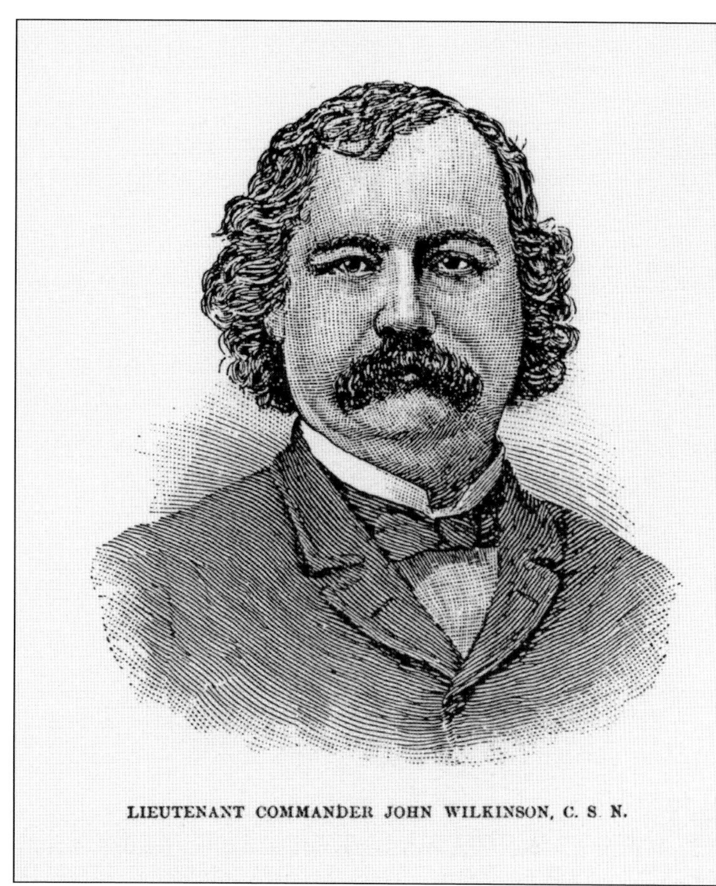

LIEUTENANT COMMANDER JOHN WILKINSON, C. S. N.

Lt. Comdr. John Wilkinson was the *Chickamauga*'s captain during her only raid against enemy shipping along the New England coast in the fall of 1864. He was away on a blockade running mission during both battles at Fort Fisher.

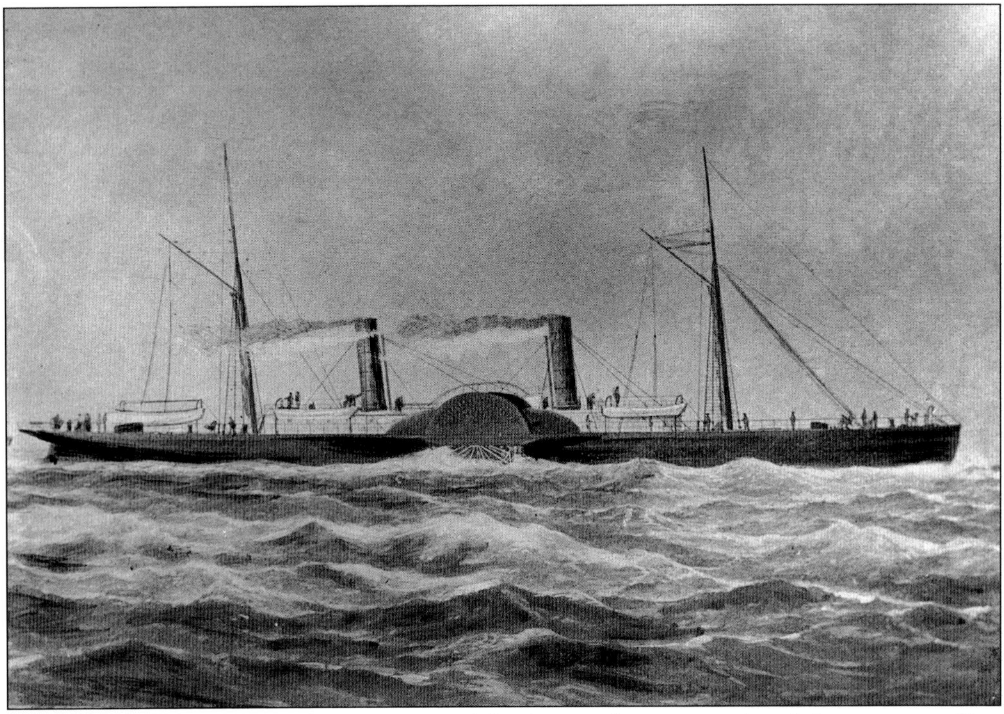

The blockade runner *Colonel Lamb* was named for the popular commander of the garrison at Fort Fisher. (US Naval History and Heritage Command.)

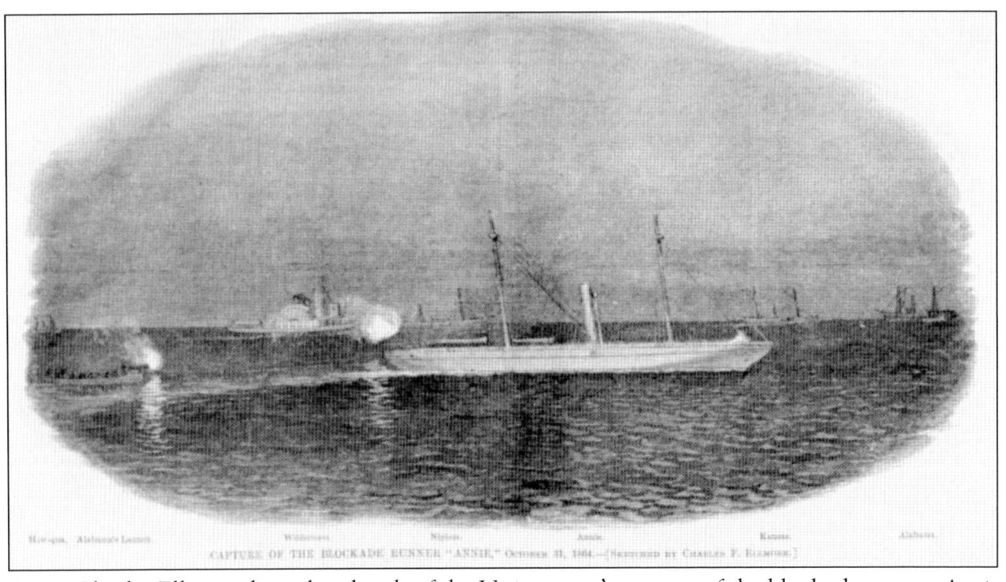

Artist Charles Ellmore drew this sketch of the Union navy's capture of the blockade runner *Annie* off New Inlet on October 31,1864. The sketch appeared in *Harper's Weekly*.

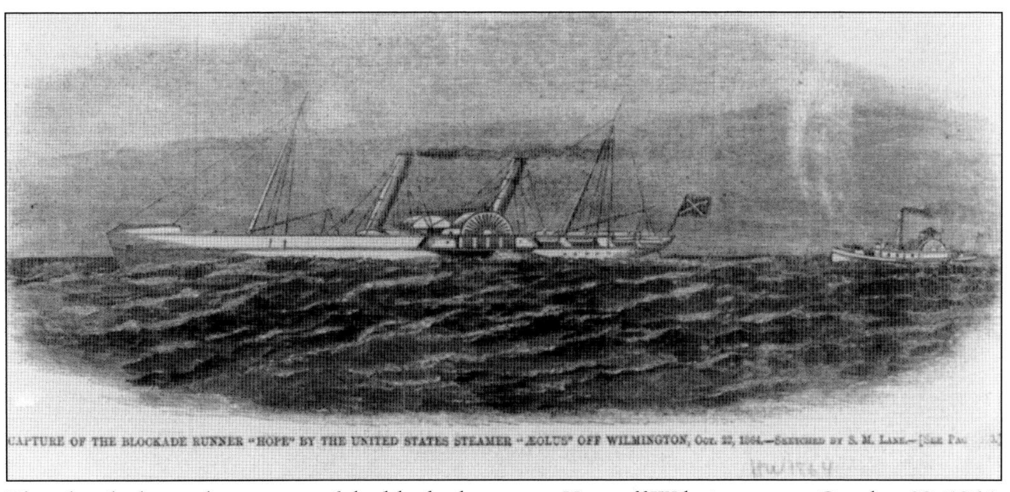

This sketch shows the capture of the blockade runner *Hope* off Wilmington on October 22, 1864, by the USS *Aeolus*. (LOC.)

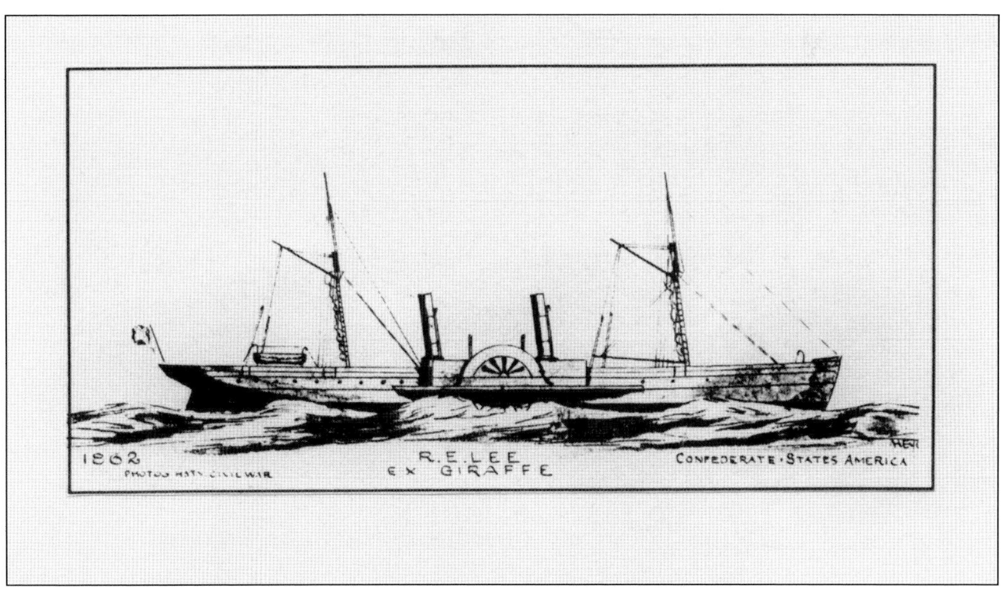

The blockade runner *R.E. Lee* was named for the popular general of the Army of Northern Virginia. (North Carolina Archives and History.)

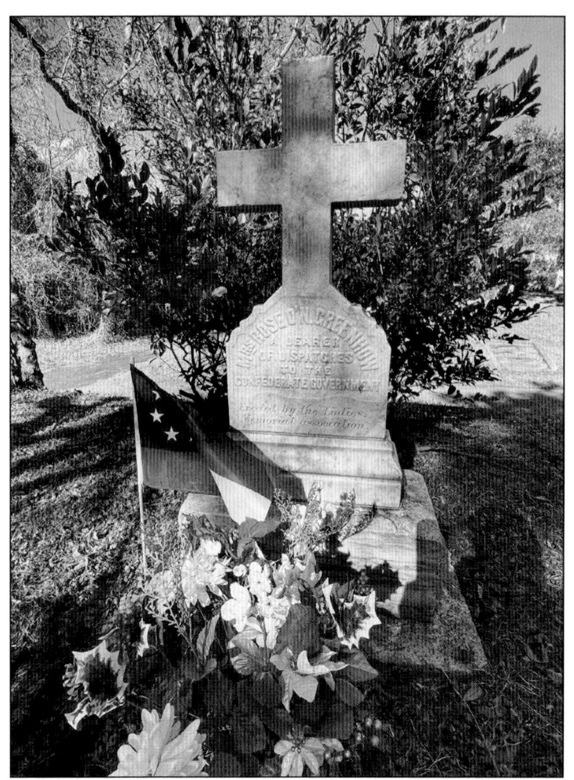

Following her funeral in St. Thomas the Apostle Church, the remains of Rose O'Neill Greenhow were buried here in Oakdale Cemetery. Her grave was later marked by the Ladies Memorial Association with the marble cross shown here.

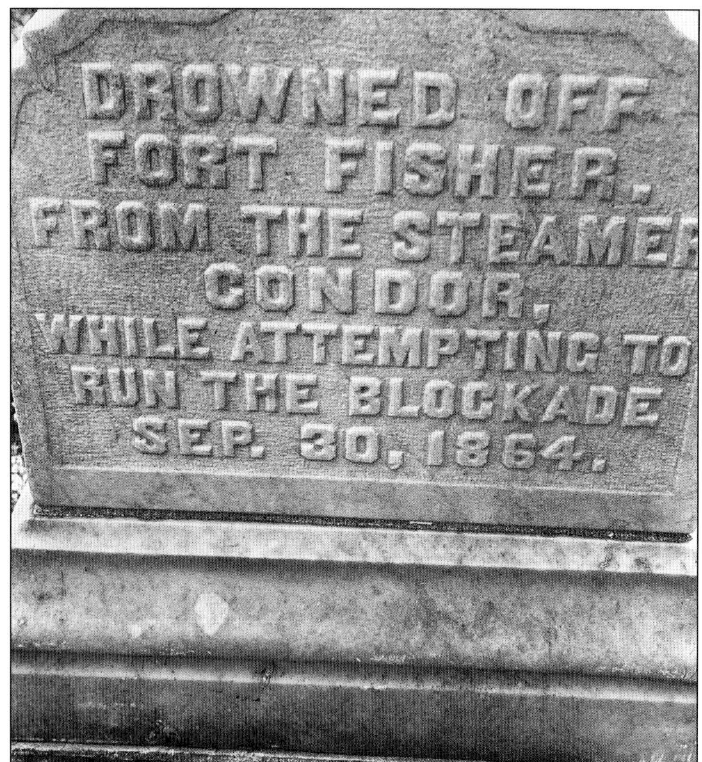

The reverse of Rose O'Neill Greenhow's tombstone gives a few details of how the famed Confederate spy met her end off Fort Fisher.

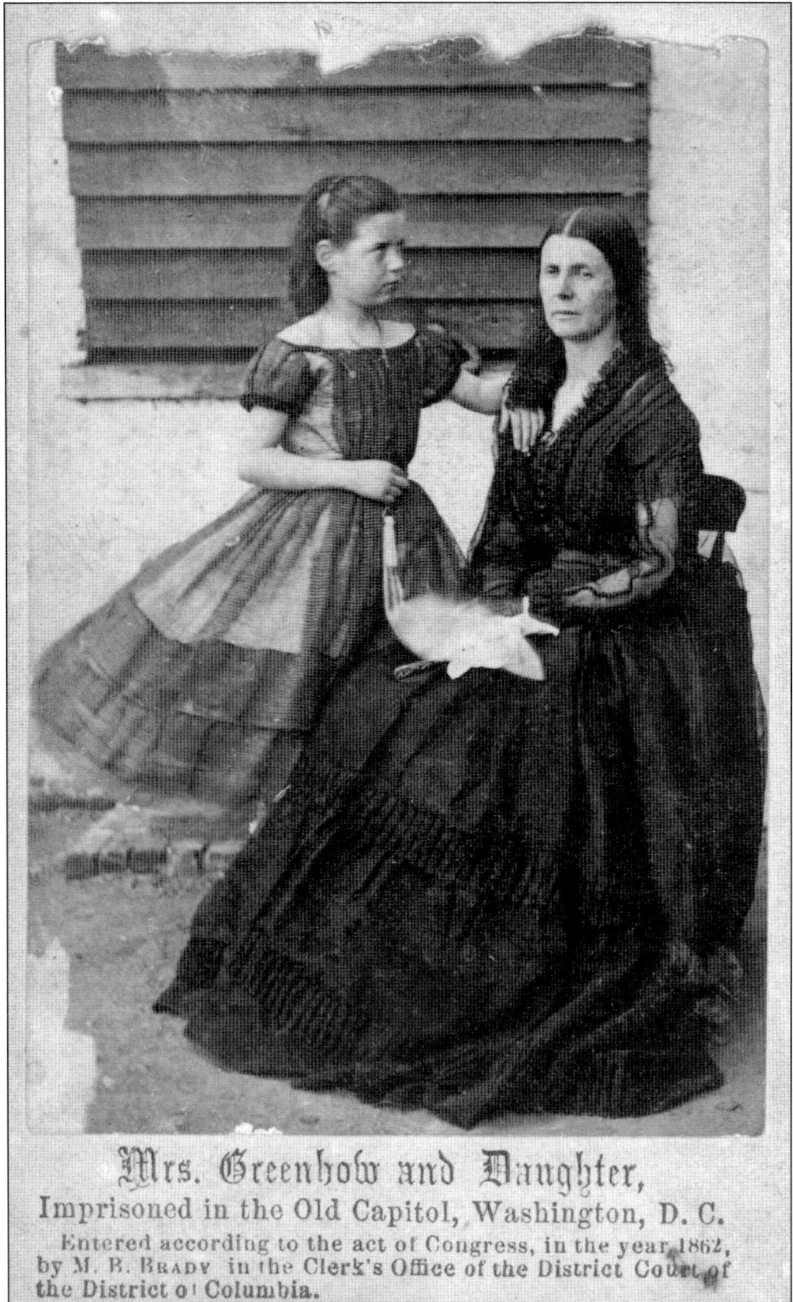

The famous Confederate spy Rose O'Neill Greenhow is shown here in a photograph with her daughter Little Rose in the Old Capital Prison in Washington, DC. Though she mainly operated in Maryland and Northern Virginia, Greenhow made a trip to Europe to raise funds for the war effort as well as to promote her own literary endeavours. Her adventurous life came to a tragic end off Fort Fisher when the blockade runner upon which she was returning home to the Confederacy, the *Condor*, wrecked just off New Inlet in the wee hours of the morning of October 1, 1864. According to local legend, she was unable to swim because she had sewn gold into the lining of her dress. (LOC.)

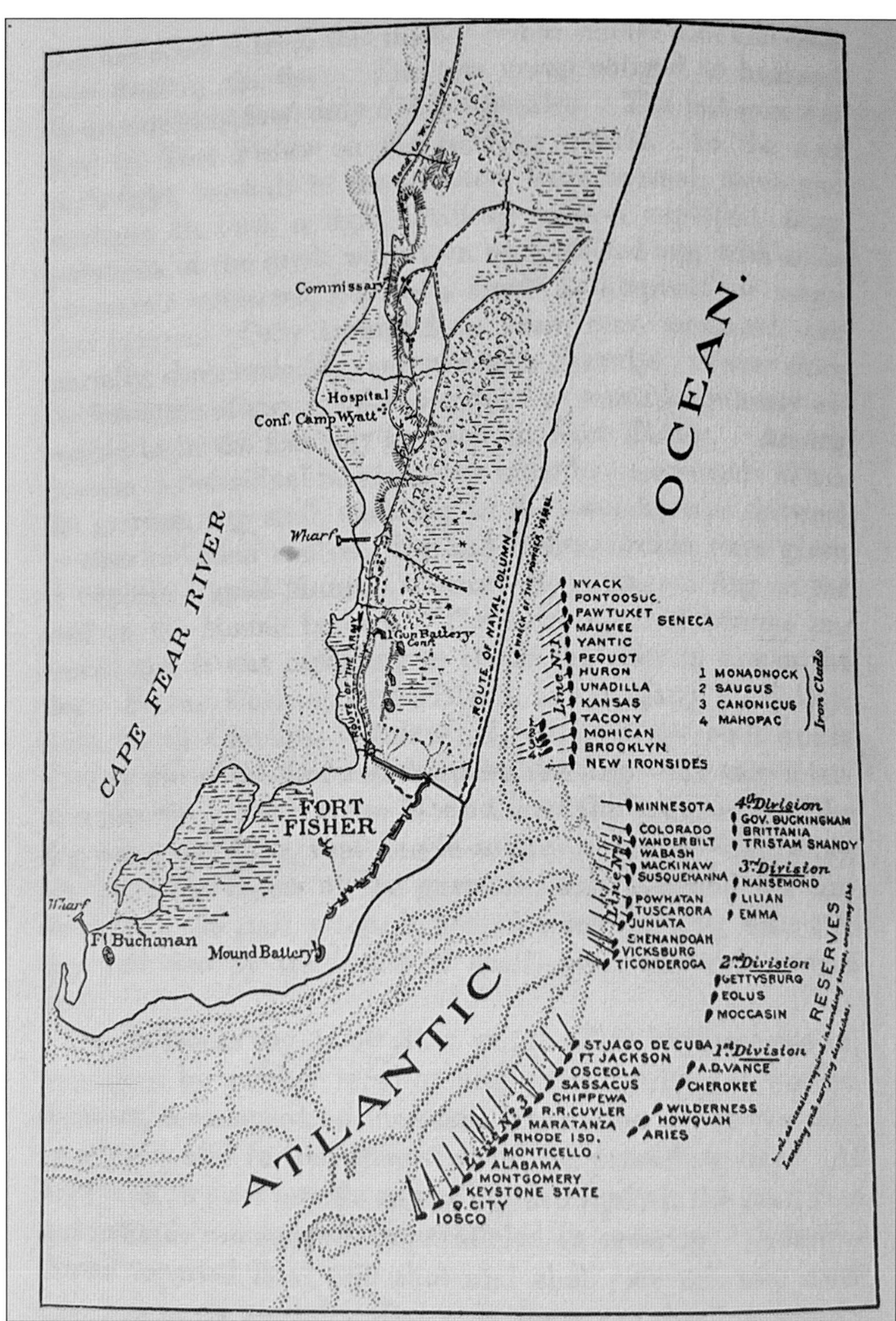

Walter Clark included this map of the attack on Fort Fisher in his book *Several Regiments and Battalions from North Carolina in the Civil War.* Note the position of the powder vessel adjacent to the fort. (Clark's *Regiments.*)

Three

First Battle of Fort Fisher in December 1864

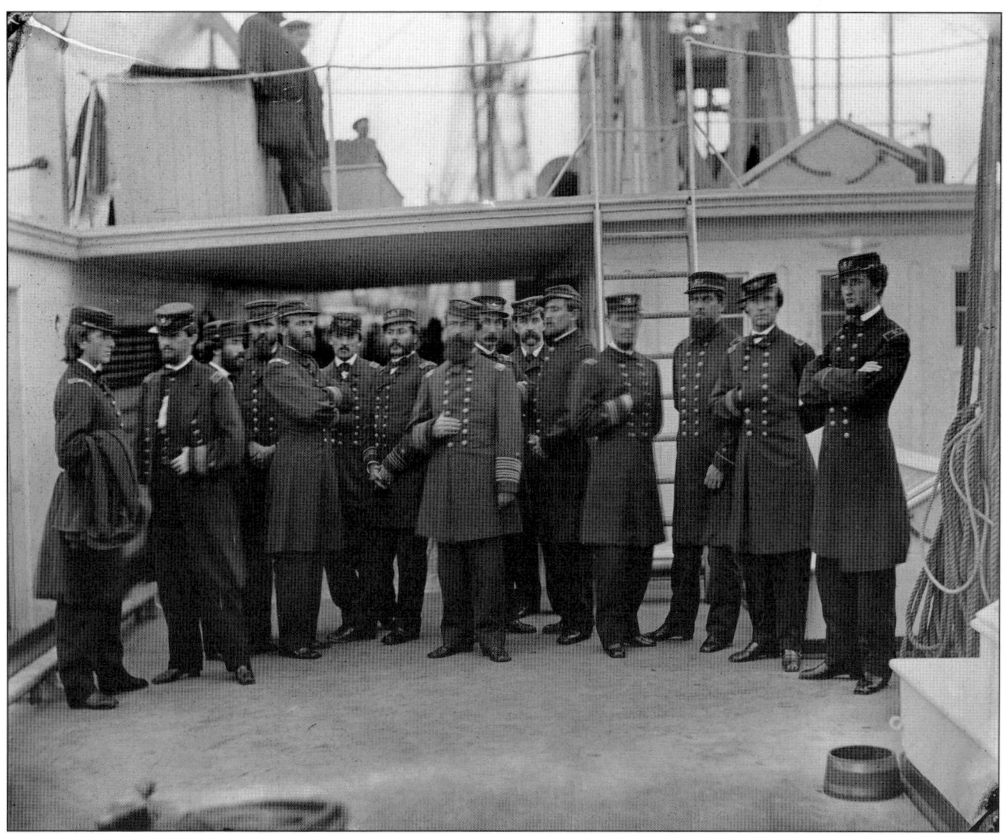

Rear Adm. David Porter is meeting with his staff in December 1864 aboard his flagship, the USS *Malvern*, at Hampton Roads, Virginia. The Union high command decided it was time to close the Confederacy's main outlet to the sea, so he put together a joint army/navy expedition to take out Fort Fisher. (LOC.)

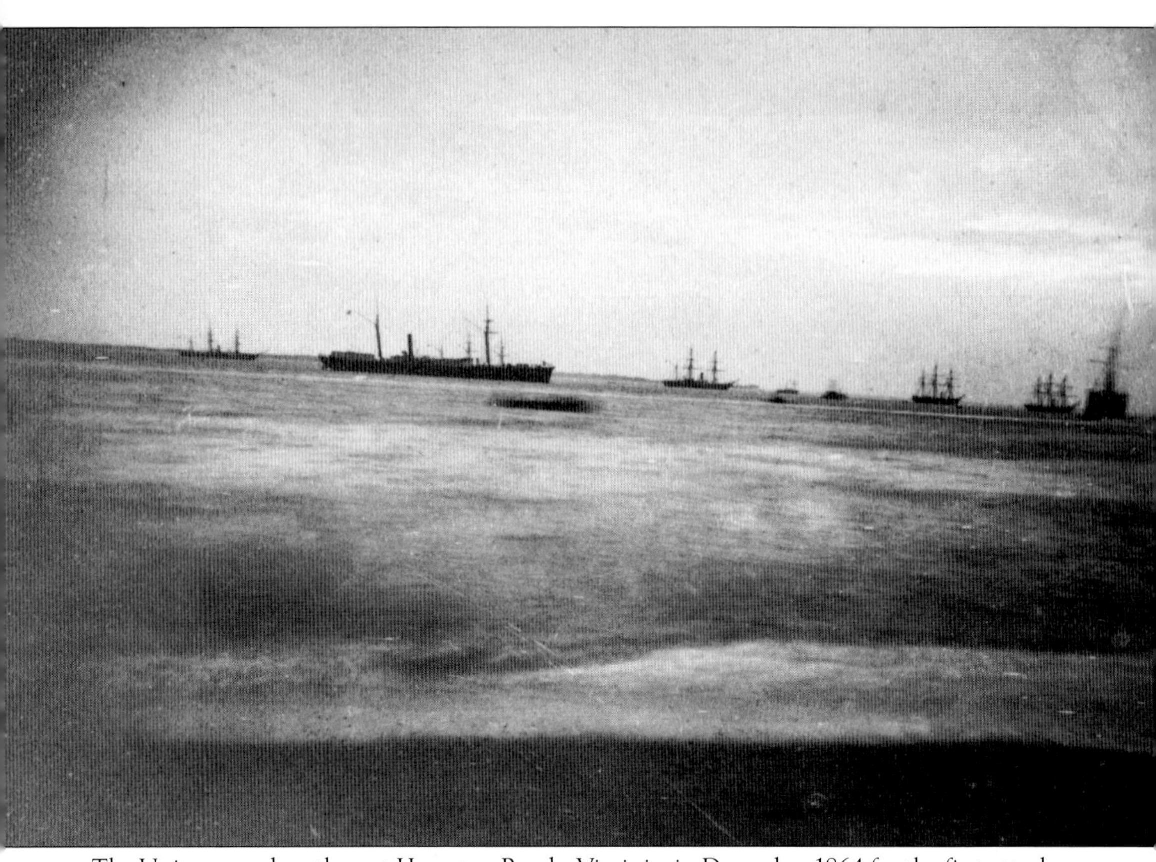

The Union armada gathers at Hampton Roads, Virginia, in December 1864 for the first attack on Fort Fisher. (National Archives.)

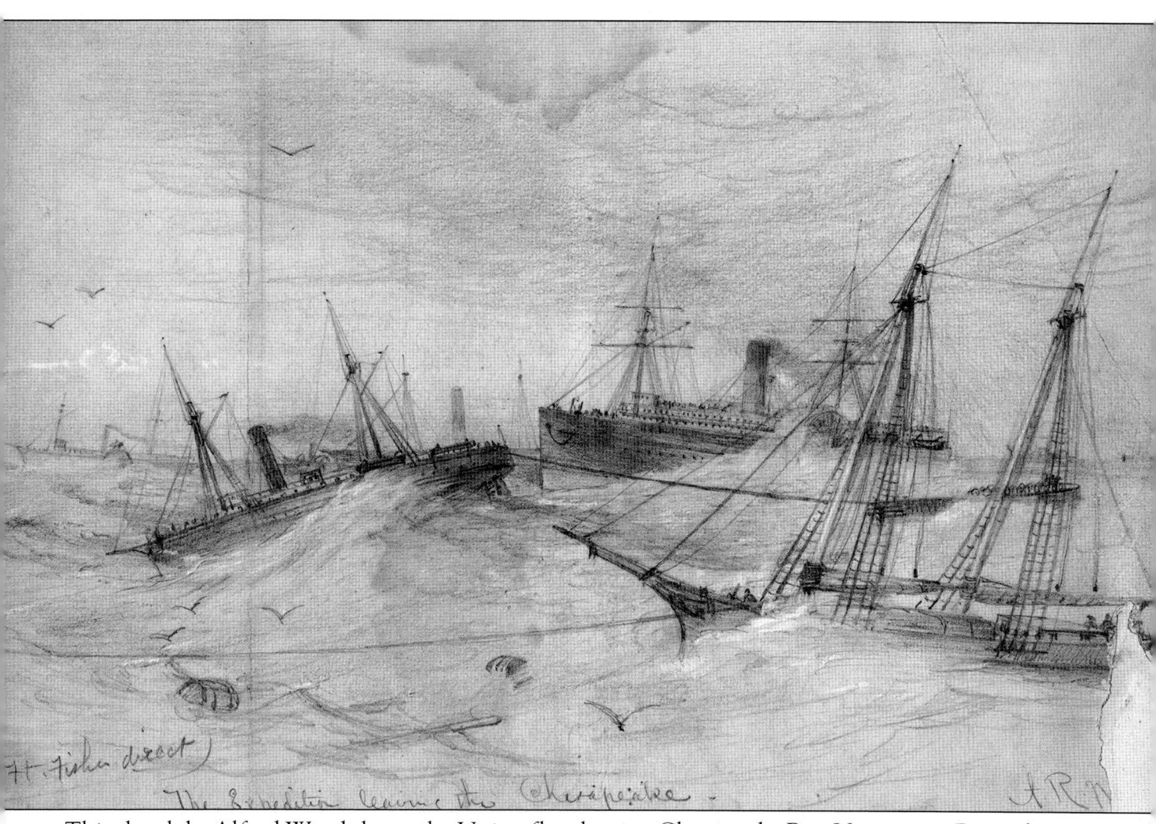

This sketch by Alfred Waud shows the Union fleet leaving Chesapeake Bay, Virginia, in December 1864 on its way to attack Fort Fisher. The armada was buffeted by the high seas from a fierce nor'easter that brewed up before they took their positions off the Cape Fear coast. (LOC.)

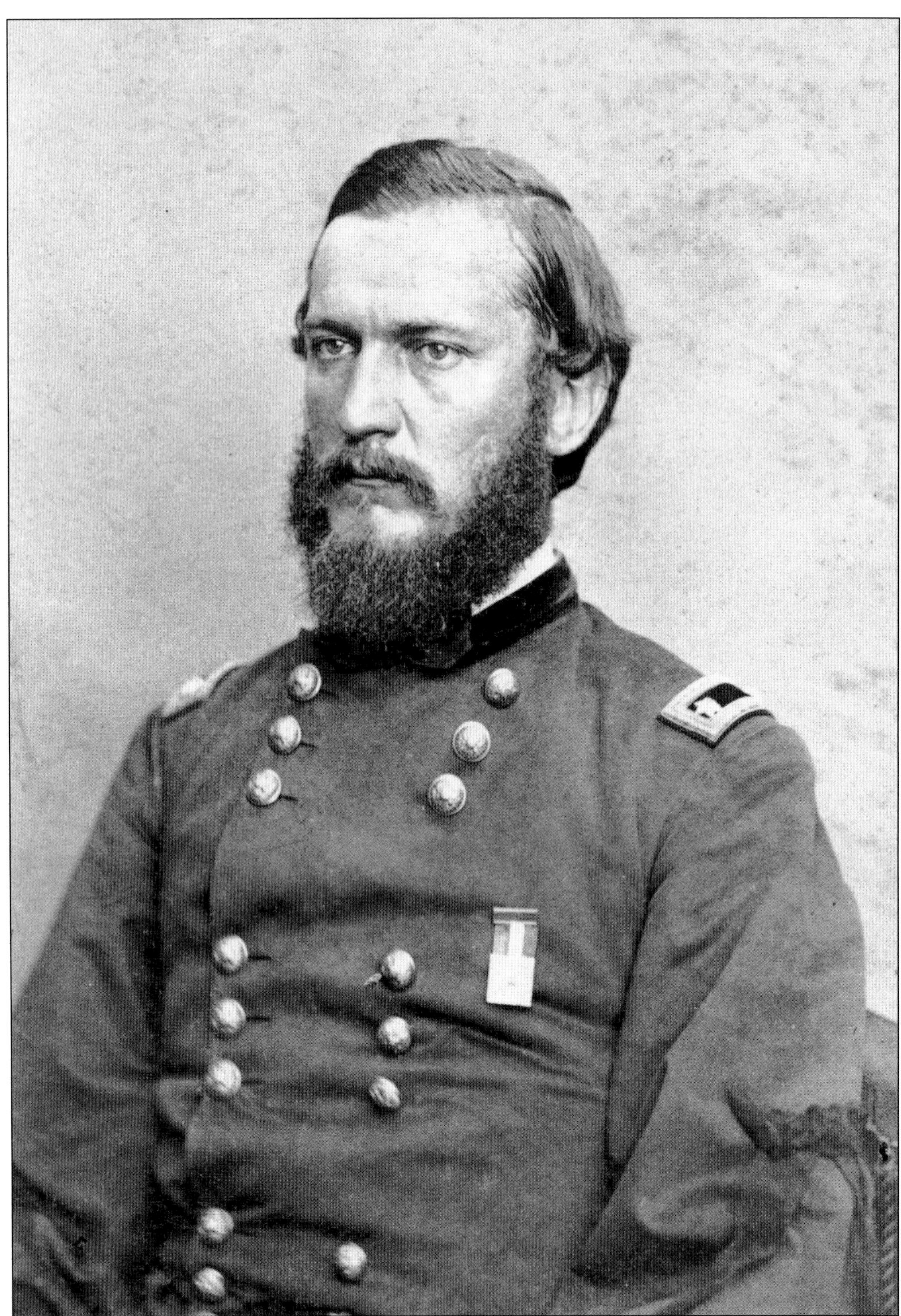

Maj. Gen. Godfrey Weitzel was a skilled army engineer whom Gen. Ulysses S. Grant sent to scout the Cape Fear coast in September 1864. Weitzel came back with a healthy respect for the defenses guarding the river, especially those along New Inlet. (LOC.)

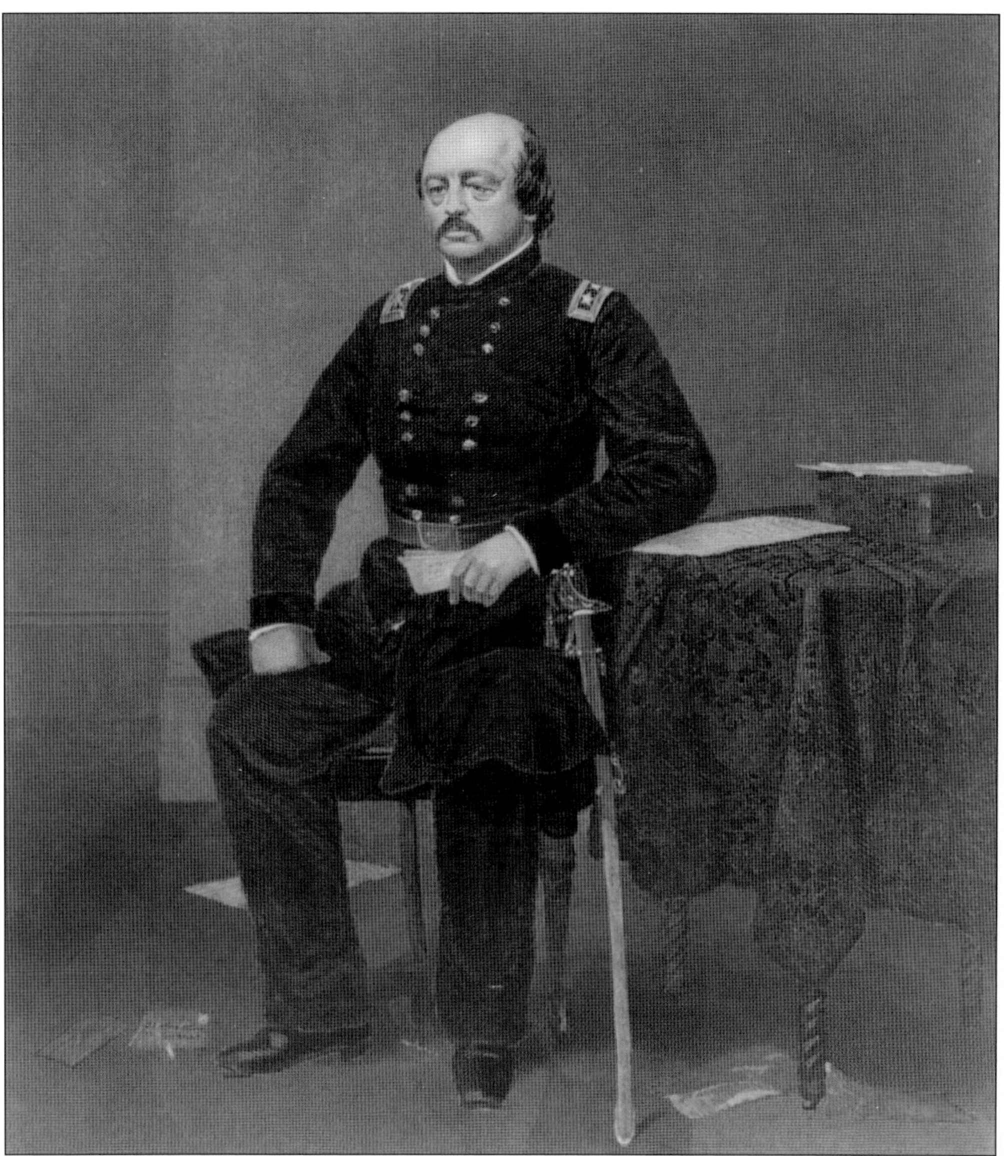

Even though from the ocean the forts did not look like much, reports from spies and deserters about the Confederate defenses along New Inlet told a different story. The Union high command was therefore willing to take a chance on Gen. Benjamin Butler's idea to destroy the works before the main Union landing parties ever got to the beach. They decided to see if, as Butler theorized, such a large explosion would indeed blow down what appeared from the offshore vantage point of the Union blockading fleet to be merely a collection of sand dunes. (LOC.)

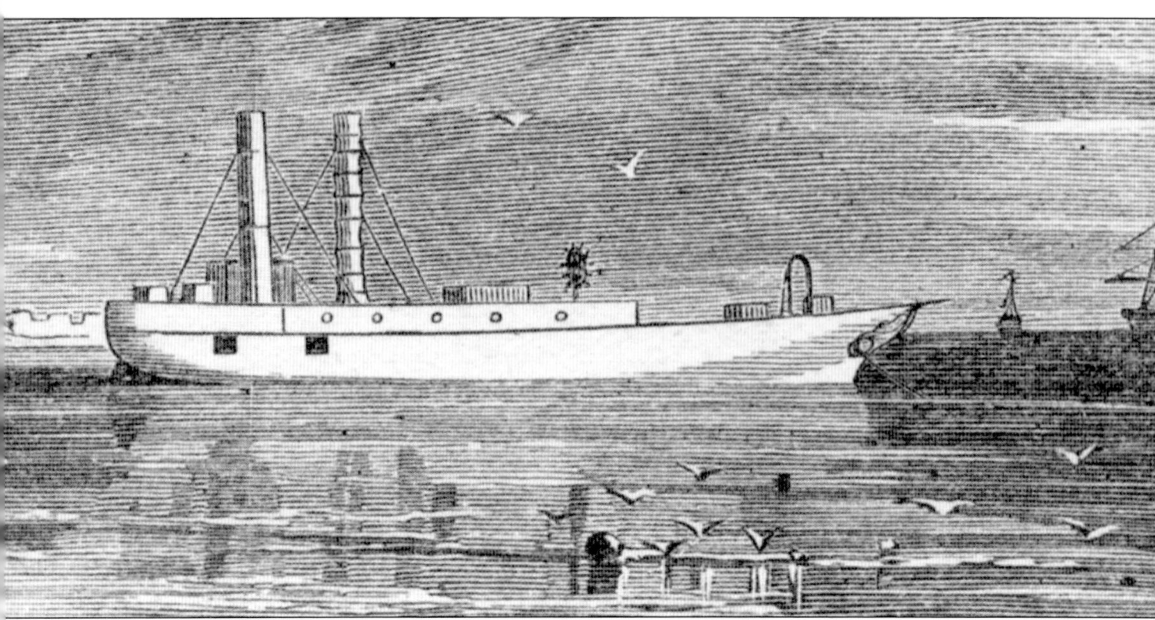

This sketch drawn by C.F. Ellmore shows the powder ship *Louisiana* just before she was blown to smithereens in the effort to level Fort Fisher on Christmas Eve 1864. The drawing appeared in *Harper's Weekly* on January 28, 1865.

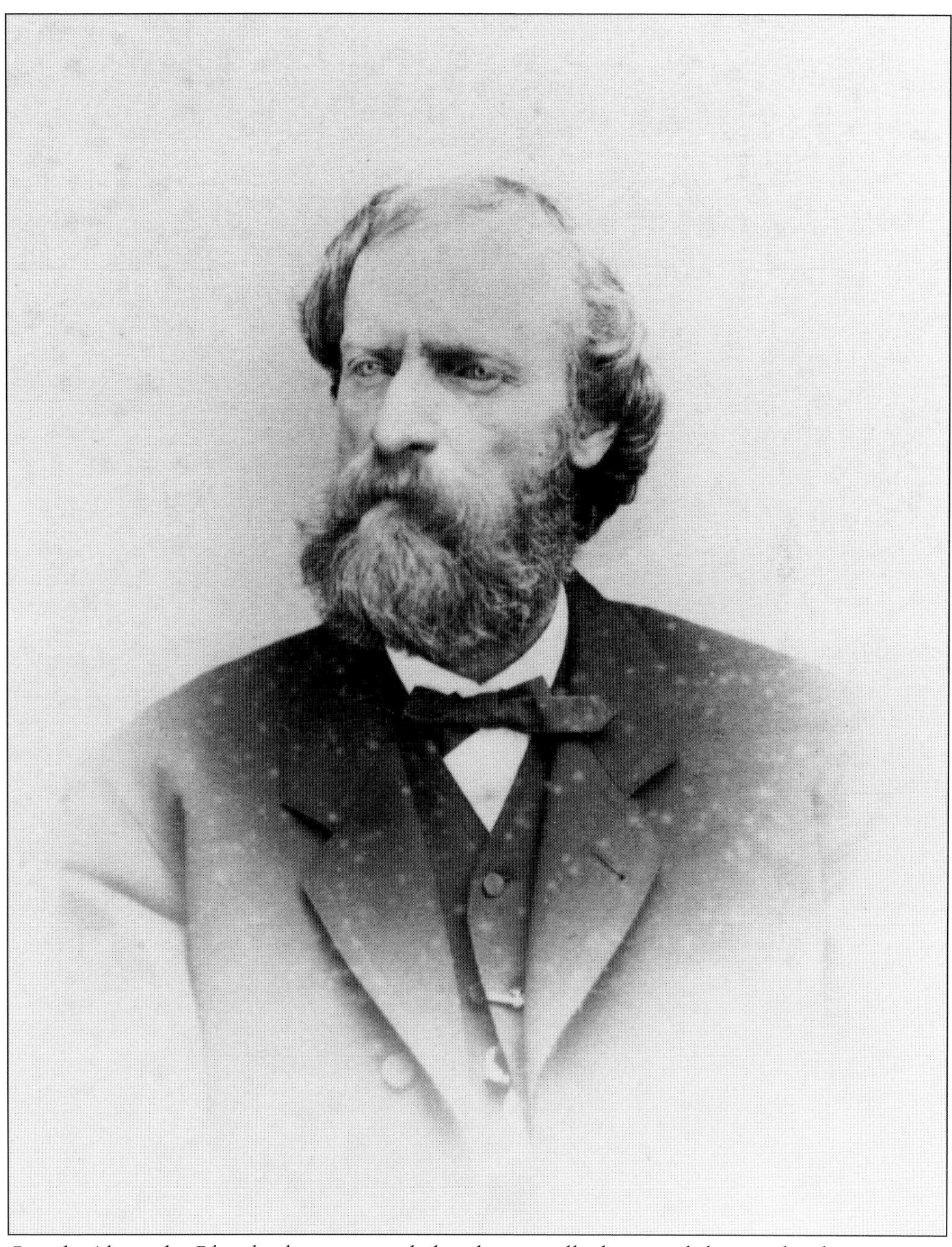

Comdr. Alexander Rhind, who commanded and personally detonated the powder ship *Louisiana* commencing the First Battle of Fort Fisher on Christmas Eve 1864, is pictured in 1867. (US Naval History and Heritage Command.)

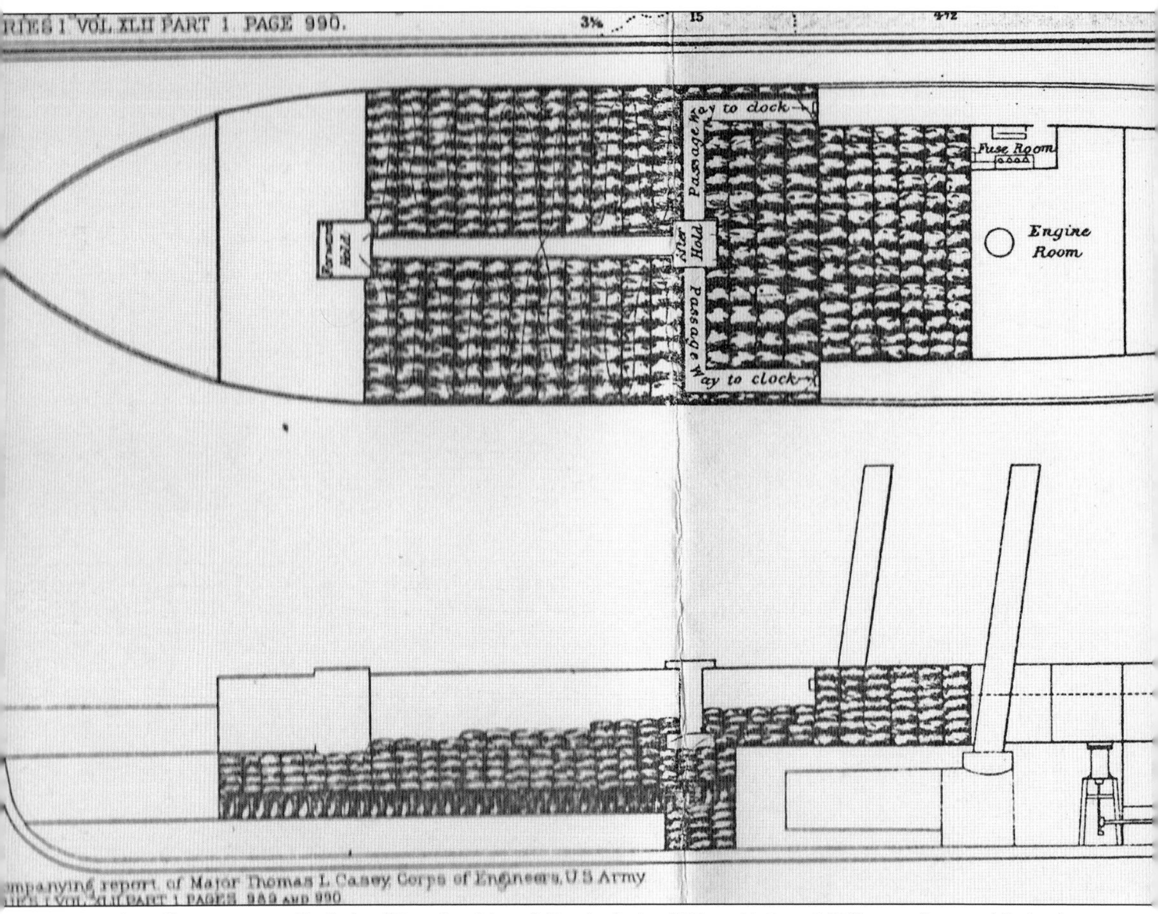

This illustration called the "Powder Vessel Exploded off Fort Fisher, NC" was first published in the *Atlas to Accompany the Official Records of the Union and Confederate Armies.* (US Naval History

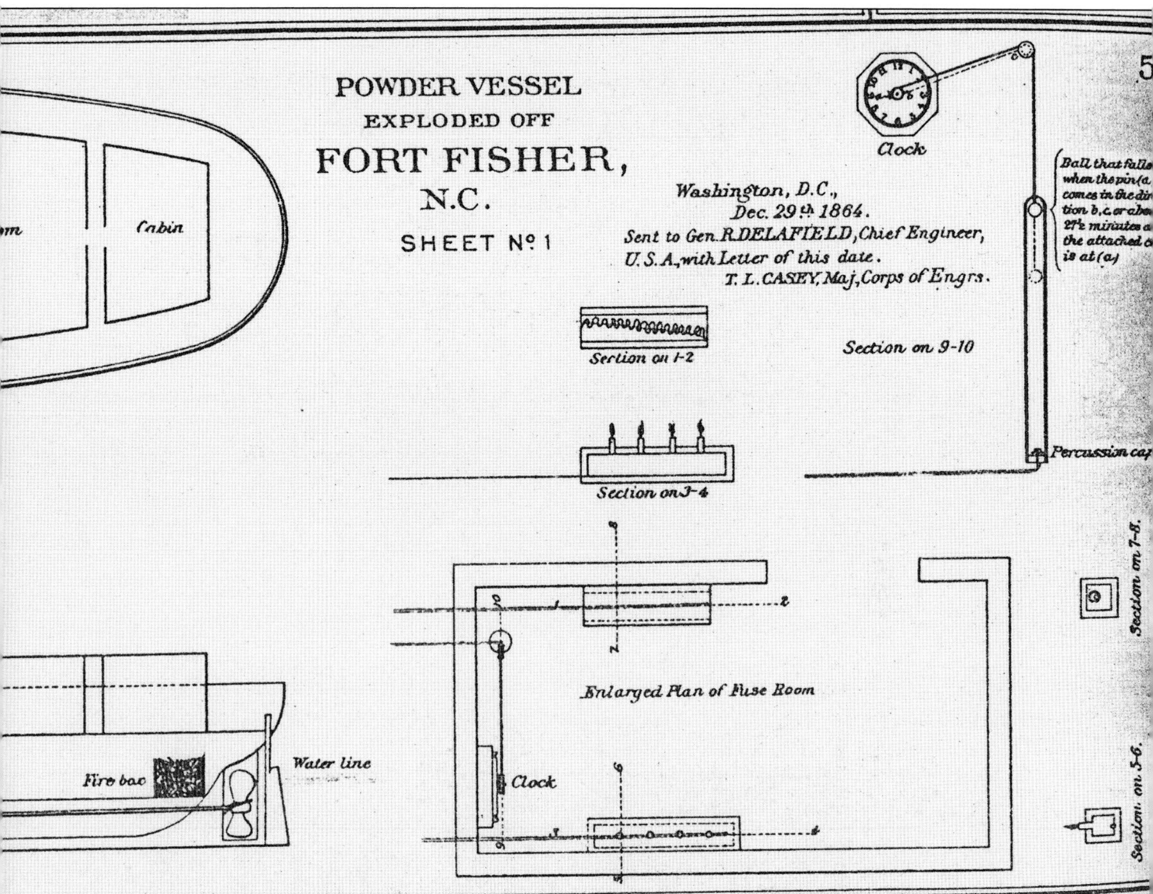

and Heritage Command.)

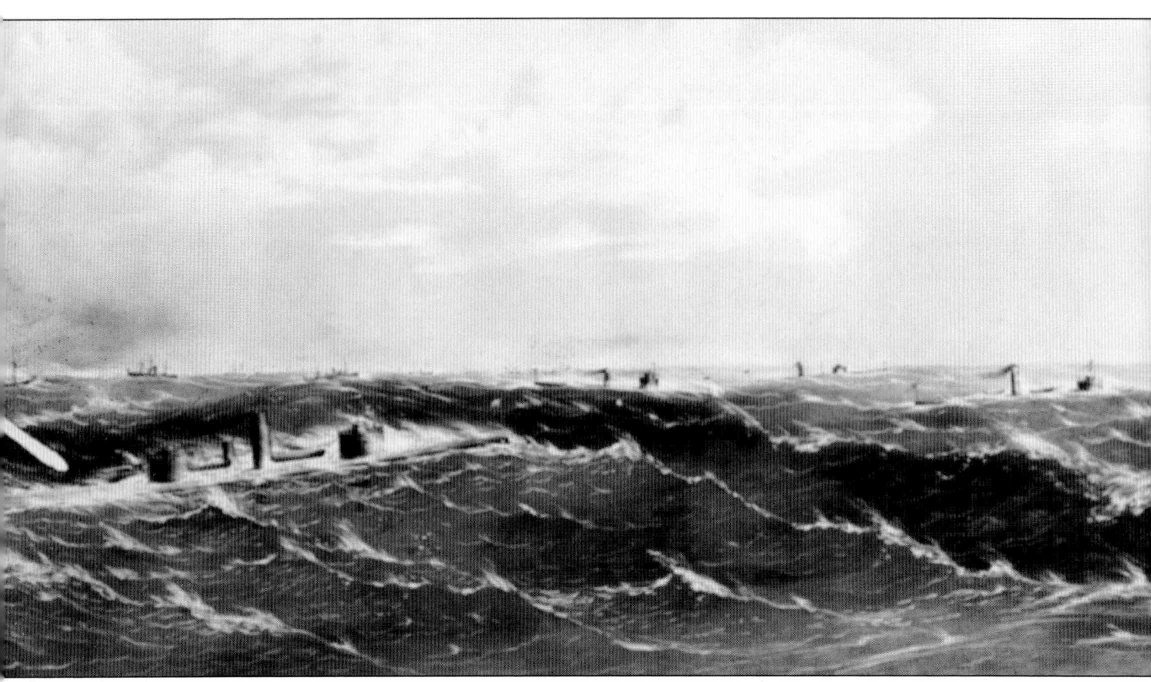

This lithograph, "Monitor Iron-Clads and the *New Ironsides*, forming part of the Fleet of Rear Admiral D.D. Porter, U.S.N. riding out a Gale of Wind, at Anchor off Fort Fisher, Coast of North Carolina, December 21, 1864" was created by Endicott & Company, New York, around 1865. Seeing the fort still standing, the ships of Rear Adm. David Porter's armada resorted to a more traditional means of attack and unleashed their guns. Some of the Union navy's most advanced ships were on hand for the attack, including the following monitors in the foreground and middle distance: *Monadnock* (twin-turret), *Canonicus*, *Mahopac*, and *Saugus*. Ships in the distance are the *Brooklyn*, *New Ironsides*, *Juniata*, *Tacony*, and *Malvern*. (US Naval History and Heritage Command.)

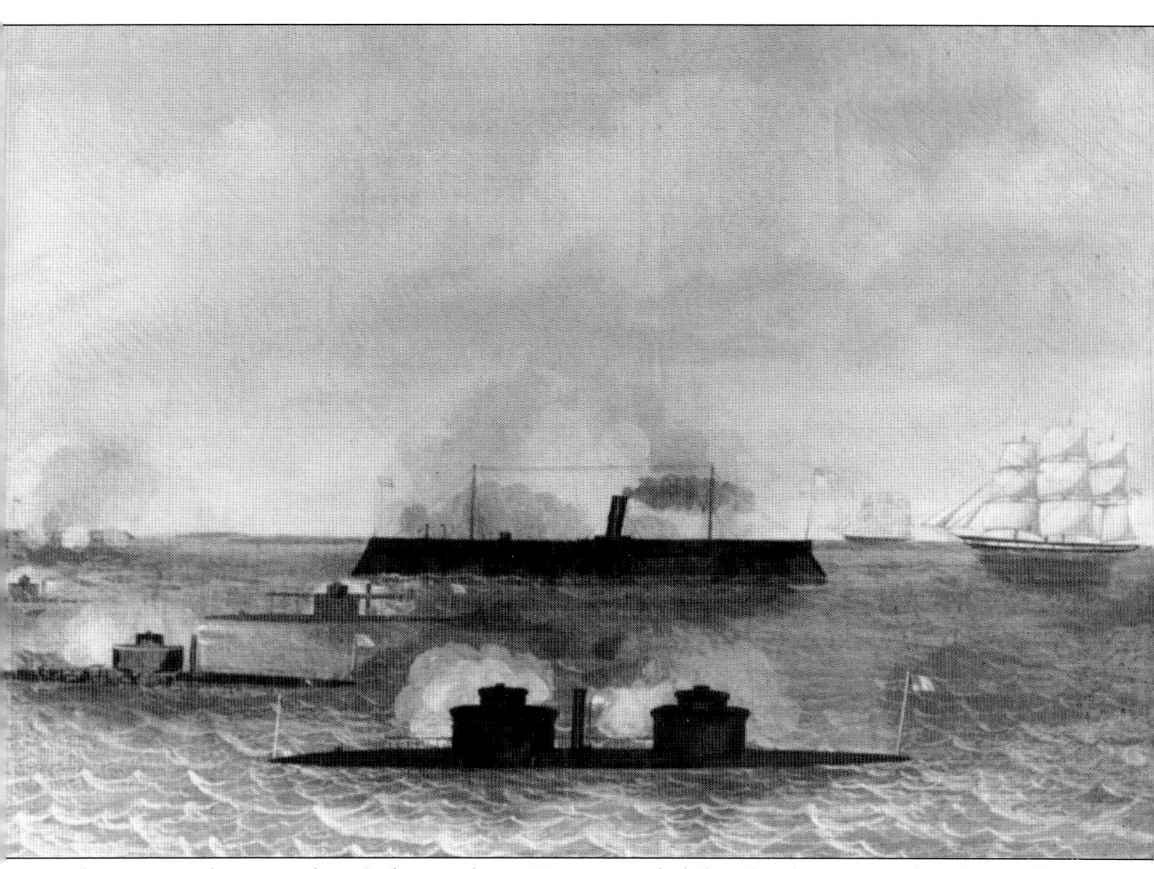

This painting by an unidentified artist shows Union ironclads bombarding Fort Fisher during the first assault on the fort in December 1864. The twin-turret monitor in the center foreground is the *Monadnock*. The large broadside ironclad beyond is the *New Ironsides*, while the three single-turret monitors are *Canonicus, Mahopac*, and *Saugus*. (US Naval History and Heritage Command.)

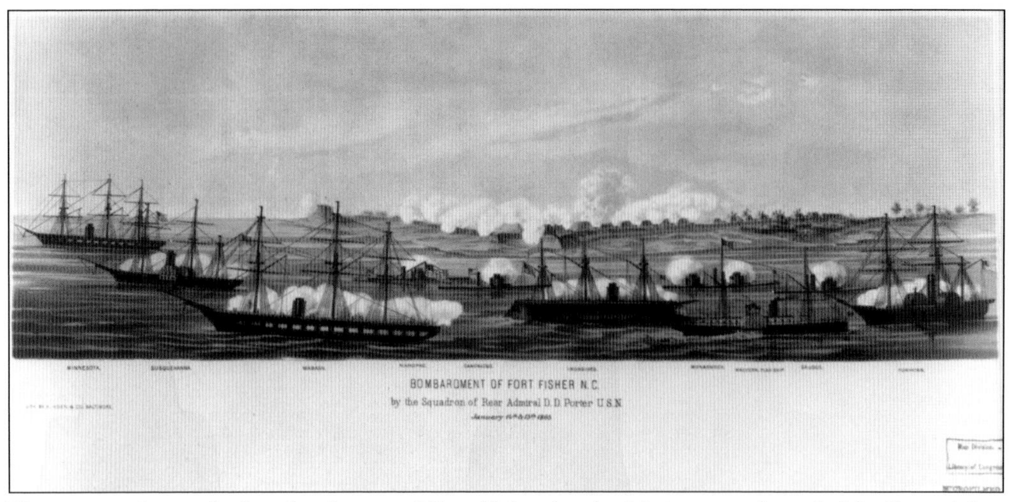

This image shows the bombardment of Fort Fisher by the Union squadron, led by Rear Adm. David Porter. (LOC.)

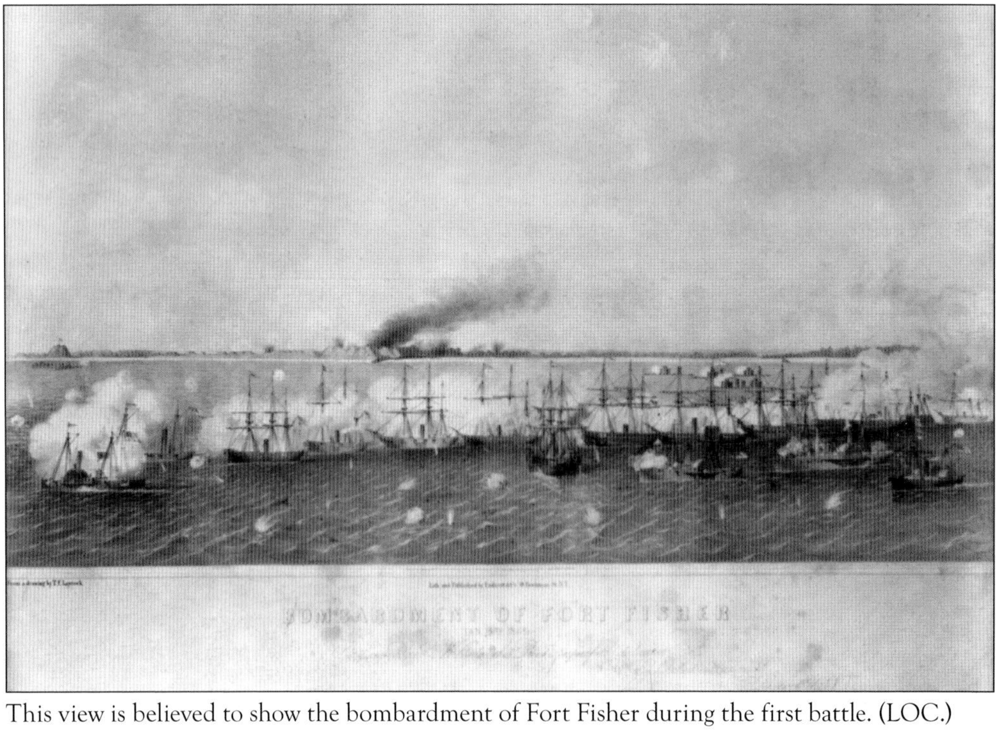

This view is believed to show the bombardment of Fort Fisher during the first battle. (LOC.)

Even though he had been relieved from his official duties prior to the first attack on Fort Fisher, Maj. Gen. W.H.C. Whiting offered his services to Colonel Lamb, who eagerly accepted his help. Whiting was pleasantly surprised to see how well the fortifications he had worked so hard designing held up under combat conditions. (LOC.)

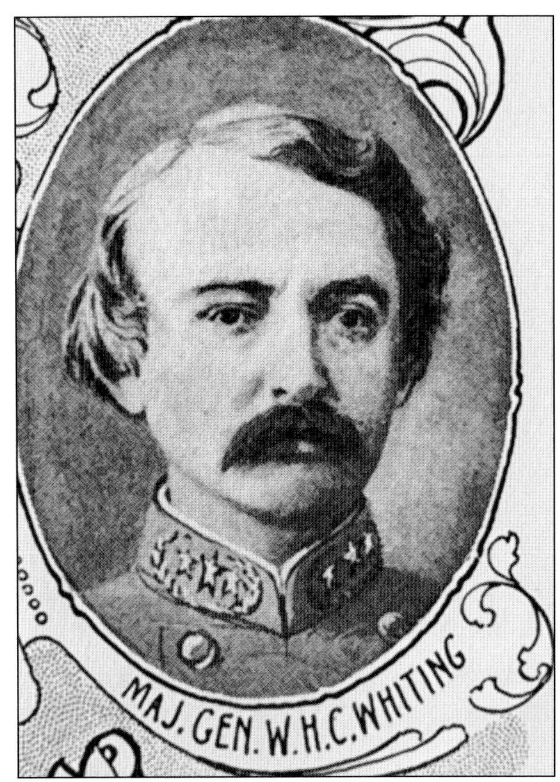

This is a close-up view of Mound Battery at Fort Fisher during the Christmas Eve battle. Mound Battery held up remarkably well not just to the effects of the explosion of the powder ship, but to the heavy guns of the Union fleet. This sketch was drawn by an unidentified artist and appeared in *Harper's Weekly* on January 28, 1865.

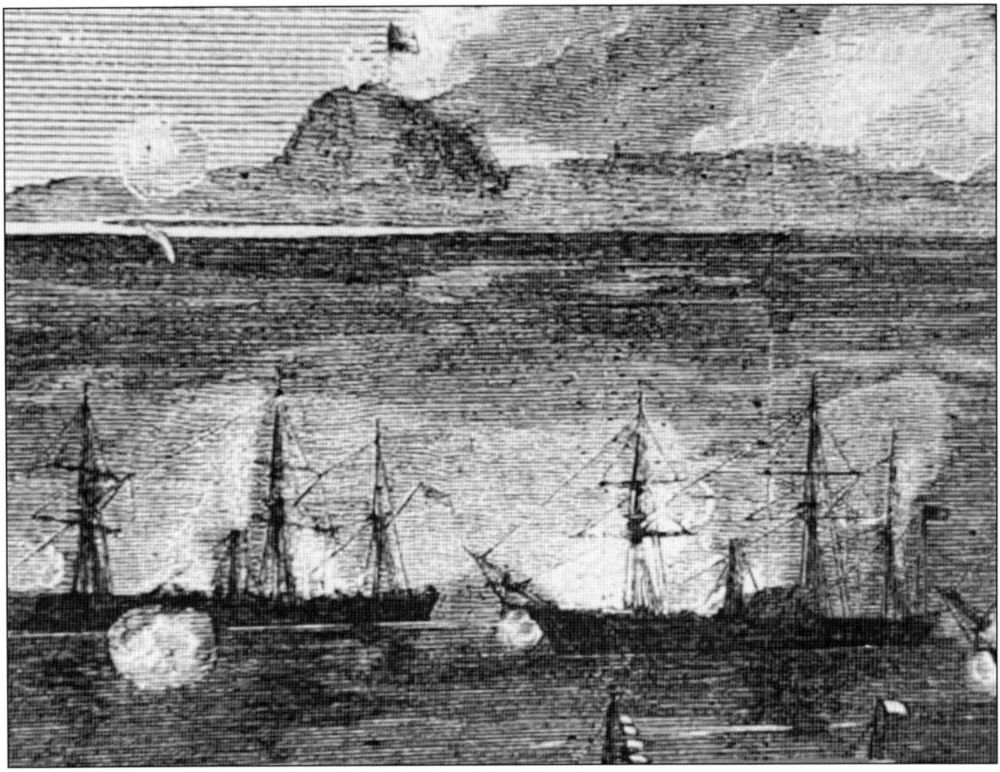

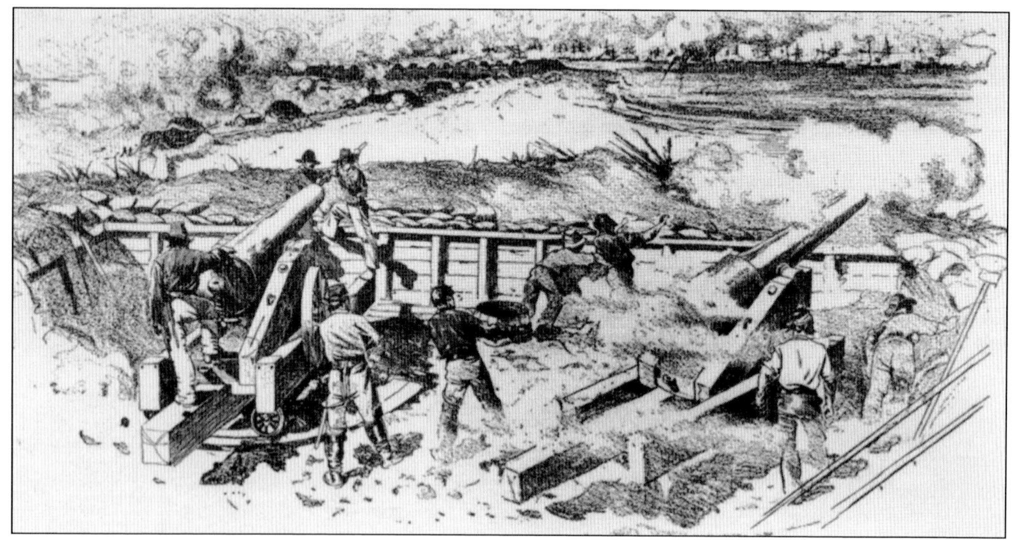

The gunners from atop the Mound Battery returned fire at the Federal ships. The great bombardment for the most part came to an end, and a Union strike force up the beach was supposed to move in and mop up whatever resistance had survived. However, they were surprised at the amount of resistance they met. This sketch of the First Battle of Fort Fisher appears in *Battle & Leaders of the Civil War.*

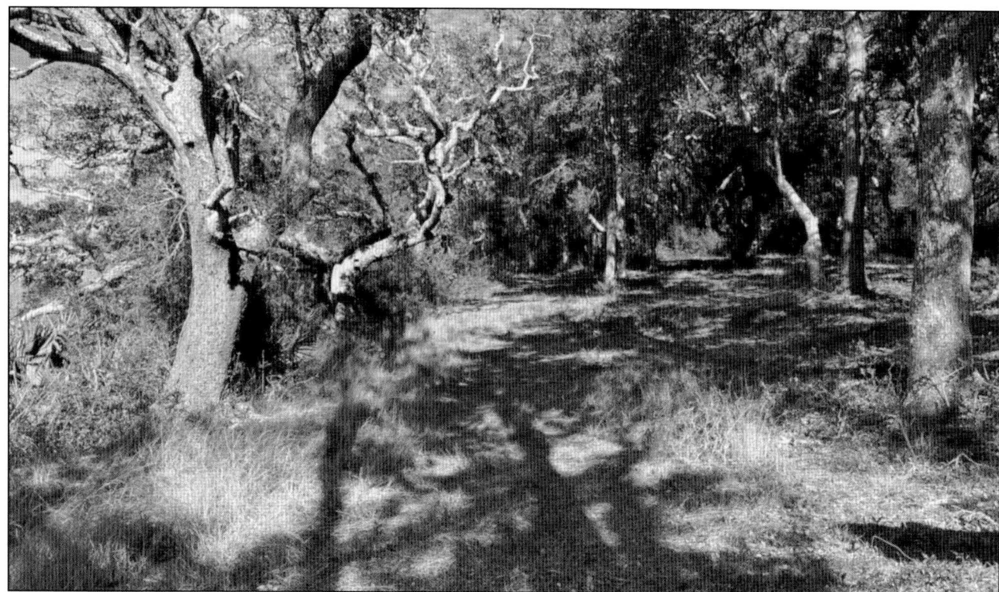

The remains of the old road leading north from the fort are pictured here. The Union strike force from the XXIV Army Corps under Gen. Godfrey Weitzel moved in from the north, roughly following the route of this old road all the way to the very gates of the fort. Their scouts told them this was the weakest link in the fortifications; however, they were unable to penetrate this place when their attack finally got underway on Christmas Day. They did manage to make it to the very ramparts of the fort but were repelled by the defenders. They were unable to regroup for another major attack, and the weather started to deteriorate with sleet and freezing rain, making conditions uncomfortable for soldiers from both sides, especially the wounded lying exposed in the cold. They soon found it necessary to pull back up the beach to await evacuation to their ships offshore.

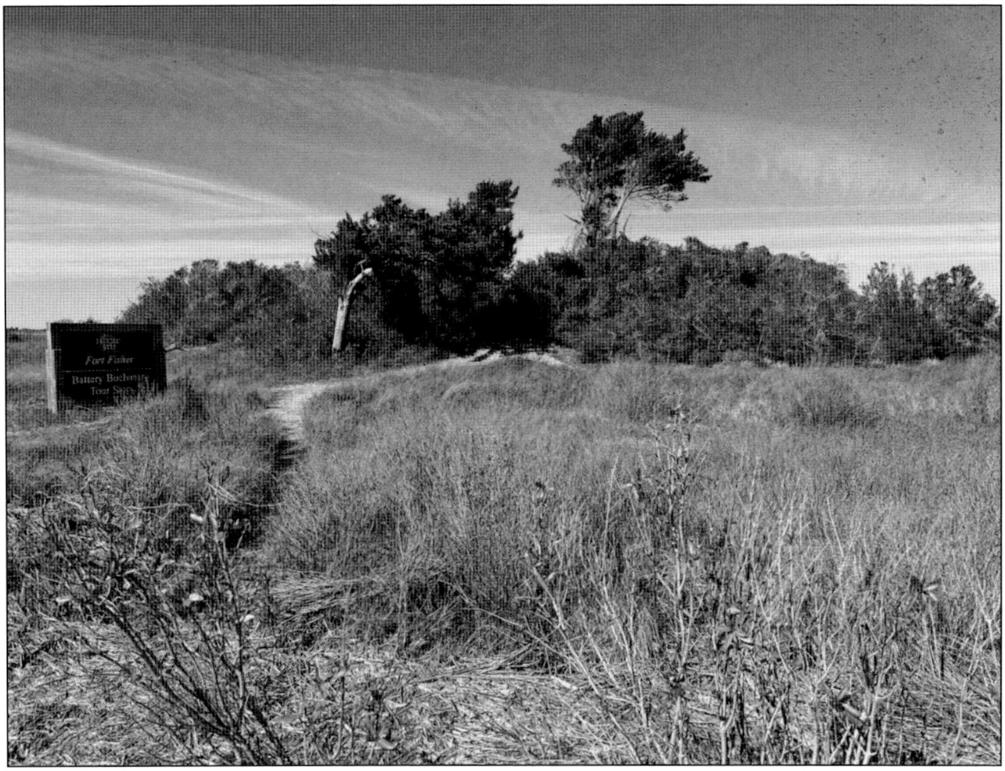

Battery Buchanan was a key part of the defenses of Fort Fisher. The naval contingent manning the defenses at Battery Buchanan played a valuable role in the First Battle of Fort Fisher, with several sailors helping Lamb and his men fire the rifled Brooke cannons, which were artillery pieces meant for use on ships and not static fortifications.

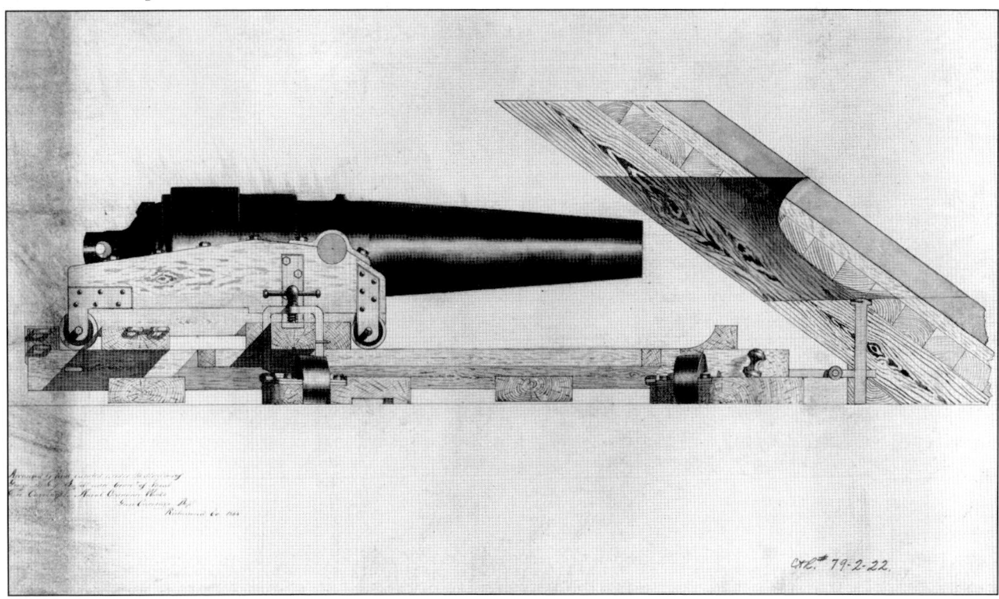

This is a diagram of a Brooke rifled cannon mounted onboard a ship. (US Naval History and Heritage Command.)

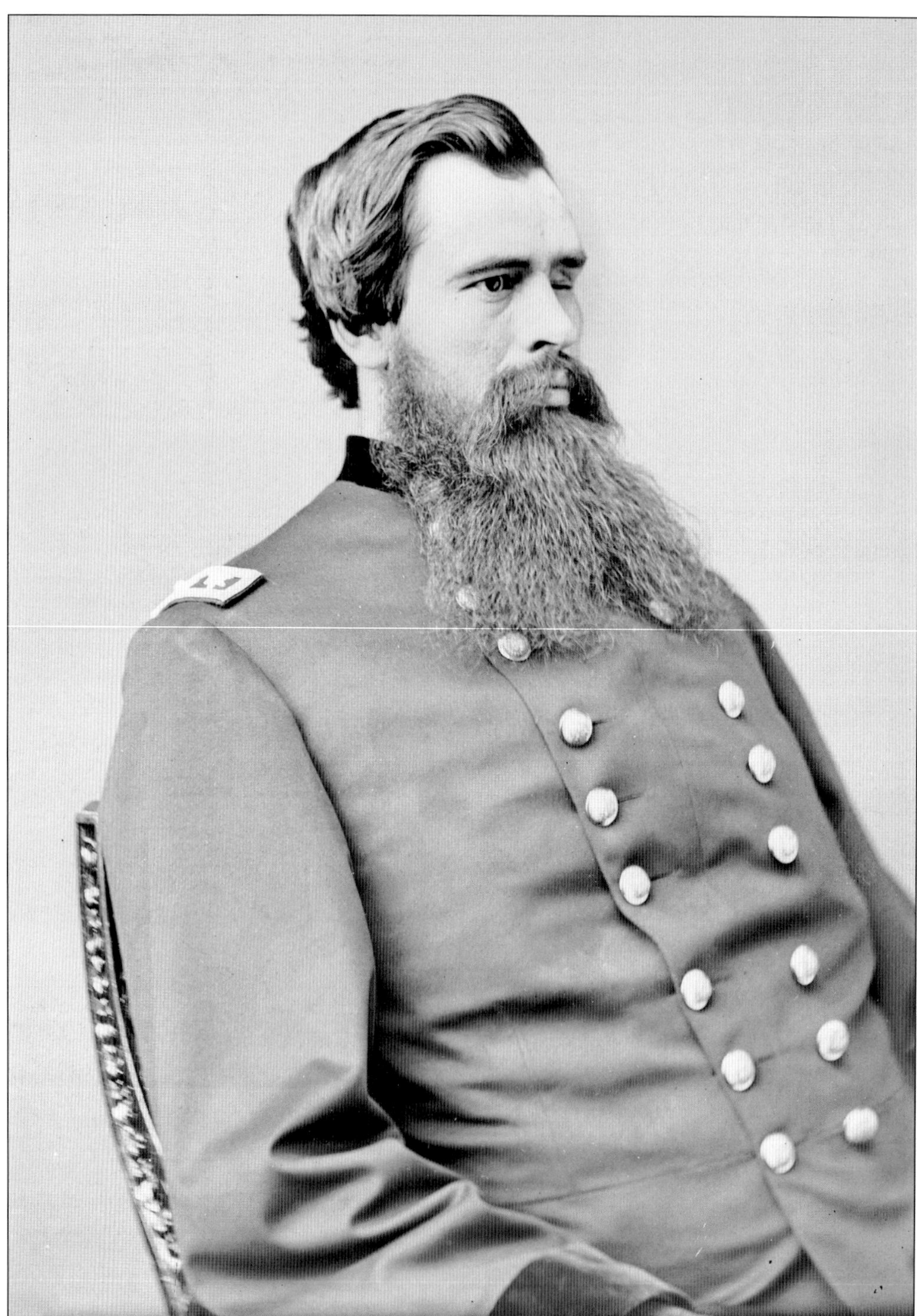

Brig. Gen. N. Martin Curtis, a six-foot, seven-inch New Yorker, and his men paid the price for Gen. Benjamin Butler's incompetence, nearly being stranded on the beach during the landing operations just north of Fort Fisher. Fortunately, he was able to extricate his men back to the ships offshore before Confederates were able to drive them into the Atlantic. (LOC.)

Gen. Benjamin Butler drew the ire of both friend and foe alike because of his heavy-handed treatment of the civilian population across the South, earning him nicknames such as "Beast Butler" or "Bluebeard of New Orleans," but he always seemed able to rely on his political connections to help maintain his command in the Union army. However, not even his most loyal backers back in Washington could save him after the embarrassing defeat of the Union forces at Fort Fisher. (LOC.)

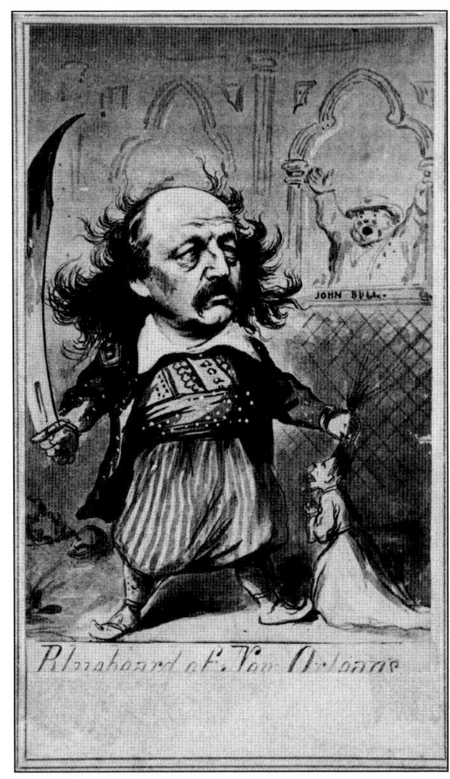

The northwest side of Fort Fisher is shown here. Though the attack from the north made its way to the ramparts before being repulsed by Confederate defenders, Union leaders did not have time to exploit any weaknesses they might have found. They were fortunate to make it back to their ships before the weather broke.

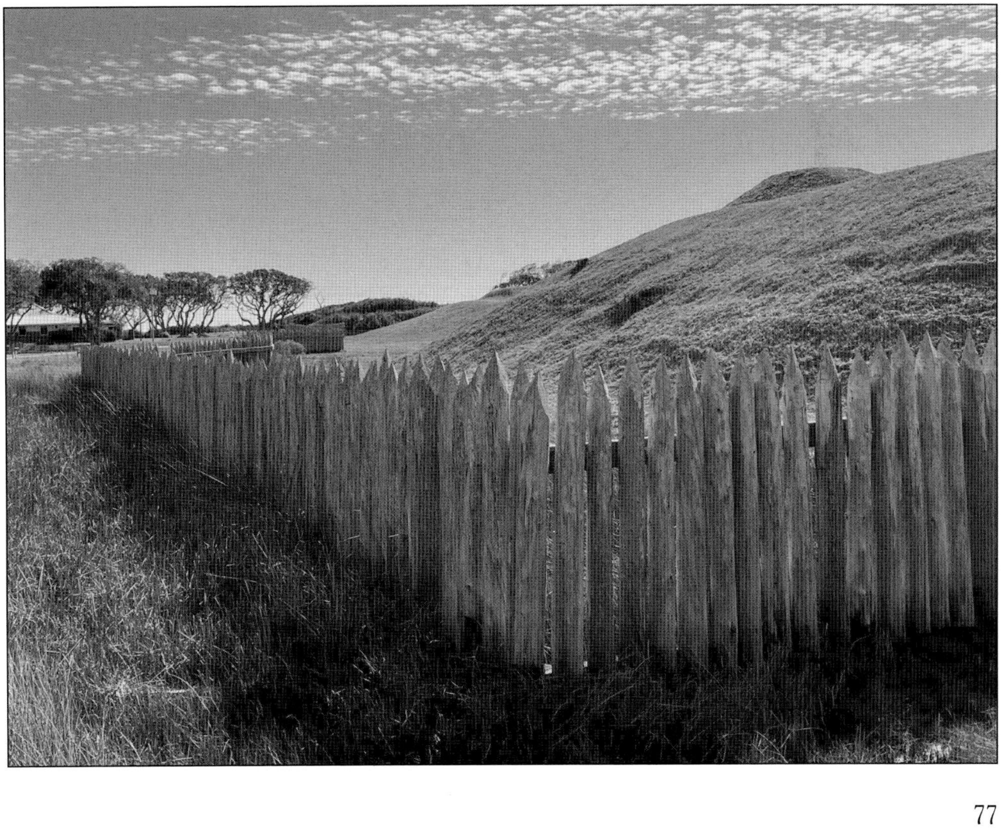

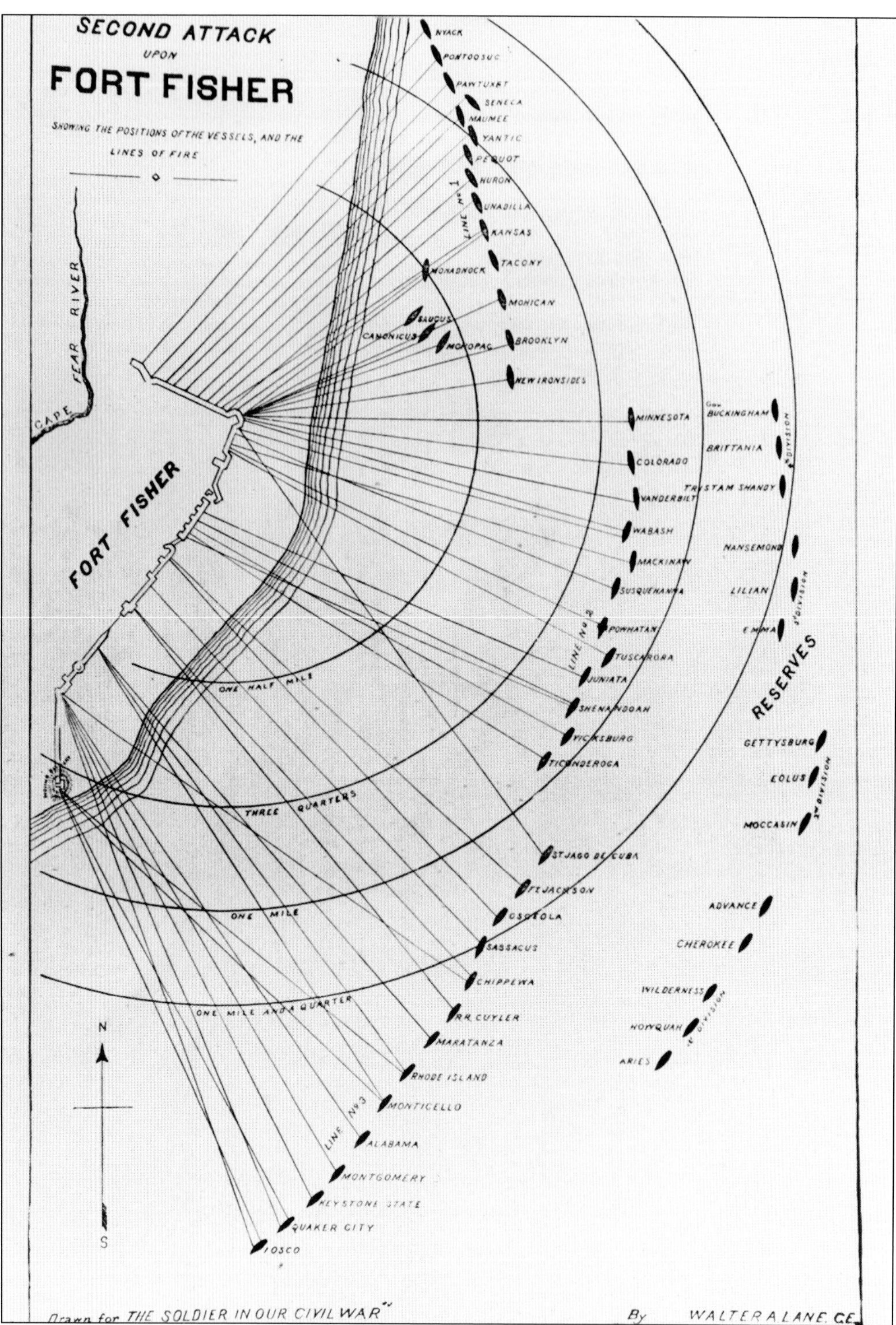

Walter A. Lane prepared this chart, "Second Attack upon Fort Fisher, NC, January 13th–15th, 1865," showing where each vessel was positioned in relation to Fort Fisher. (US Naval History and Heritage Command.)

Four

The Fall of Fort Fisher in January 1865

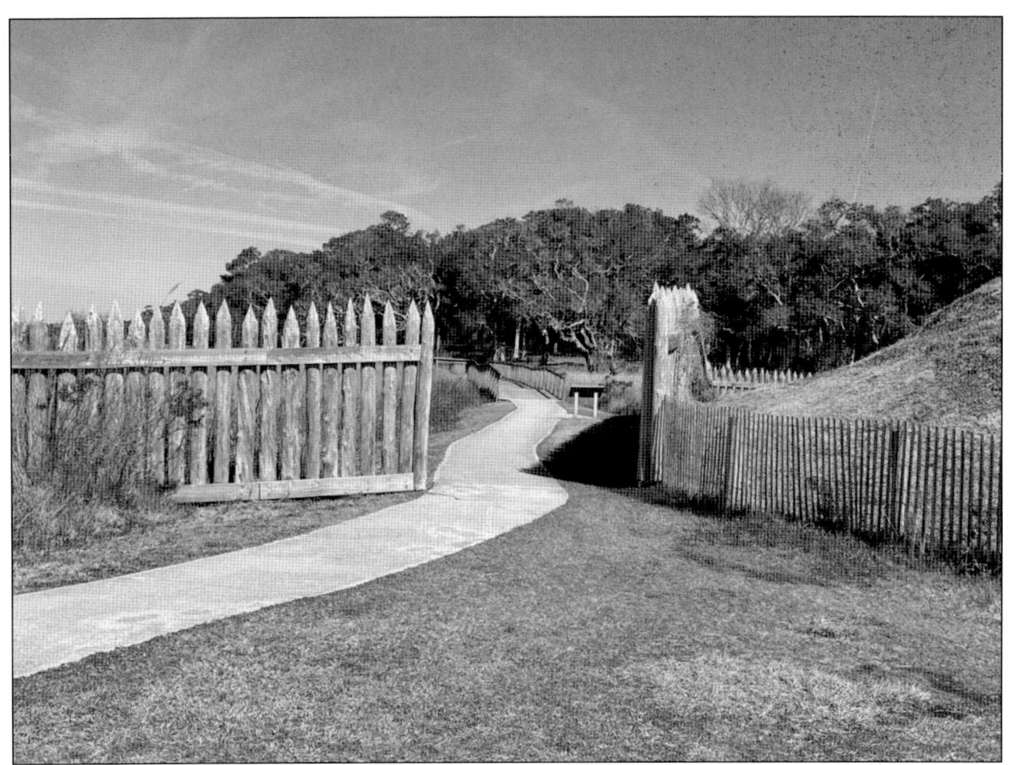

A reconstruction of the "The Bloody Gate" is shown here. This spot between the left salient of the breastworks and the low ground to the river was considered by Colonel Lamb to be the weakest spot in the fort. Events during the second Union attack in January 1865 proved him to be correct.

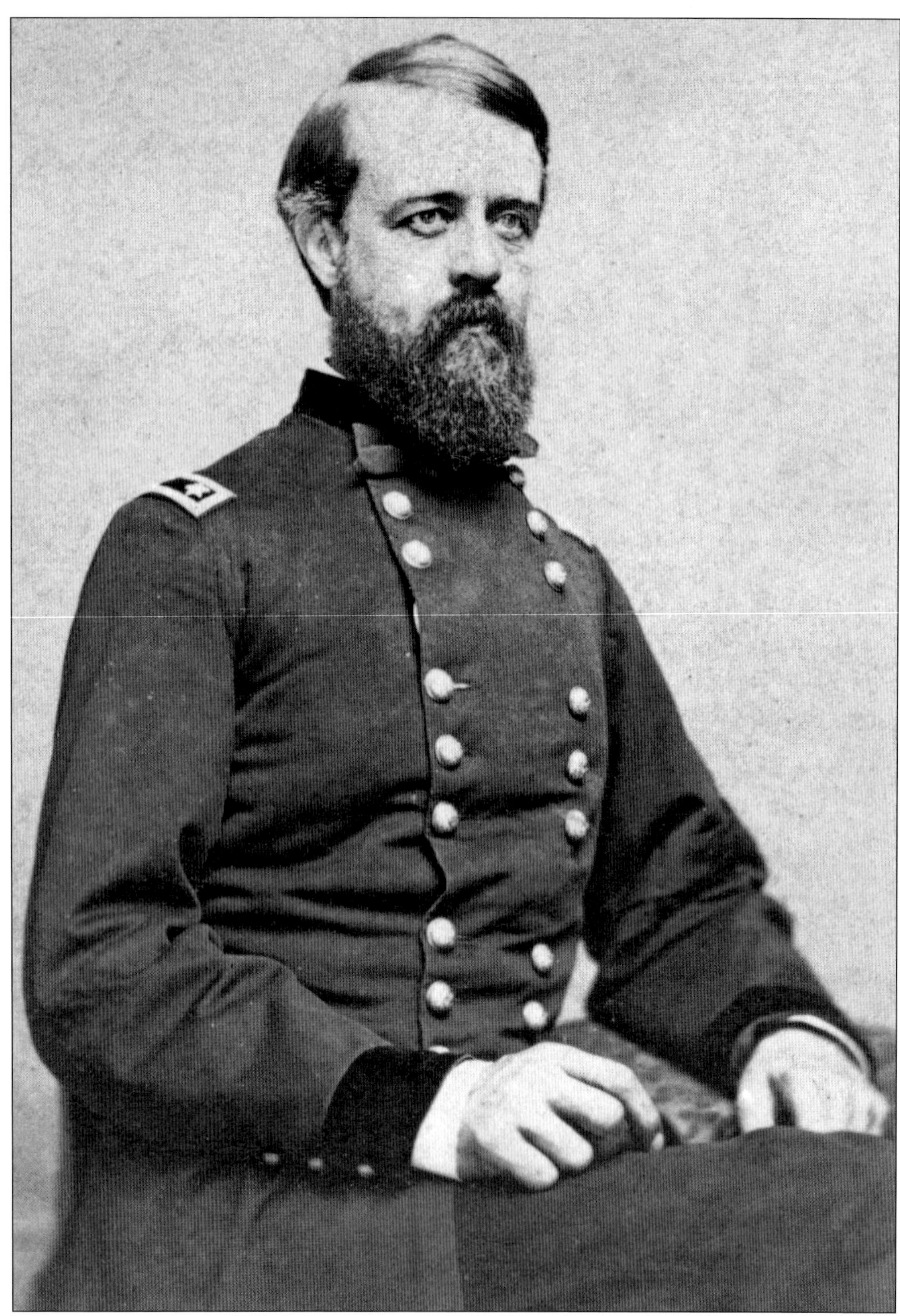

Maj. Gen. Alfred Terry, pictured here, took over the army portion of the expedition after General Grant relieved Gen. Benjamin Butler following the Union's embarrassing defeat during the First Battle of Fort Fisher. (LOC.)

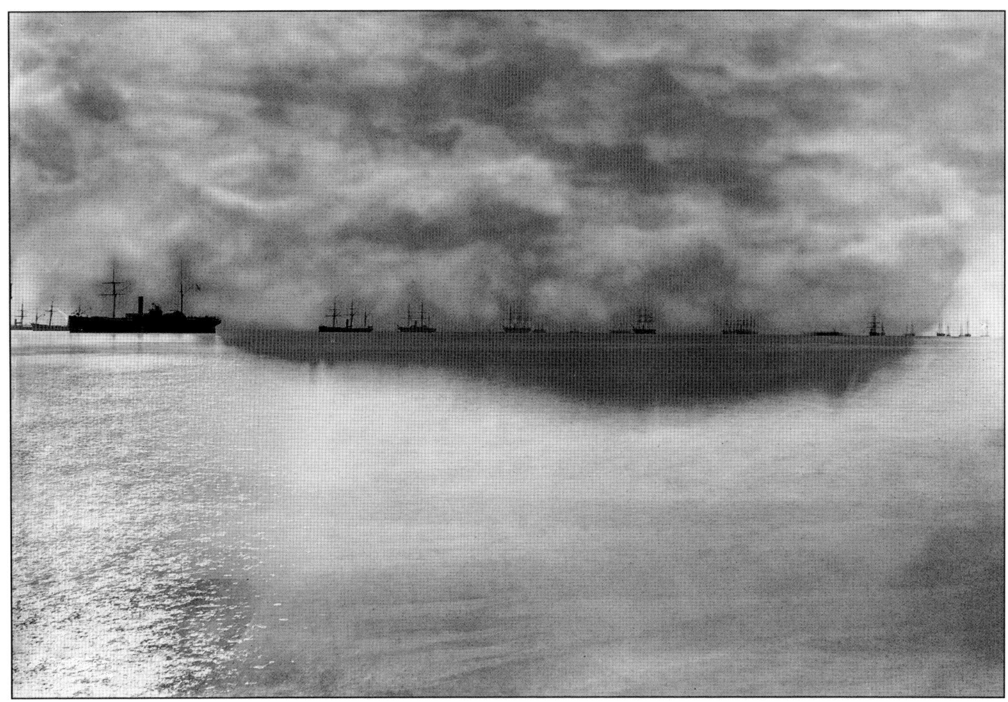

Timothy O'Sullivan took this photograph showing the Union fleet in Chesapeake Bay before its departure for the second attack upon Fort Fisher in January 1865. (LOC.)

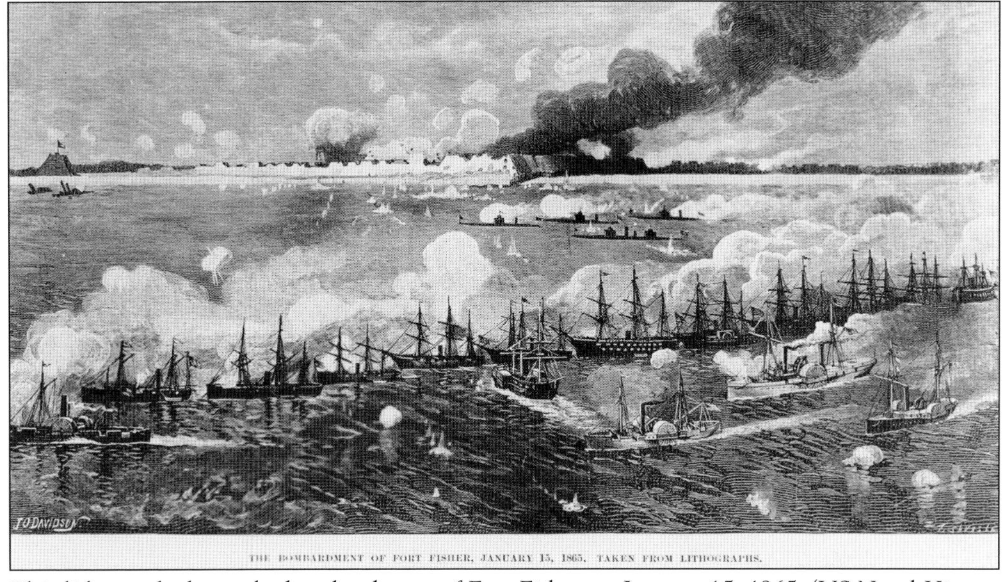

This lithograph shows the bombardment of Fort Fisher on January 15, 1865. (US Naval History and Heritage Command.)

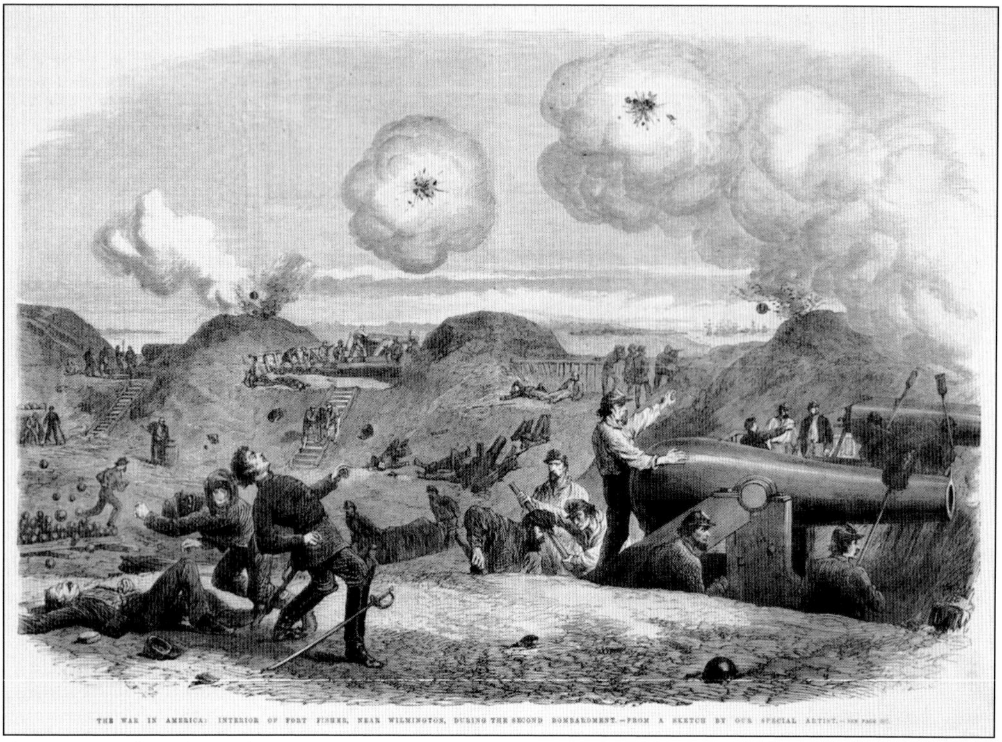

A correspondent from the *Illustrated London News* recorded conditions inside Fort Fisher during the January 15, 1865, bombardment. (North Carolina Collection Photographic Archives, Wilson Special Collections Library, University of North Carolina at Chapel Hill, the Bruce Cotten Image Collection.)

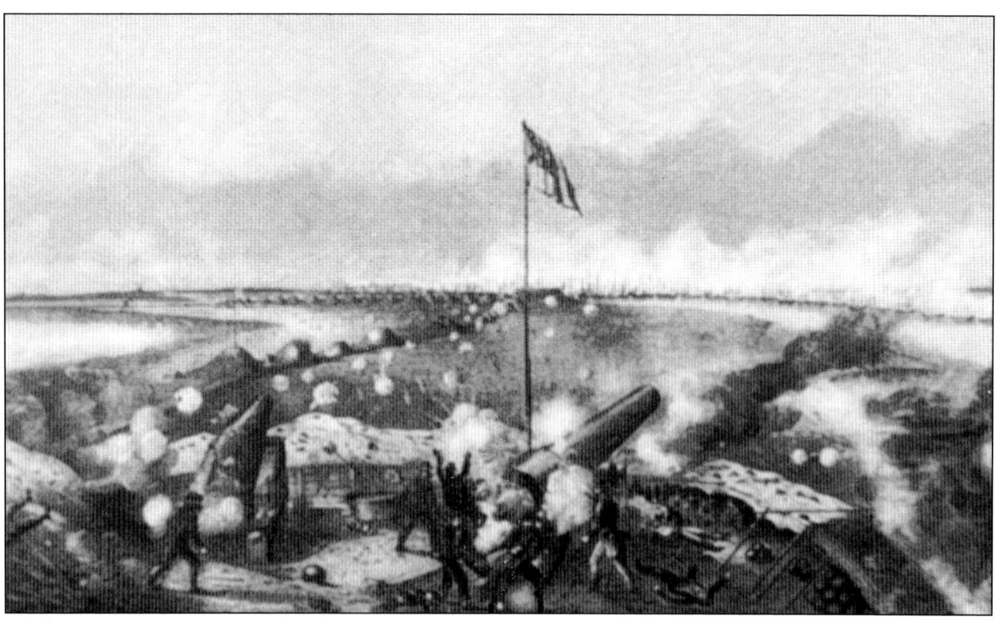

This scene of the Second Battle of Fort Fisher is taken from Walter Clark's book *Several Regiments and Battalions from North Carolina in the Civil War.*

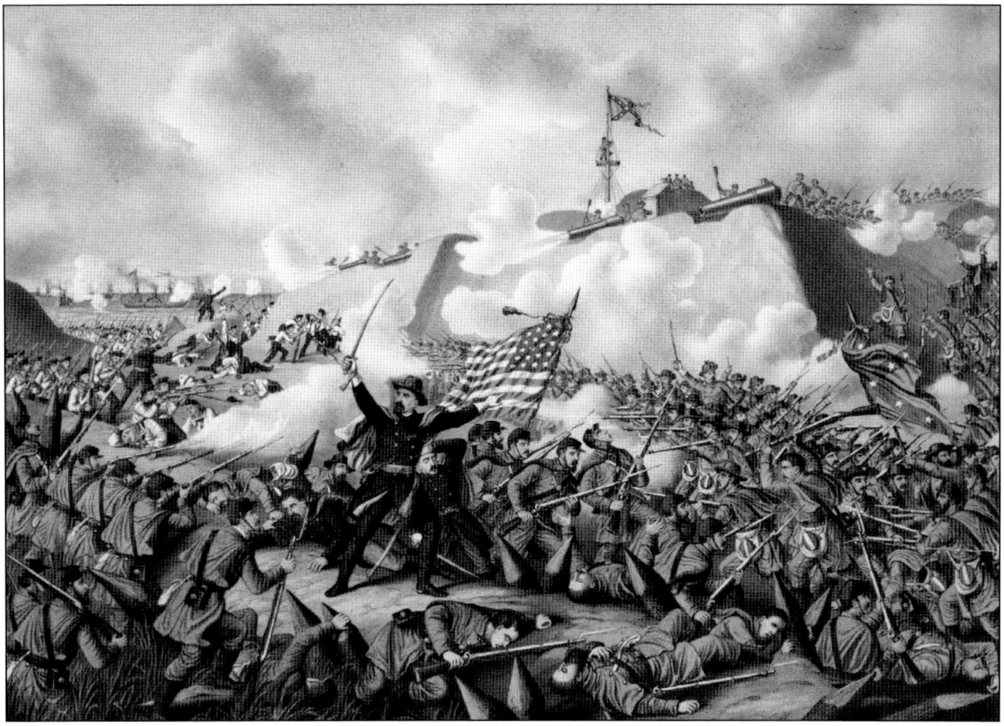

This Kurz and Allison lithograph shows the capture of Fort Fisher. (LOC.)

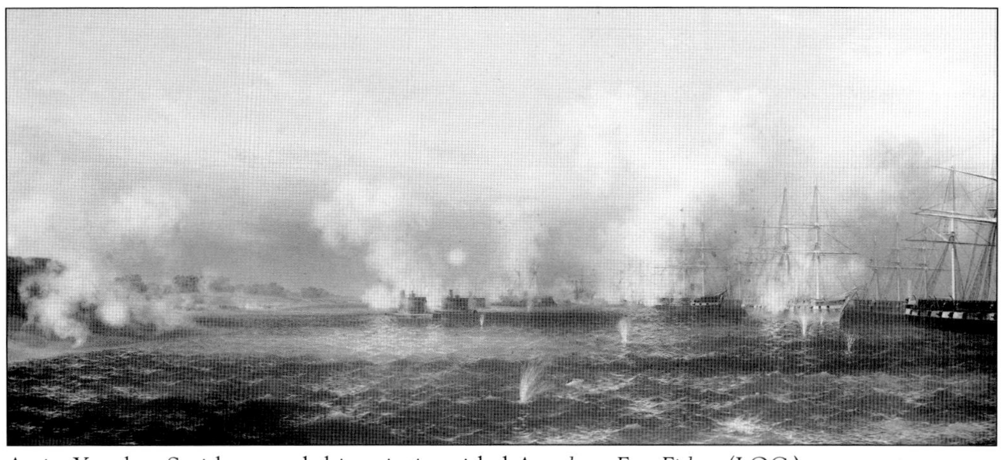

Artist Xanthus Smith created this painting titled *Attack on Fort Fisher*. (LOC.)

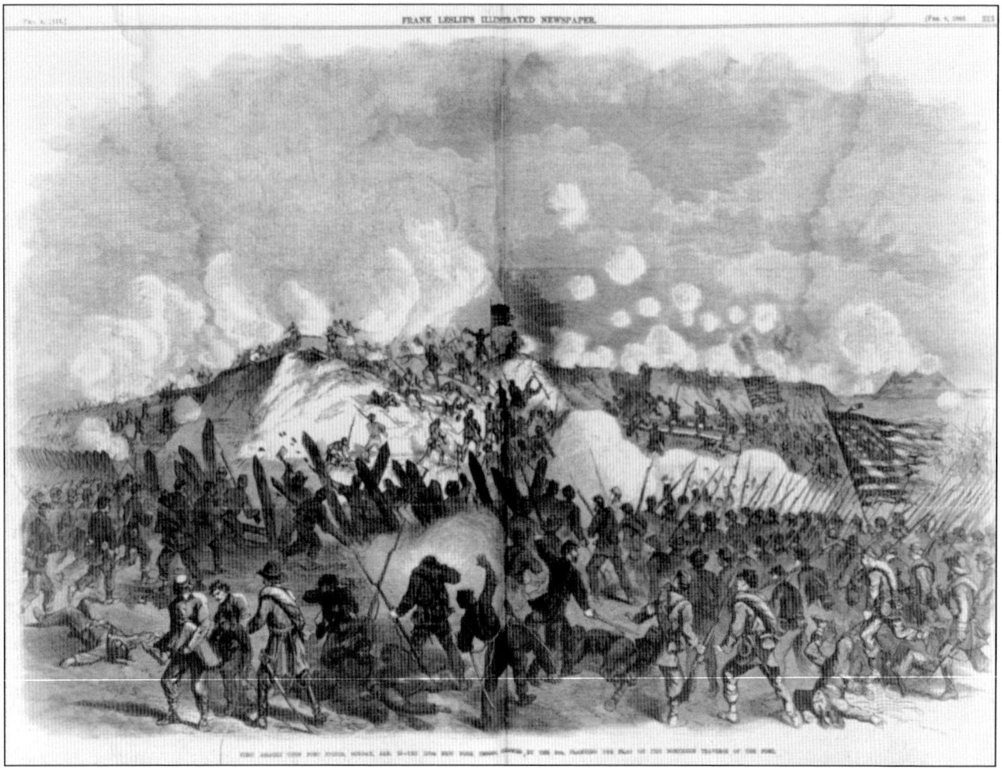

Shown here is the second assault on Fort Fisher on January 15, 1865, with New York troops planting their colors upon the northern traverse. (LOC.)

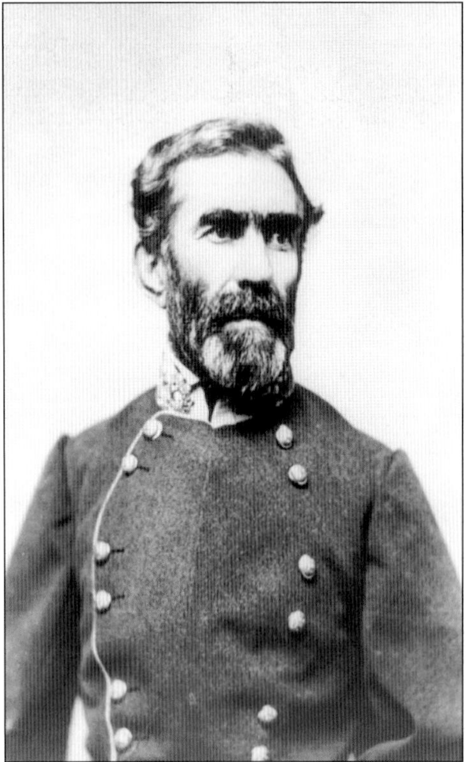

Gen. Braxton Bragg refused to authorize reinforcements for the beleaguered fort, abandoning them to sure annihilation. (LOC.)

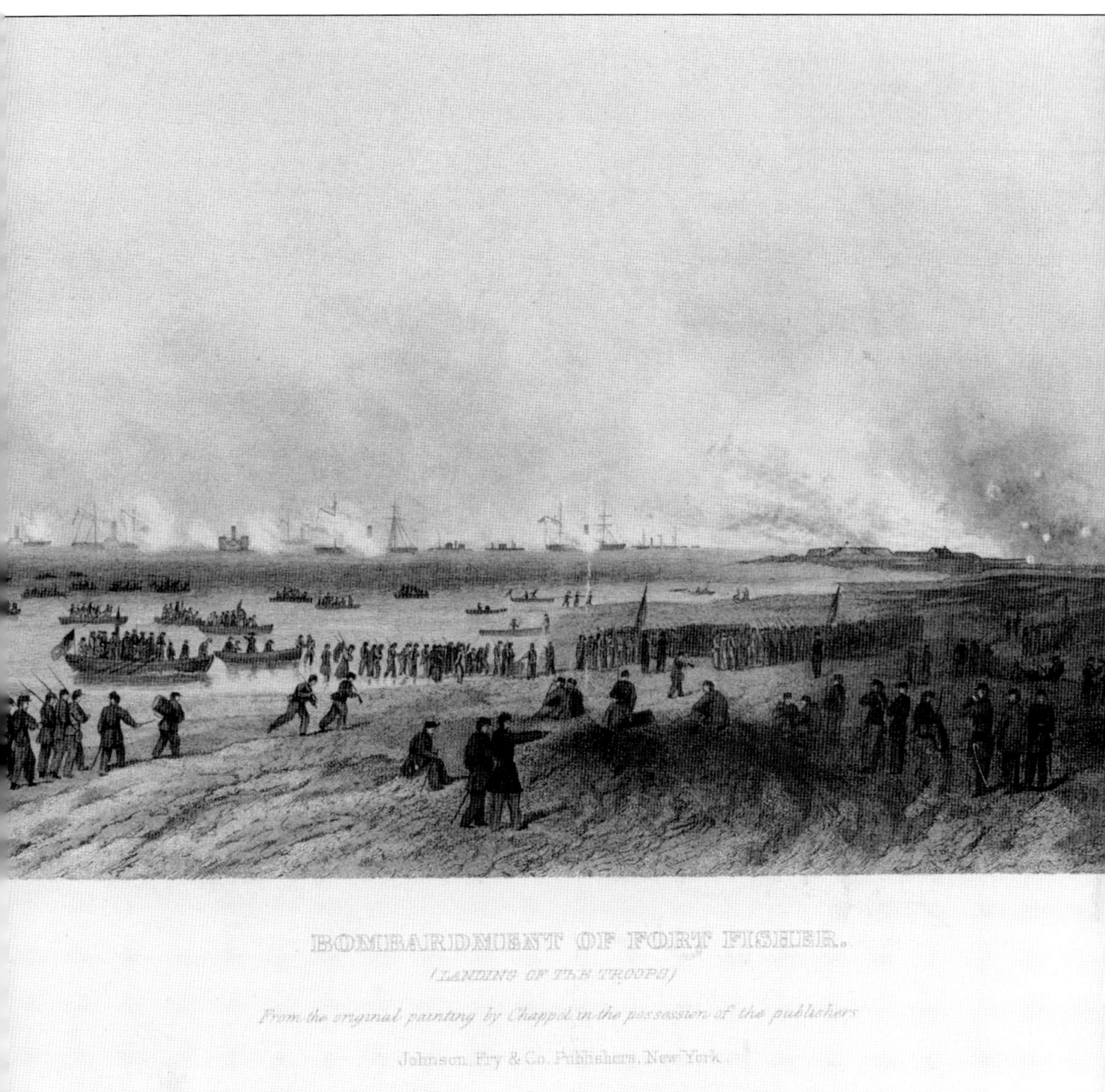

This illustration shows the Union troops gathering on the beach for the attack on January 15, 1865. (US Naval History and Heritage Command.)

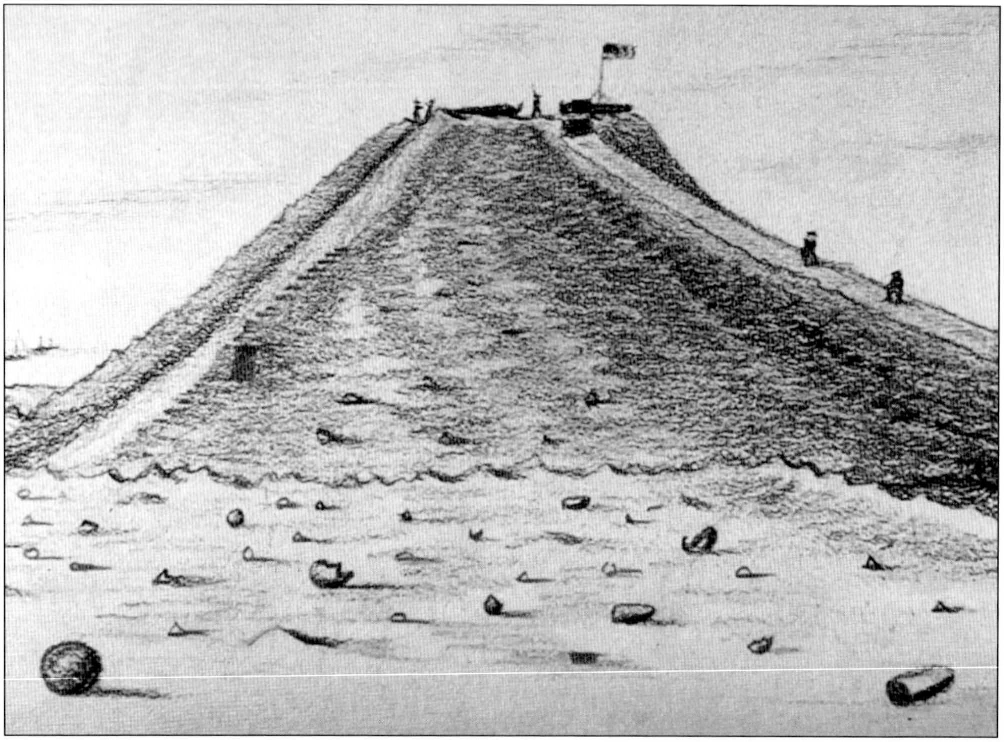

Acting ensign R.H. Sands of the USS *Gettysburg* drew this image of the Mound Battery shortly after the battle on January 15, 1865. (ORN.)

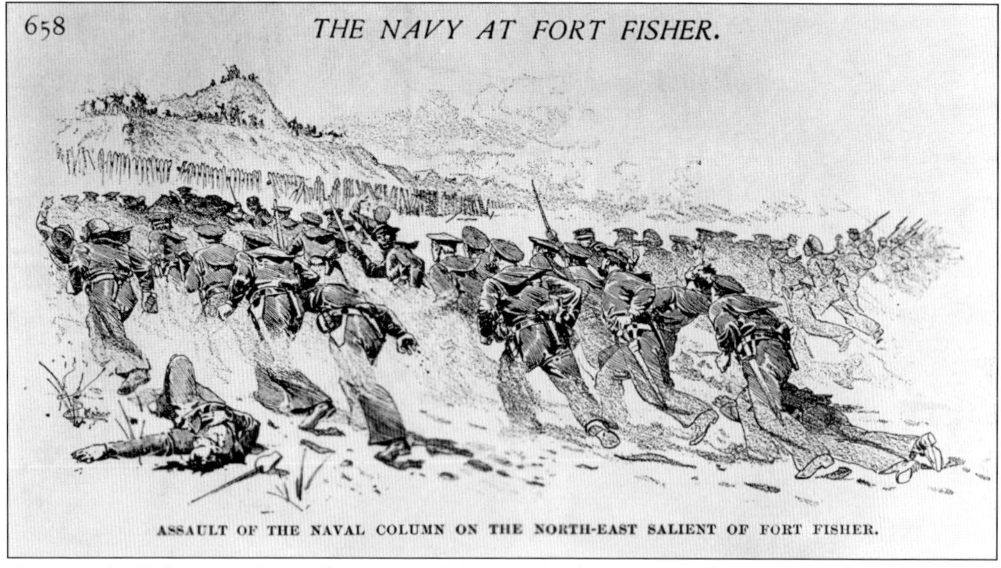

A pen-and-ink drawing shows the attack of the naval column upon the fort's northeast bastions. (US Naval History and Heritage Command.)

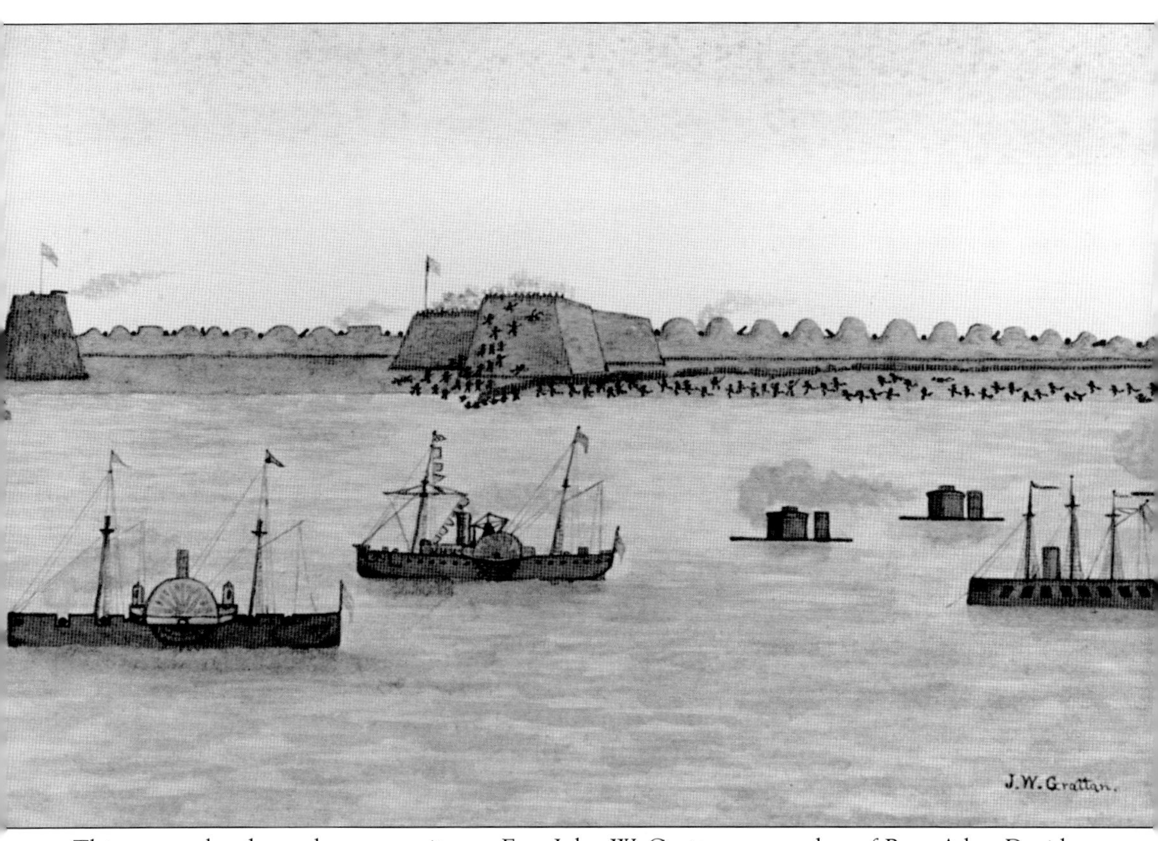

This watercolor drawn by an eyewitness, Ens. John W. Grattan, a member of Rear Adm. David Porter's staff, shows the storming of the fort while the Union fleet stands offshore. The side-wheeler in the center flying signal flags is Porter's flagship, the USS *Malvern*, while the USS *New Ironsides* is at right. (US Naval History and Heritage Command.)

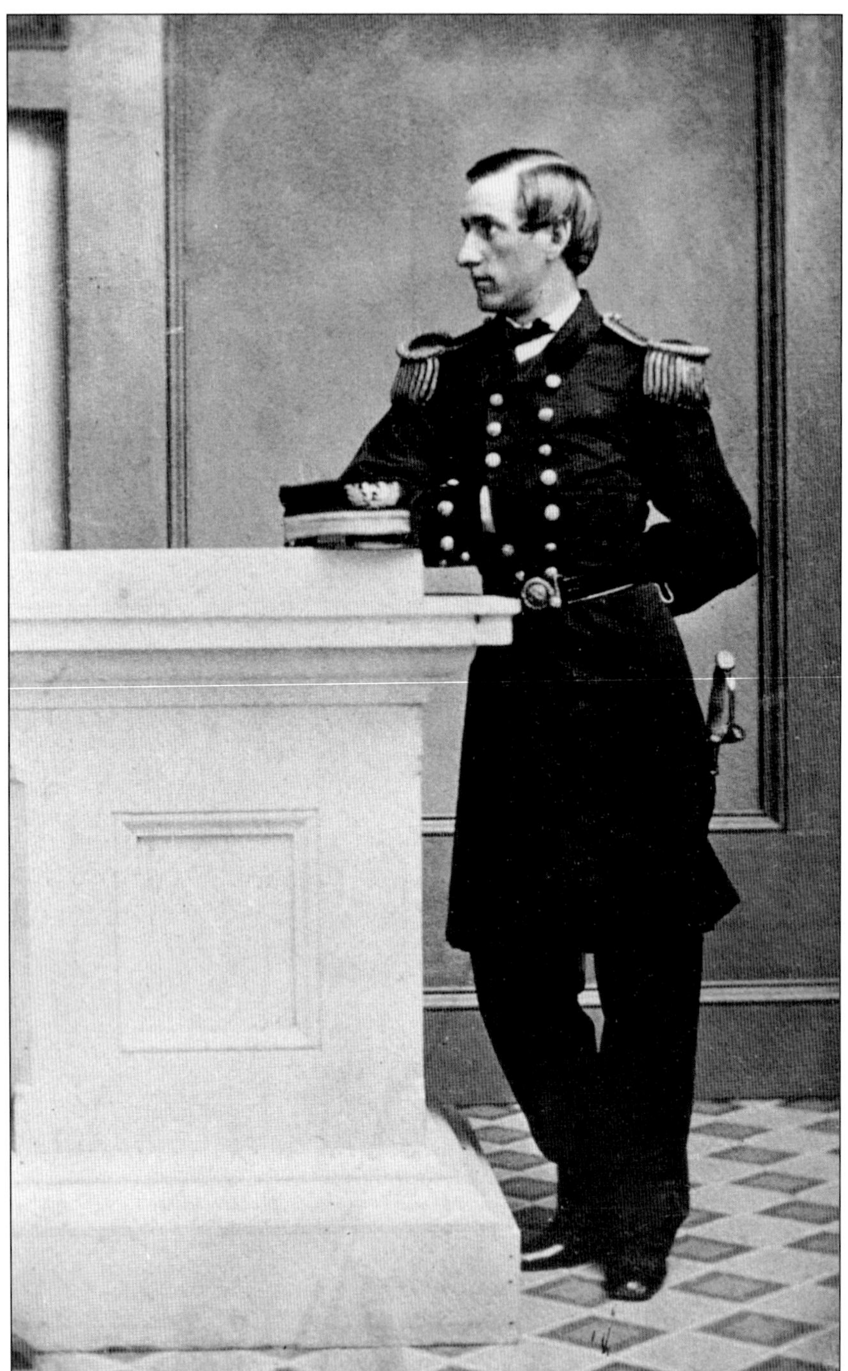

Lt. Samuel L. Preston was active throughout both battles of Fort Fisher. He was Commander Rhind's second in command on the powder ship *Louisiana*, helping ignite the explosion that started the first battle. Tragically, he was struck down while leading part of the naval column after they met stiffer resistance than anticipated when they reached the ramparts of the fort, dying within minutes of his best friend, Lt. Benjamin Porter, both members of the US Naval Academy's class of 1861. (US Naval History and Heritage Command.)

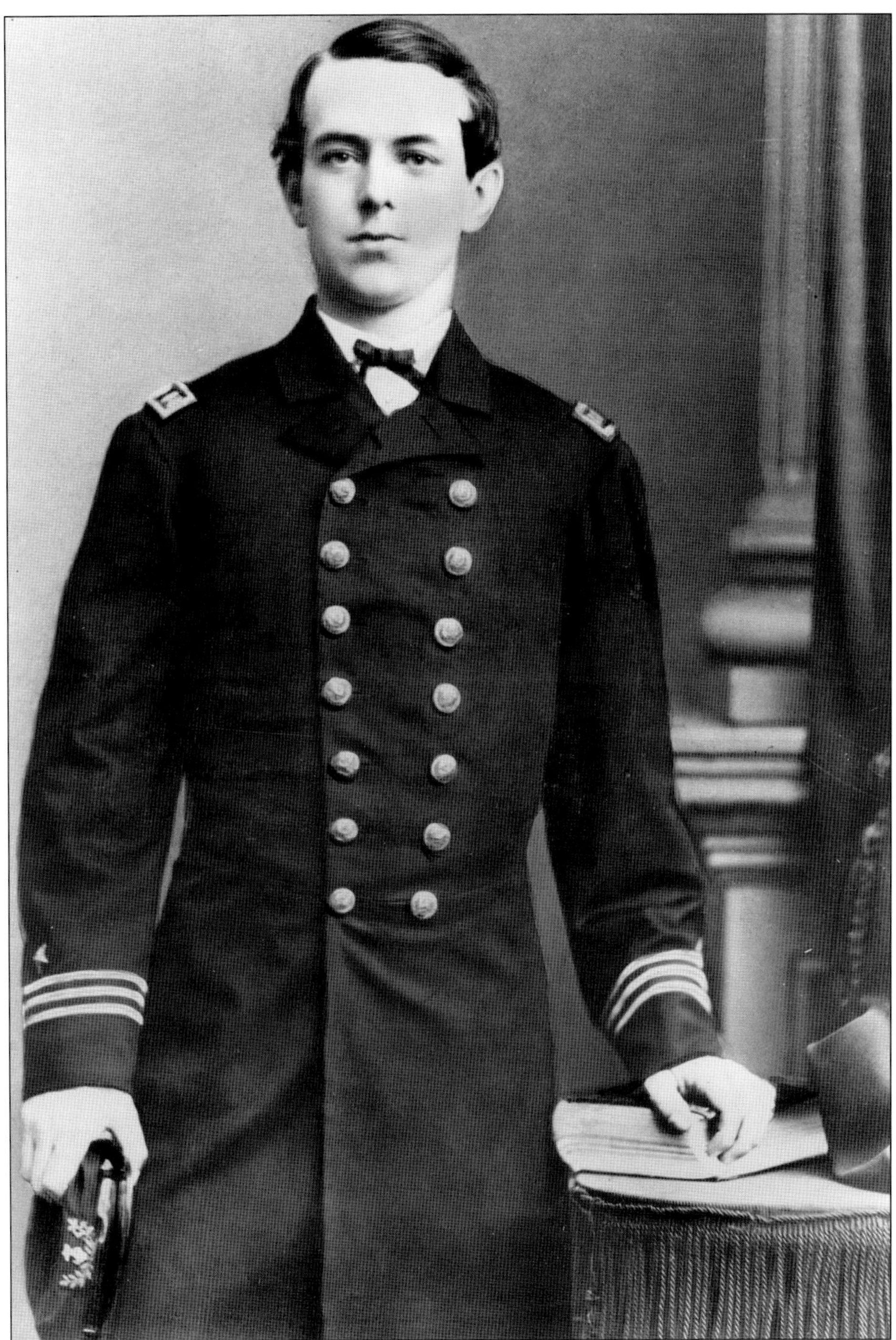

Lt. Benjamin Porter was struck down within moments of his best friend and former classmate at the US Naval Academy, Lt. Samuel L. Preston. The two served together throughout the war, being thrown into the conflict early. They were incarcerated together after being captured at Fort Sumter in South Carolina in 1863 and upon being exchanged rejoined the action just in time for the operations up the coast at Fort Fisher, North Carolina. (US Naval History and Heritage Command.)

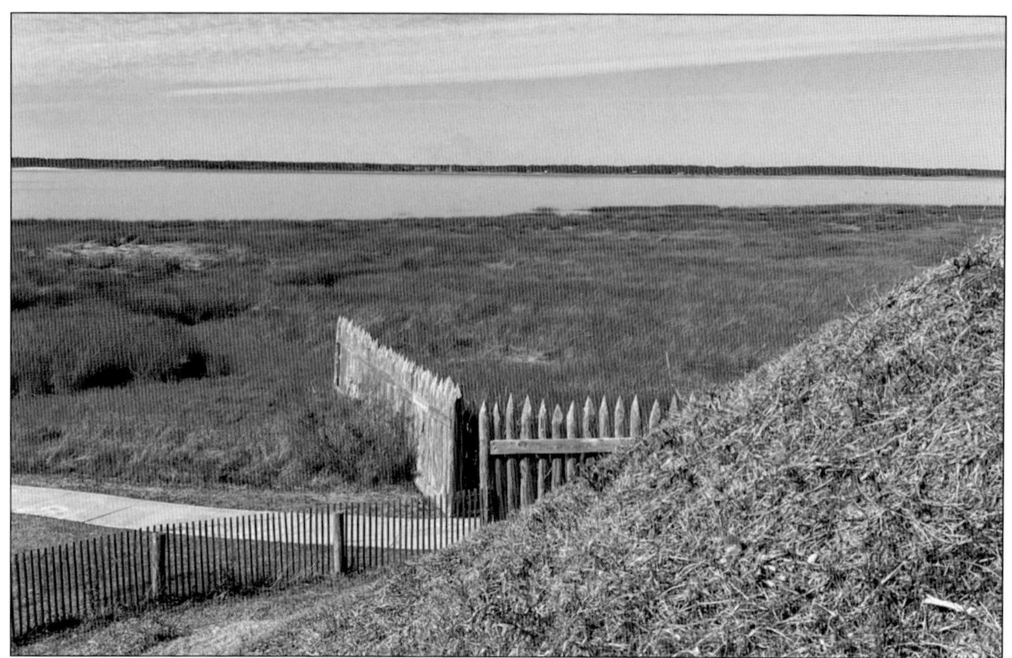

This is the main entrance to the fort, as seen from Shepherd's Battery. Union forces were able to finally penetrate the perimeter of Fort Fisher after forcing their way through the gates, something they had not been able to do in the first battle. The fighting, which raged near this landmark, gave it the nickname "The Bloody Gate."

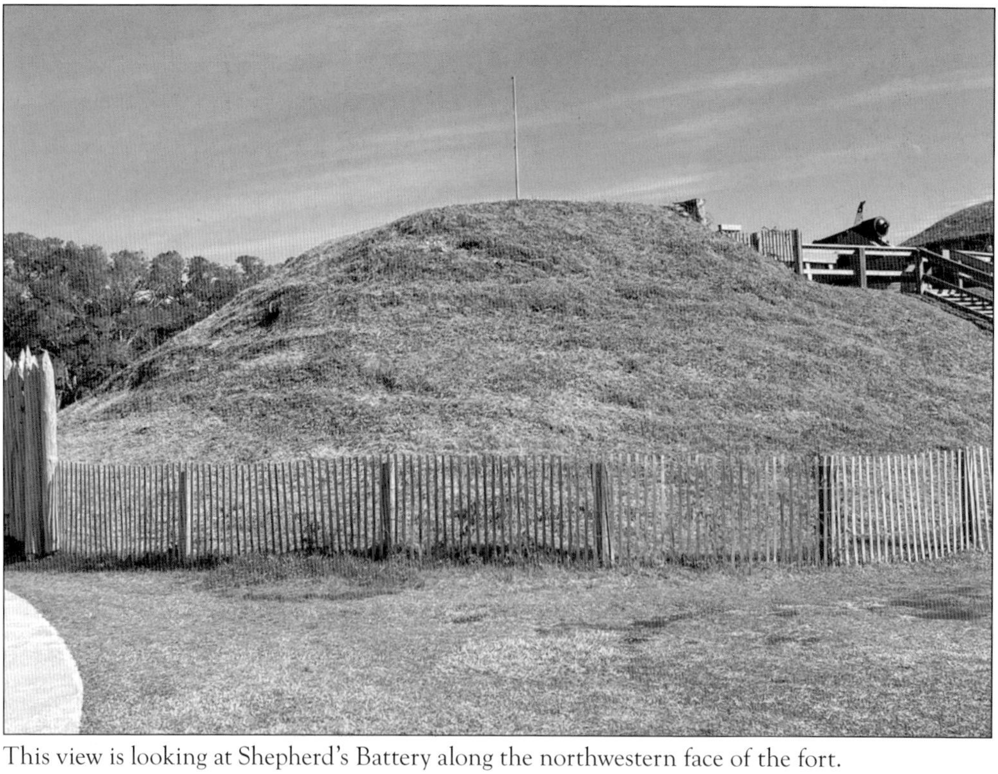

This view is looking at Shepherd's Battery along the northwestern face of the fort.

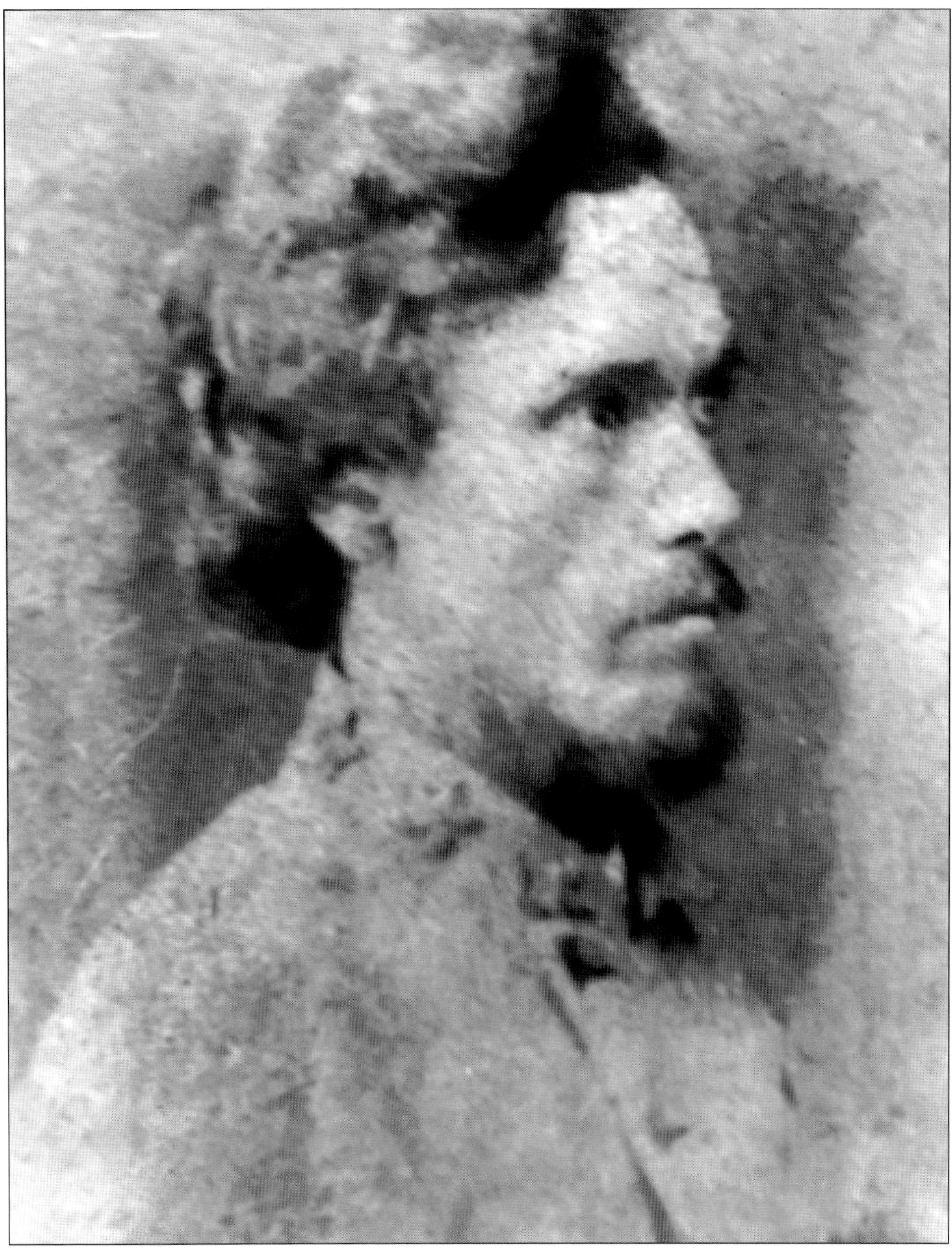

Col. William Lamb fought on after the Union forces penetrated the perimeter of the fort. He ordered the giant Armstrong guns to be directed inside the fort to clear the grounds of enemy fighters. Lamb went down shortly after Whiting, being knocked out of commission by several wounds, the most serious of which was a broken hip bone. The Virginian expressed extreme disappointment after the surgeons told him he was unable to return to the fray, but the excruciating pain emanating from what he thought was a minor wound proved the surgeons were accurate in their diagnosis. Lamb turned over command to Maj. James Reilly, the highest-ranking member of his staff still in the field. (Author's collection.)

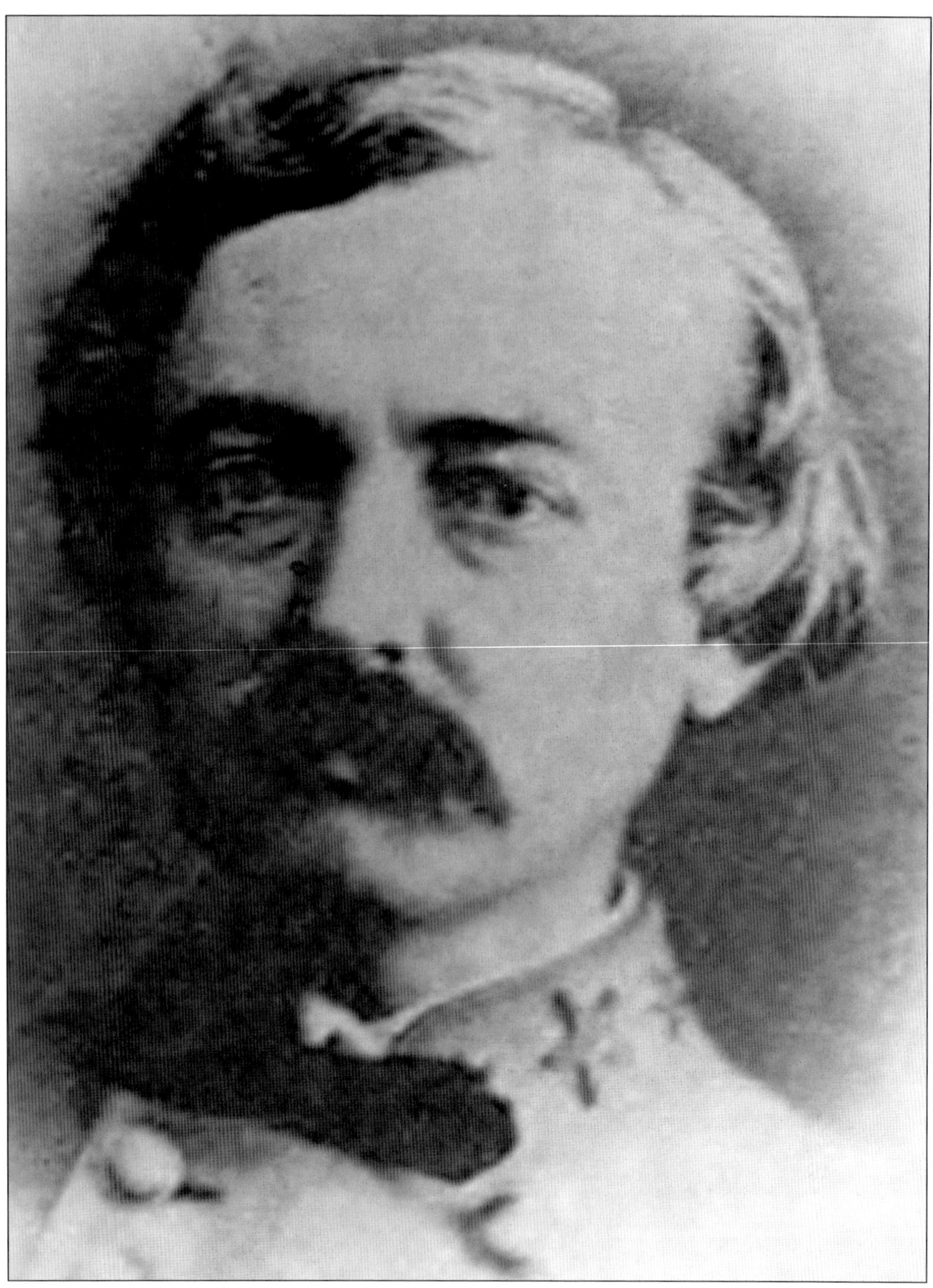

Gen. W.H.C. Whiting is shown here in an undated image. Despite being disrespected by the Confederate high command in Richmond, Whiting did not go home and sulk. Instead, "Little Billy," as his men affectionately called him, went to Fort Fisher and before the first battle offered his services to Colonel Lamb, who gratefully accepted. Whiting fought bravely in both battles at Fort Fisher, hanging on until the bitter end and being mortally wounded as the Union forces were overwhelming the fort he spent so much of his life's energy designing. (Author's collection.)

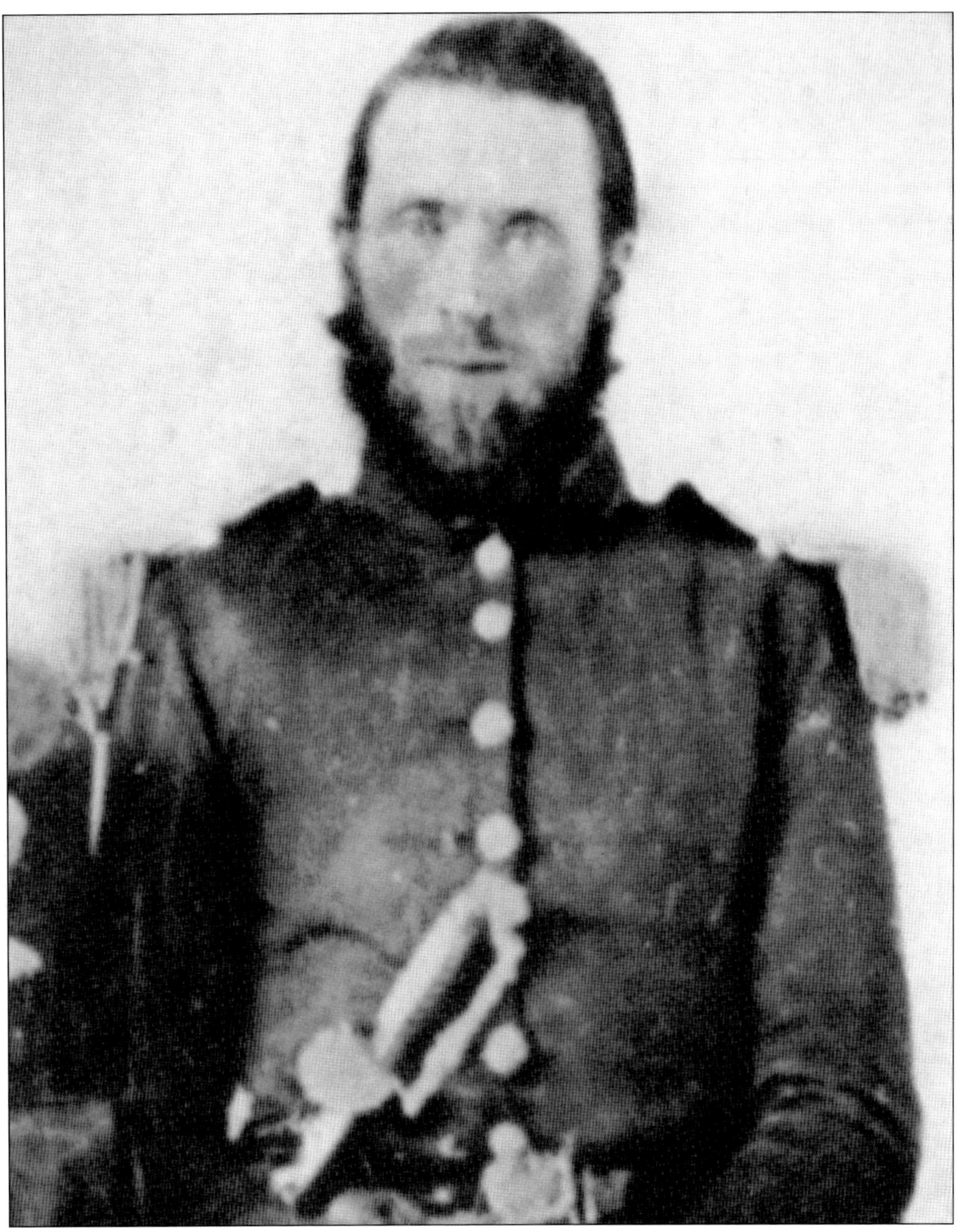

Capt. Daniel Munn of Company B, 36th North Carolina Regiment, briefly took command of the garrison immediately after Lamb was wounded, accompanying the colonel to the hospital and directing as well as he could from there, expecting Lamb to momentarily return to the fray. With his wounds worse than expected, Colonel Lamb was unable to continue and sent for Major Reilly, who assumed command. Thus, relieved of his responsibilities as the senior officer present, Captain Munn remained by Lamb and Whiting's side to the end, overseeing the evacuation of the garrison's wounded survivors who could be moved to Battery Buchanan. This photograph of Munn was taken shortly before the outbreak of the war, when he was captain of the Maysville Light Infantry Regiment of the North Carolina State Militia. (US Army Heritage and Education Center.)

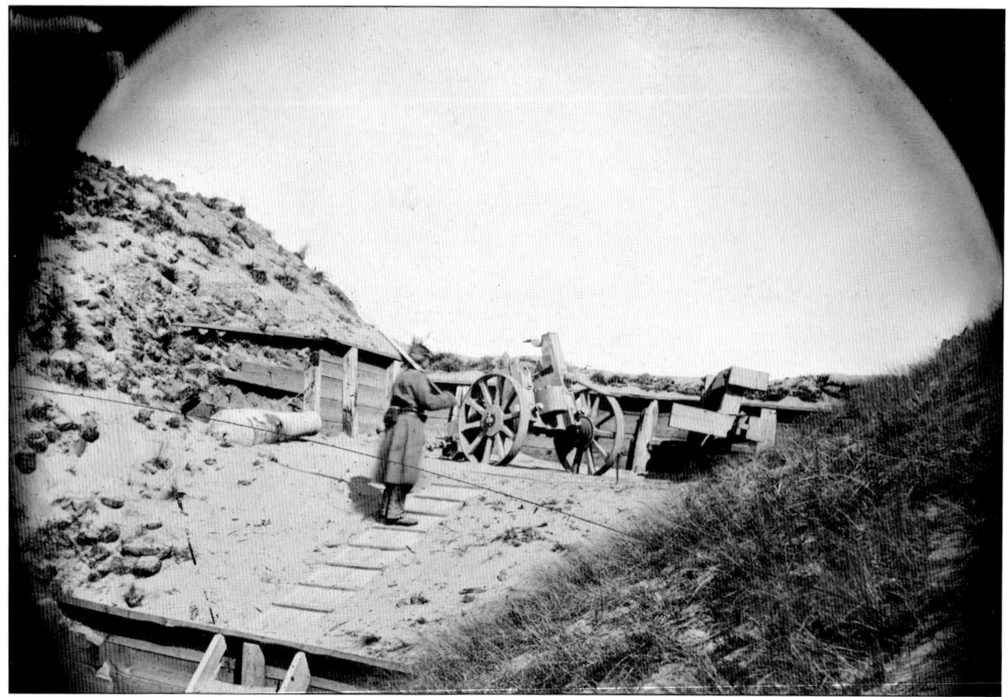

An unidentified photographer captured this image of the interior of Fort Fisher in January 1865. (LOC.)

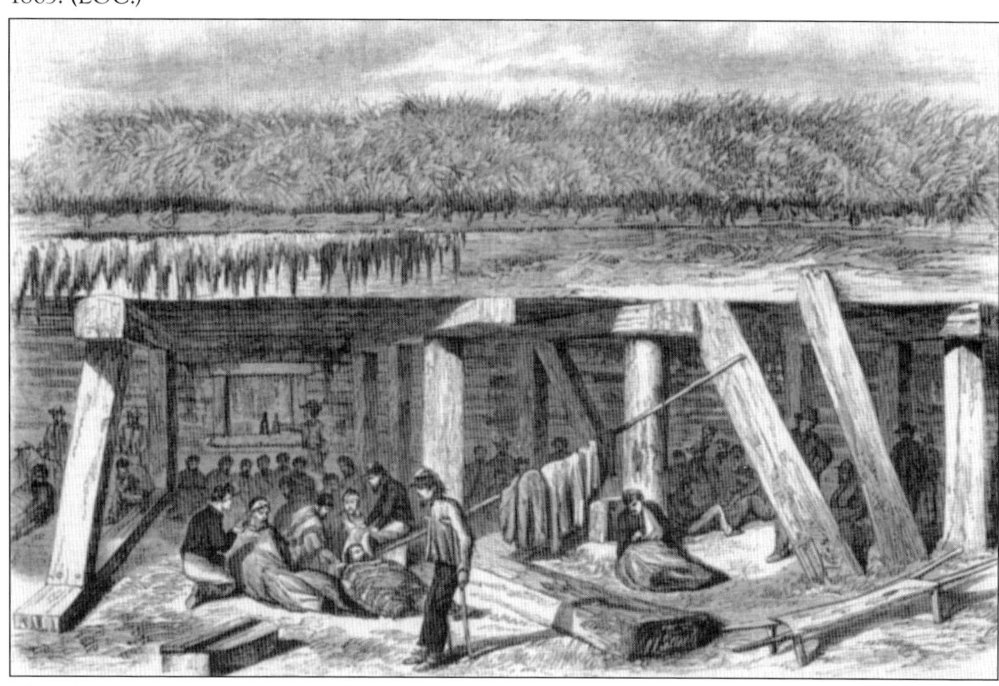

This drawing by an unidentified artist shows the Confederate wounded gathered in the fort's hospital in the Pulpit shortly after the final battle. Both Colonel Lamb and General Whiting were evacuated from this room to Battery Buchanan as Fort Fisher was being overrun. (US Army Heritage and Education Center.)

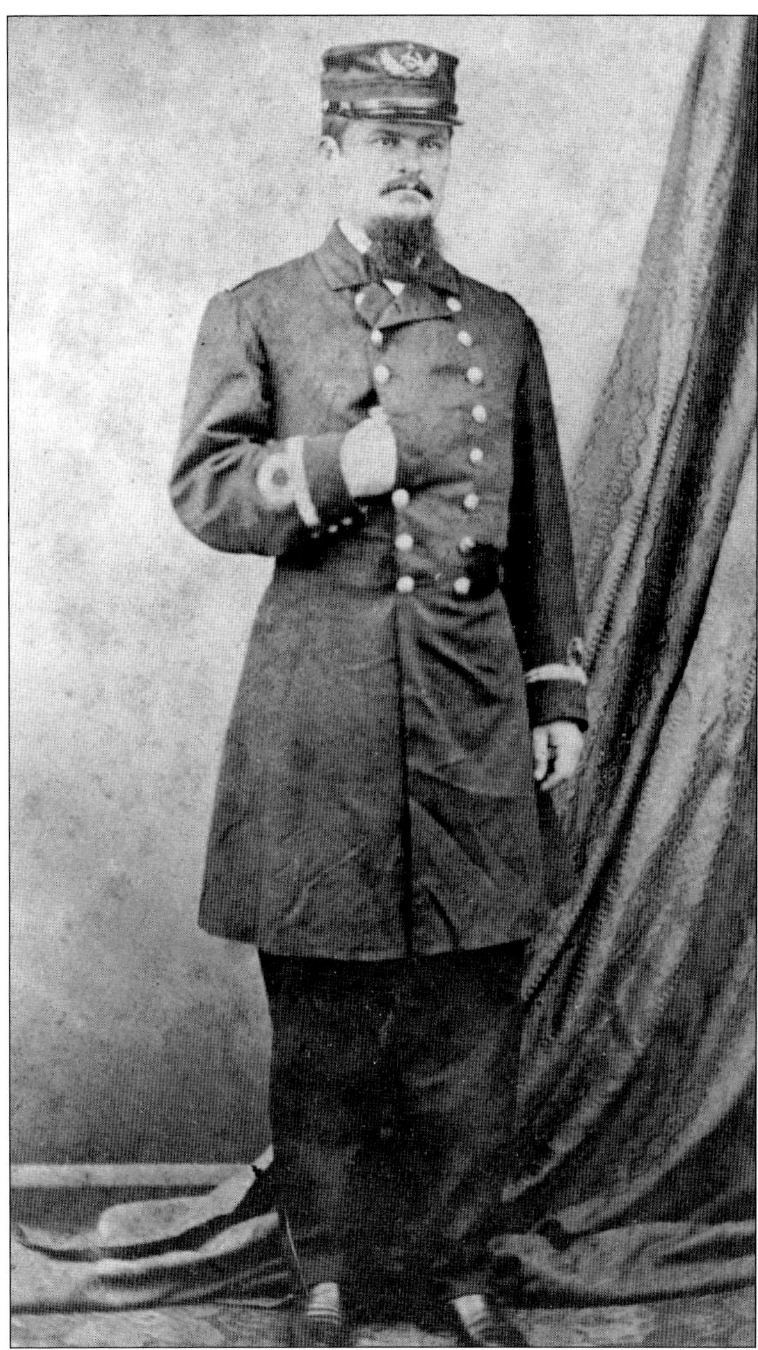

First Lt. Robert T. Chapman is shown in a photograph taken in France in 1863 while on leave from his duties aboard the CSS *Georgia*. Chapman evacuated Battery Buchanan late in the battle. Who told him to leave and exactly when to do so is unclear, but when Major Reilly arrived at Battery Buchanan with the survivors from the main garrison at Fort Fisher, he was surprised to find the place virtually empty. Even worse, they had taken the boats with them when they left, leaving the seriously wounded soldiers whom Captain Munn was guarding from Fort Fisher's main hospital before they could be taken to safety across the river. (US Naval History and Heritage Command.)

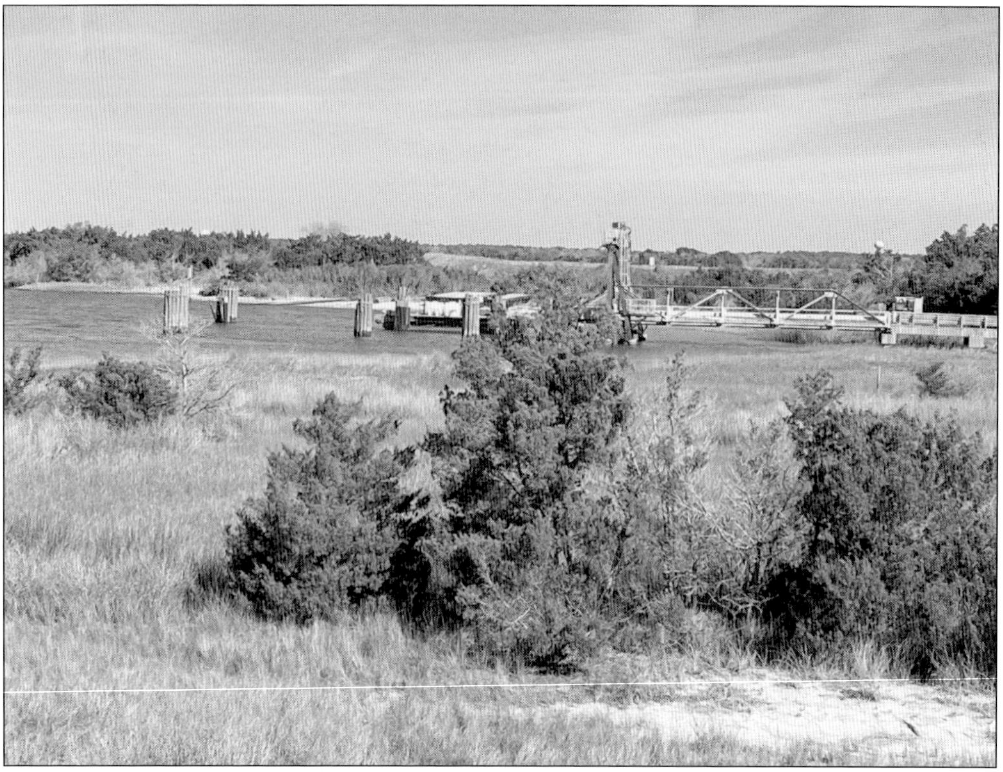

This photograph shows the view from atop Battery Buchanan, looking north toward the main defenses of Fort Fisher. The final scenes of the battle took place along this area of low ground.

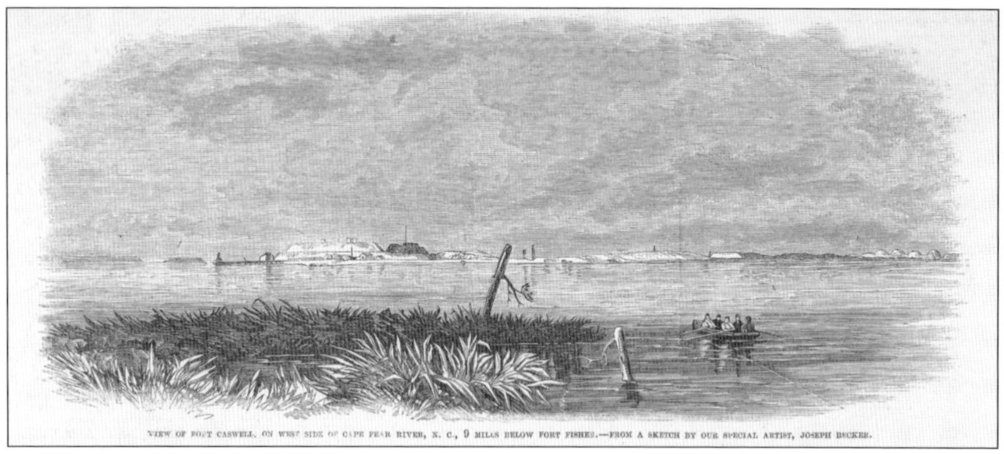

Fort Caswell, which played a key role in the defenses near the mouth of the Cape Fear River, became untenable with the fall of Fort Fisher. The fort's main magazine, said to contain over a 100,000 pounds of gunpowder, was ignited by Confederates in the wee hours of the morning on January 17, 1865, the explosion being likened by eyewitnesses to a volcano erupting. The defenders, along with those from the other defensive works at the mouth of the river, moved upstream to Fort Anderson. Fort Caswell is shown here in the March 4, 1865, edition of *Frank Leslie's Illustrated News*. (North Carolina Collection Photographic Archives, Wilson Special Collections Library, University of North Carolina at Chapel Hill.)

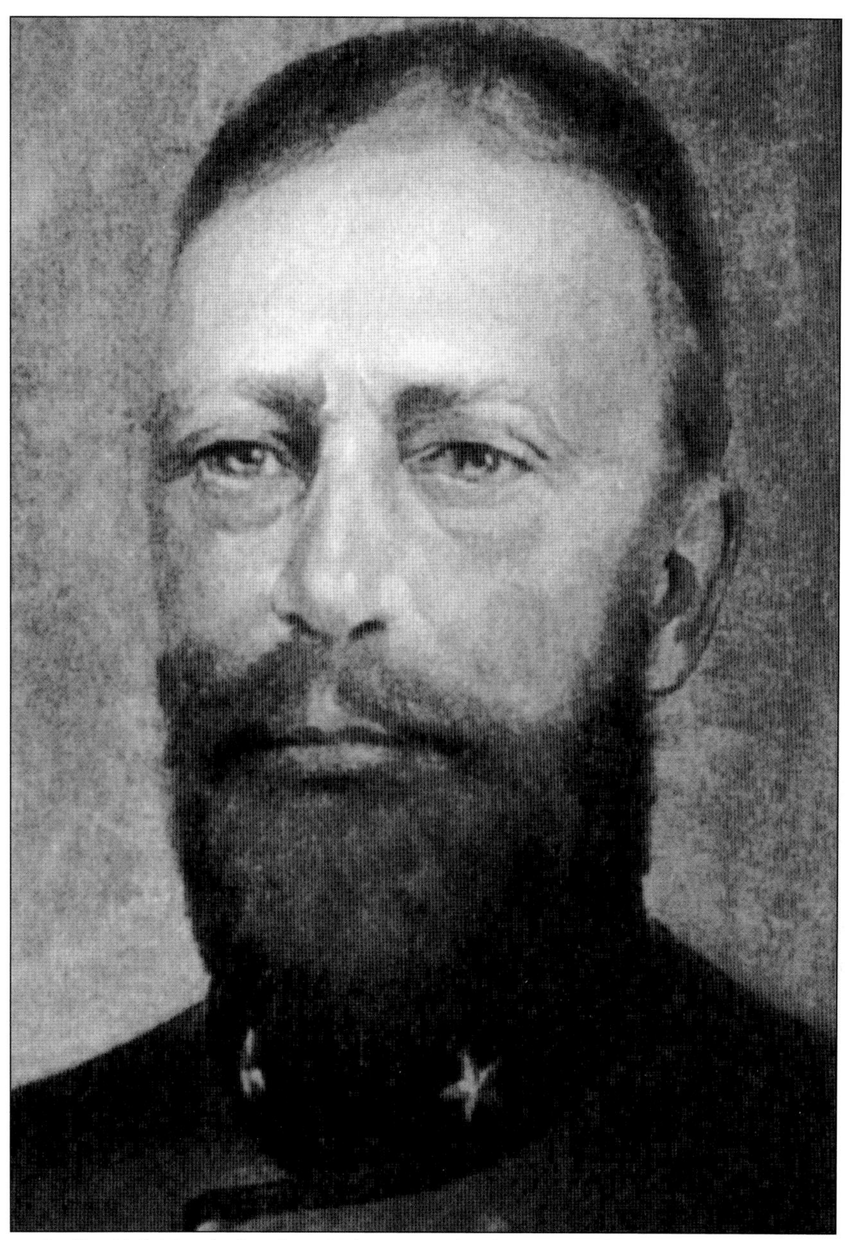

Maj. James Reilly, 10th North Carolina Volunteers, also known as the 1st North Carolina Artillery, was a native of Ireland but moved at a young age with his parents to Maryland. He served with distinction as an enlisted man in the US Army in both the Second Seminole War and later the war with Mexico. He commanded the small garrison at Fort Johnston, near the mouth of the Cape Fear, in 1861 when the War between the States broke out. His skills as an artilleryman won him a commission in the ranks of the military forces of his adopted state of North Carolina, where he served the Confederacy with distinction, becoming one of General Whiting's most trusted officers. As stated earlier, Reilly held his post until the bitter end, tenaciously holding on in the face of ever-increasing enemy forces swarming the fort. He was shocked to find that Battery Buchanan had been evacuated and that there was no way of getting the men he now commanded safely across the river. (North Carolina Archives and History.)

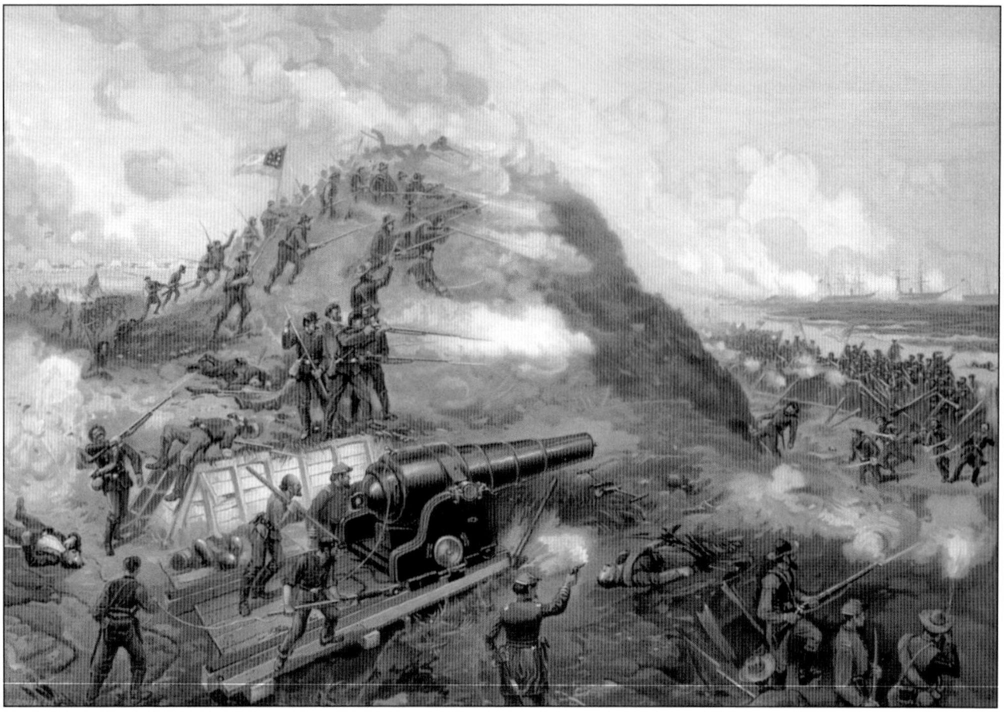

The image above is a Currier and Ives engraving showing the capture of Fort Fisher. (LOC.)

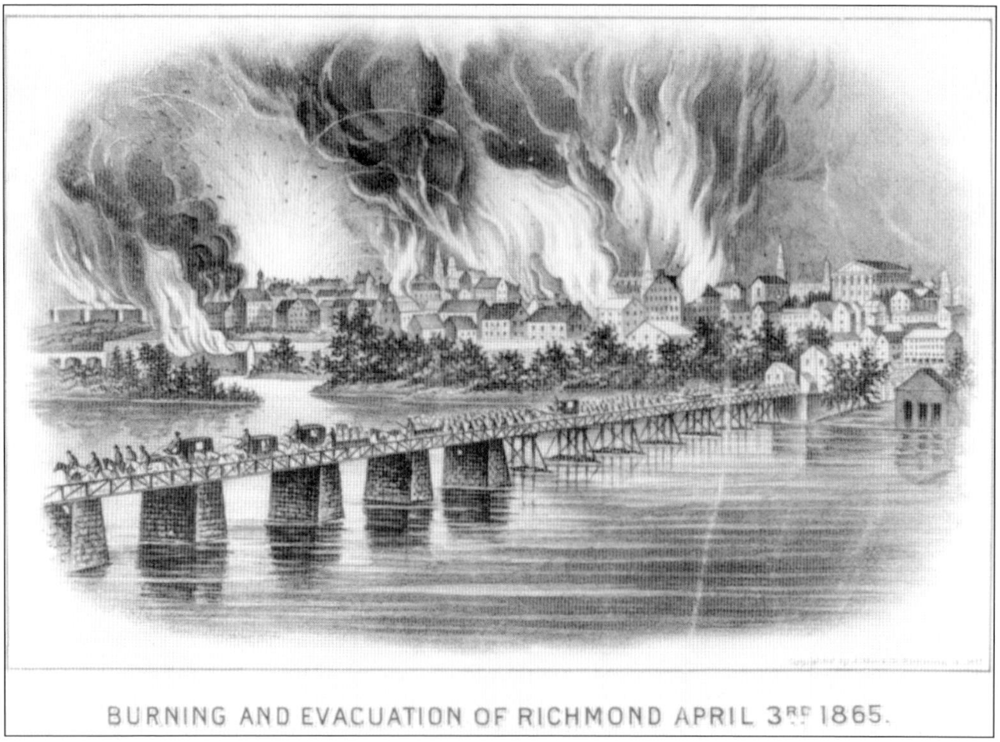

BURNING AND EVACUATION OF RICHMOND APRIL 3RD 1865.

Just as Gen. Robert E. Lee had warned, the Confederacy did not long survive the capture of Fort Fisher and the severing of its "Lifeline to the Sea." (LOC.)

Five

Aftermath

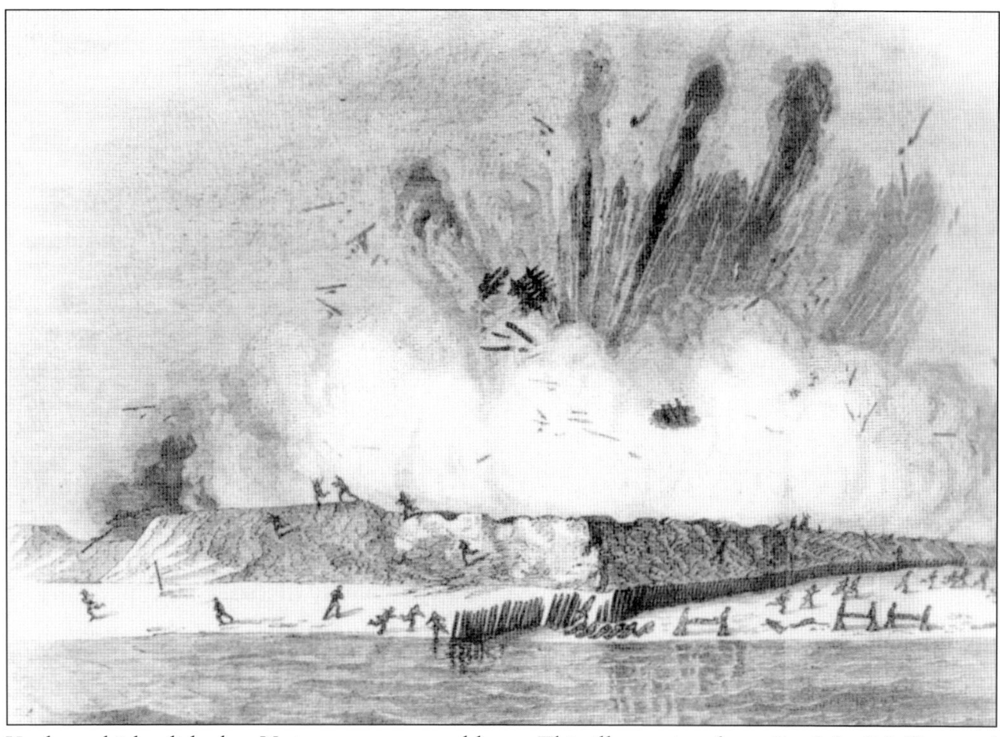

Yankee whisky did what Union gunners could not. This illustration from *Frank Leslie's Illustrated News* shows the explosion that ripped through the Pulpit on January 16, 1865. The Pulpit was the site of the Confederate powder magazine, which a drunken Union marine, staggering about in the dark with a lit cigar looking for more whisky and loot, ignited the morning after the battle. Union soldiers and sailors, along with hundreds of unarmed and wounded Confederate prisoners, were sleeping on the sandy gun emplacement, which made an ideal enclosure in which to keep prisoners temporarily housed before sending them north. The irony is that despite hurling millions of pounds of ordnance at the sandy fort, enemy gunfire failed to reach this vital spot.

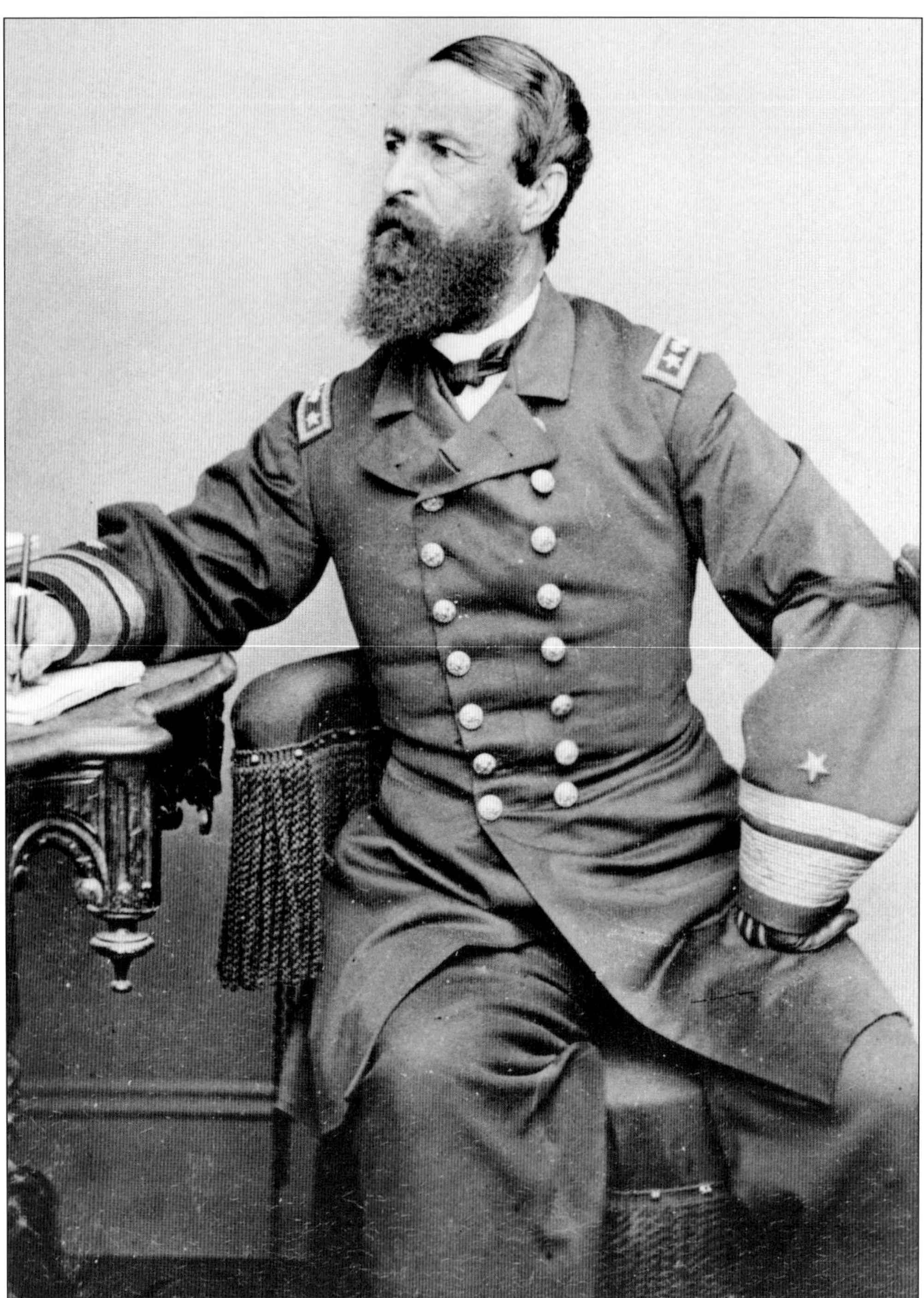

Rear Adm. David Porter developed an admiration for the handiwork of his adversaries who had taken Union forces so much blood and treasure to finally overcome. He later wrote, "No one could form the slightest conception of these works, their magnitude, strength and extent, who had not seen them, and General Whiting (the founder) must have had an abiding faith in the durability of the Confederacy when he expended so many years of labor on them." (LOC.)

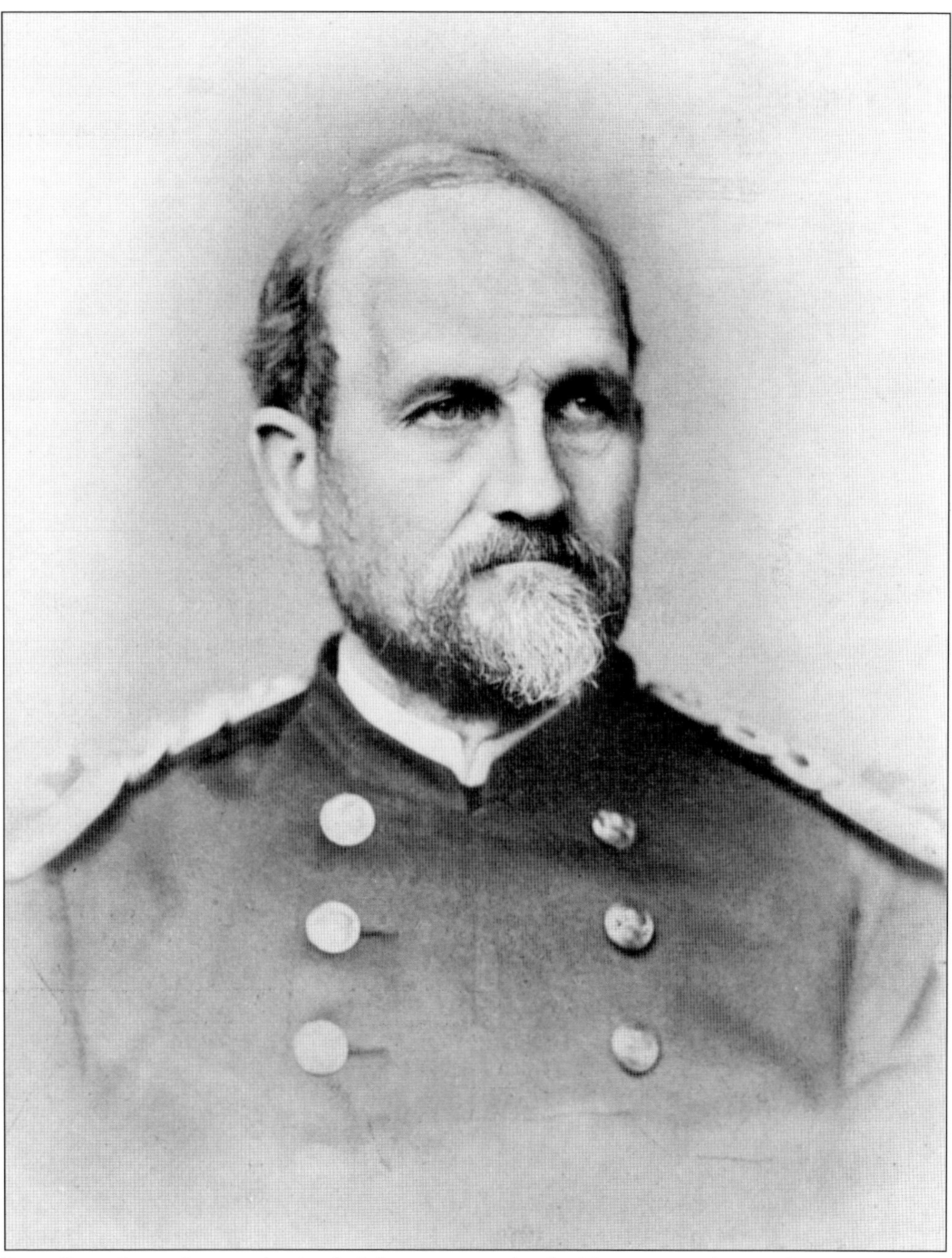

Brig. Gen. Cyrus Comstock, chief of the engineers for the Union army during the action at Fort Fisher, was very impressed with the defenses of the sandy fort and was instrumental in having the photographer Timothy O'Sullivan assigned to document the works. (LOC.)

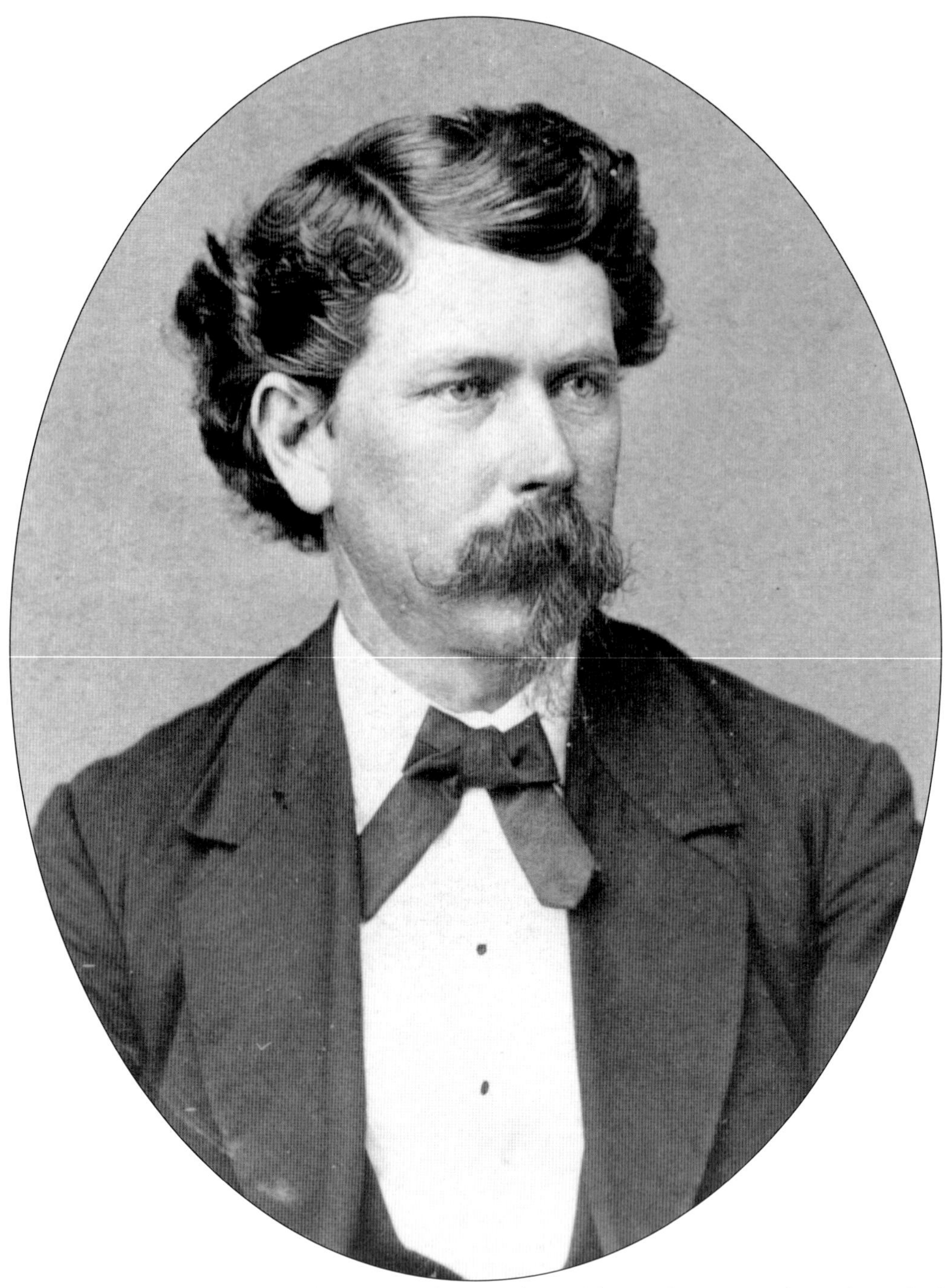

Timothy H. O'Sullivan, one of the premier photographers of the Civil War period, was dispatched to North Carolina, assigned to chronicle the aftermath of the Second Battle of Fort Fisher. (LOC.)

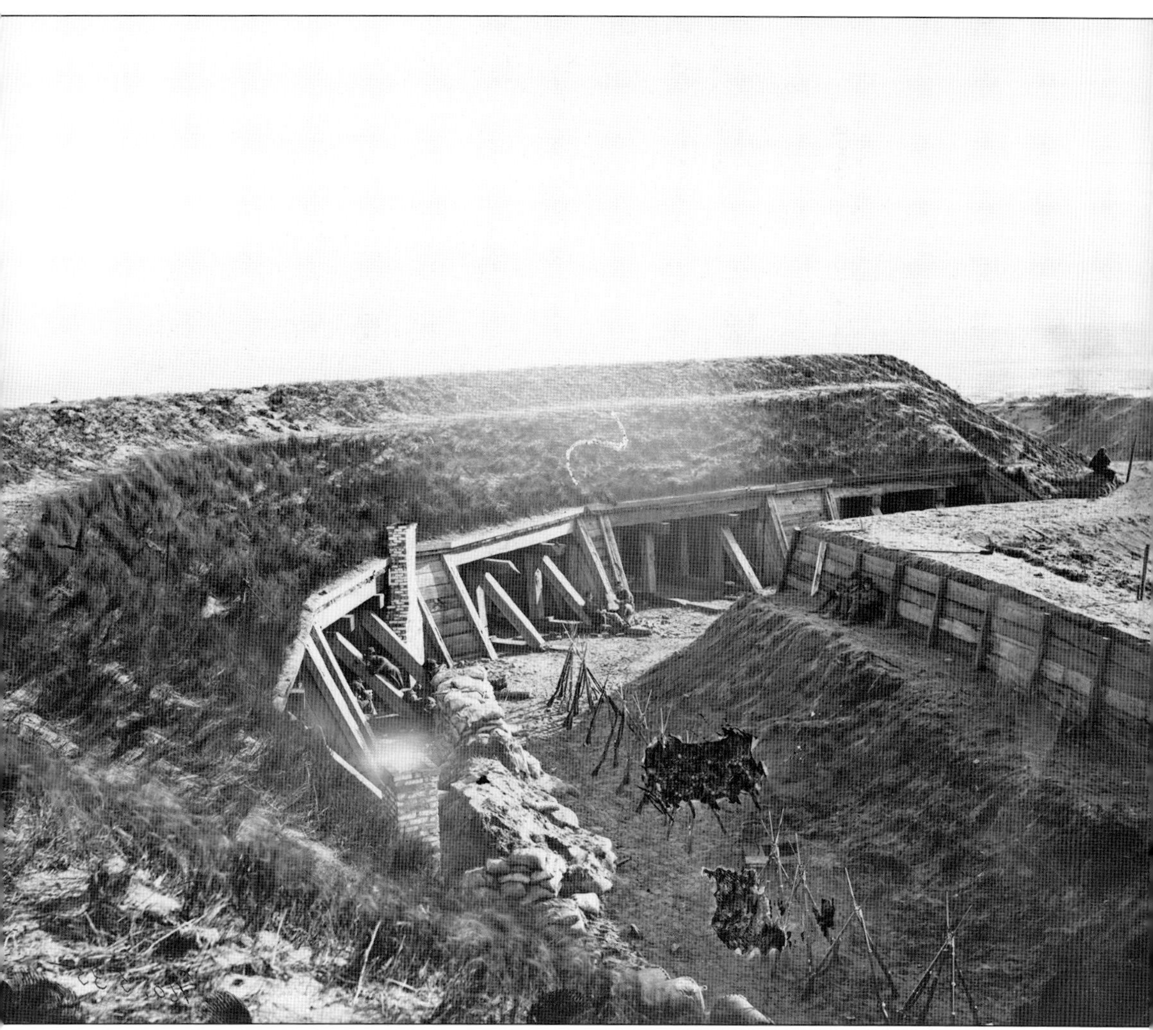

Because there was such a large loss of life due to the explosion of the powder magazine after the battle was over, there was an official investigation, of which Timothy H. O'Sullivan's photographs were a part of figuring out what happened. This is an O'Sullivan view of the inside of the Pulpit. (LOC.)

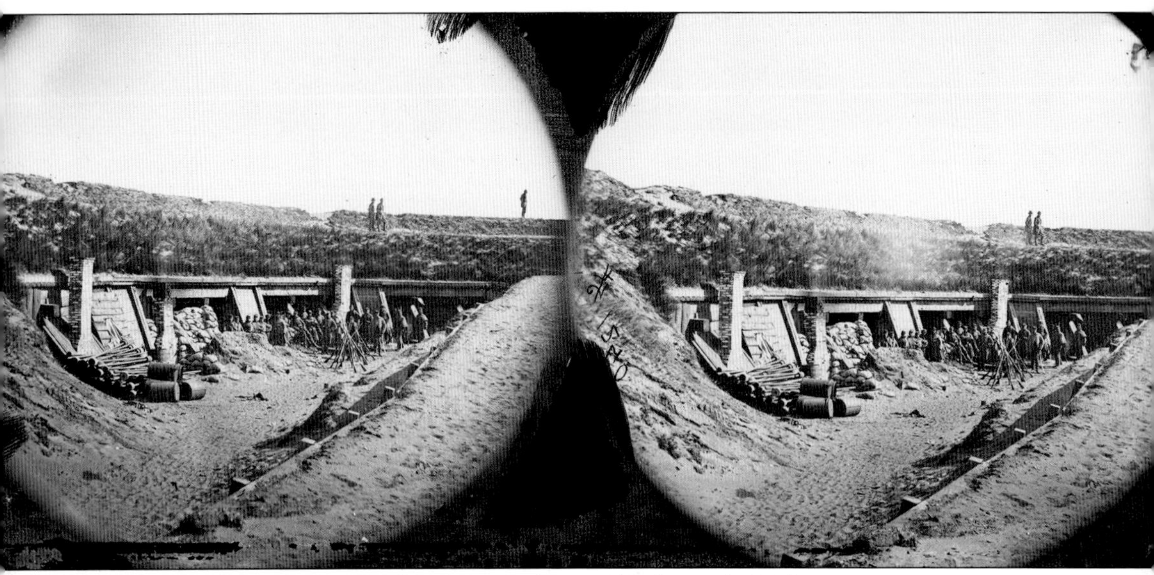

This view of the Pulpit was taken by Timothy H. O'Sullivan. (LOC.)

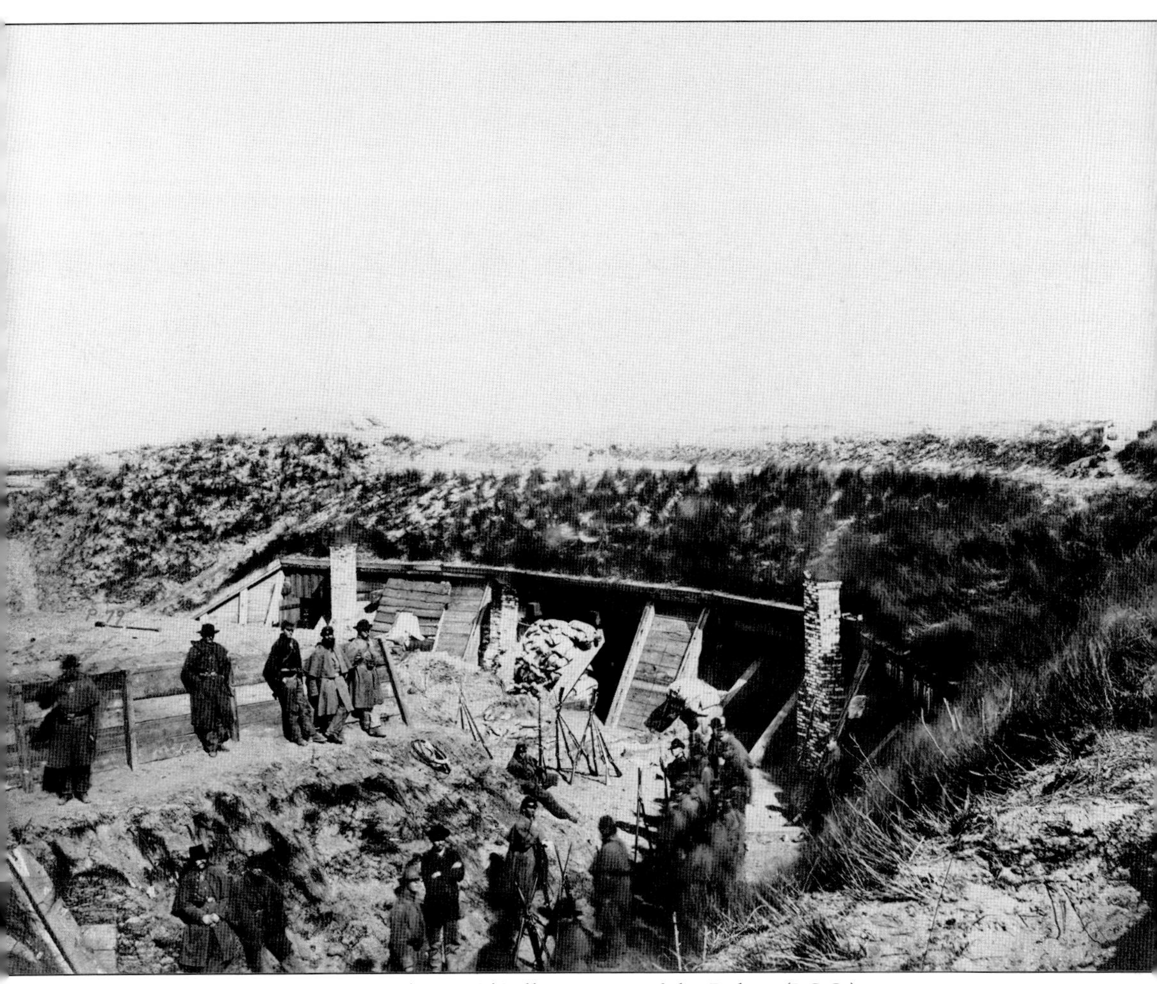

Pictured above is another Timothy H. O'Sullivan view of the Pulpit. (LOC.)

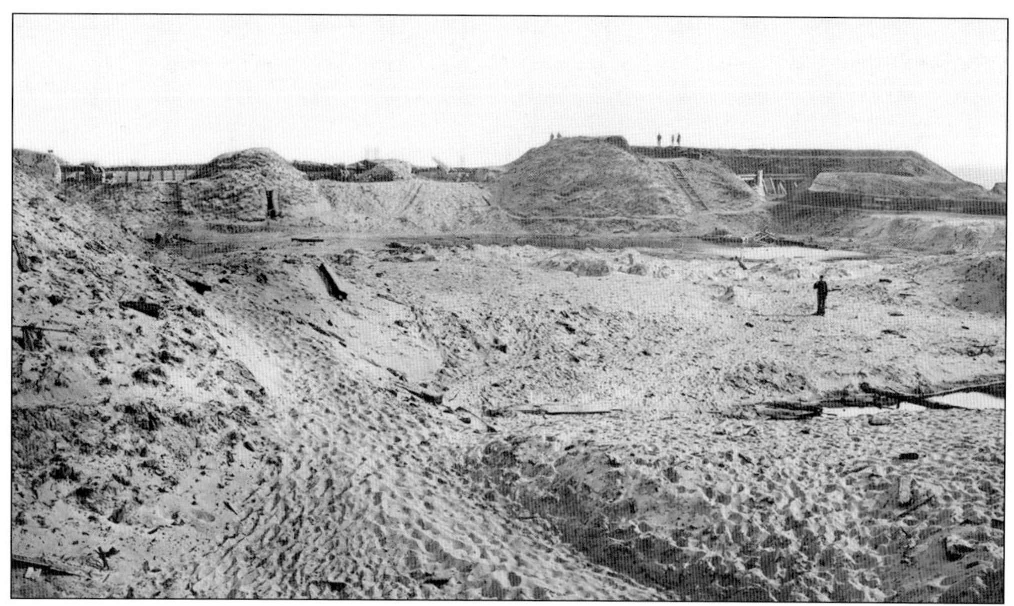

This photograph shows the main magazine inside Fort Fisher. (LOC.)

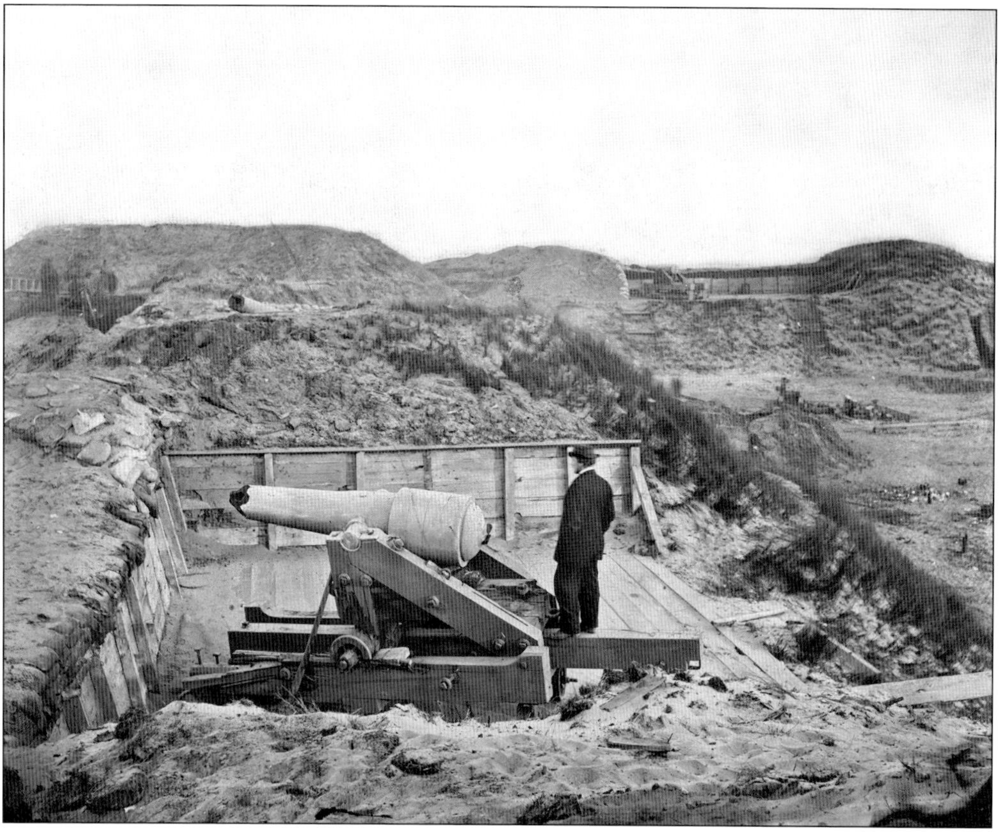

This interior view of the fort shows the damage to the heavy guns. (LOC.)

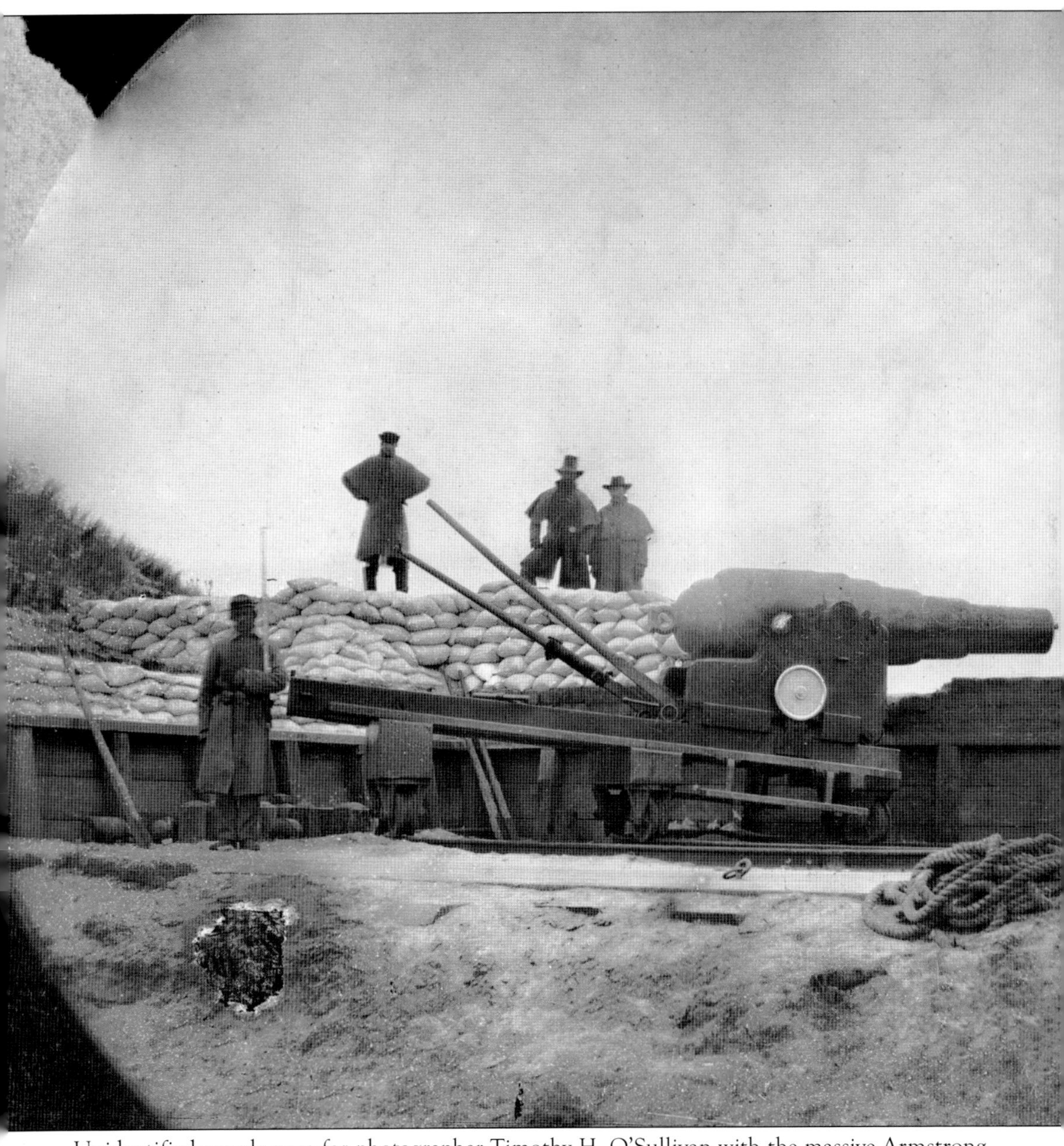

Unidentified people pose for photographer Timothy H. O'Sullivan with the massive Armstrong cannon inside the fort. (LOC.)

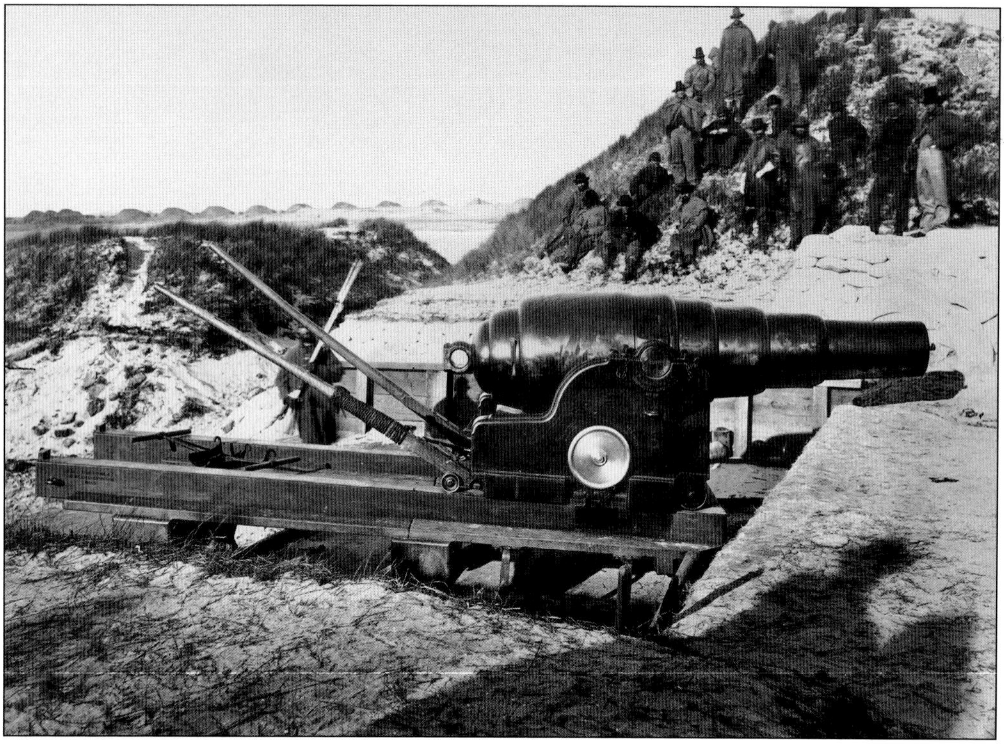

This Timothy H. O'Sullivan shot shows the Armstrong gun inside Fort Fisher. (LOC.)

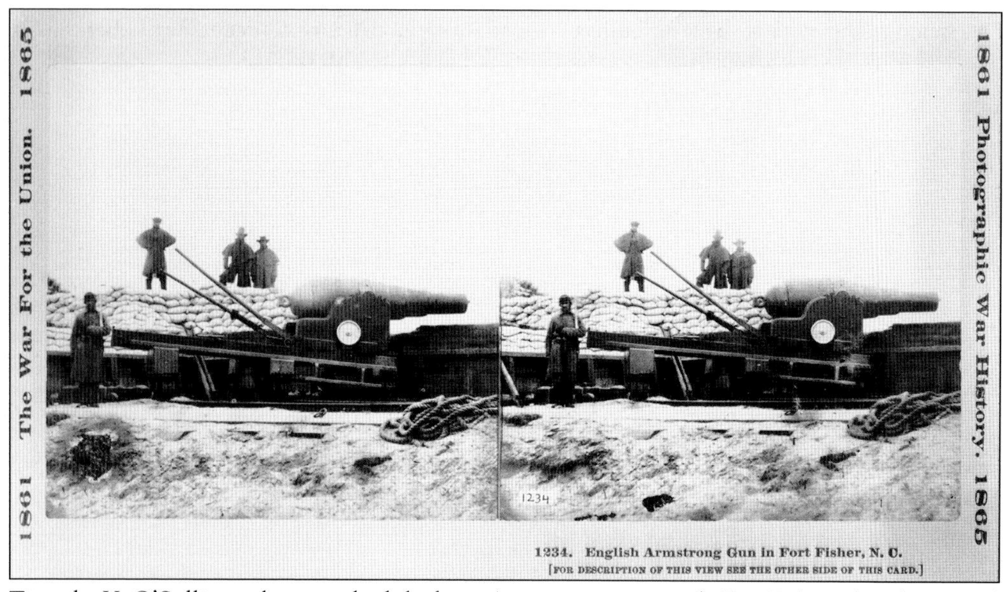

Timothy H. O'Sullivan photographed the large Armstrong gun inside Fort Fisher after the second battle. (LOC.)

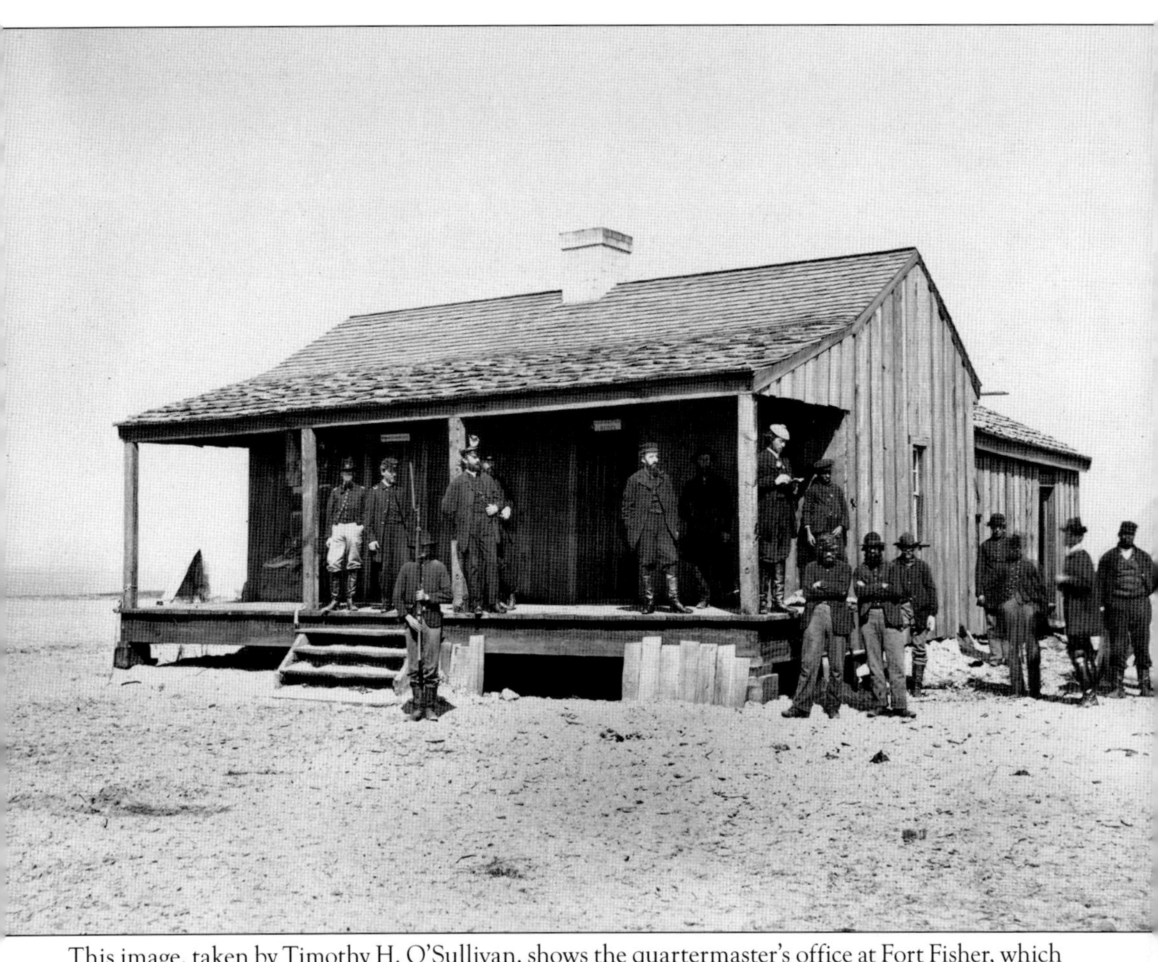

This image, taken by Timothy H. O'Sullivan, shows the quartermaster's office at Fort Fisher, which was established by the Union army shortly after the fall of the fort. (LOC.)

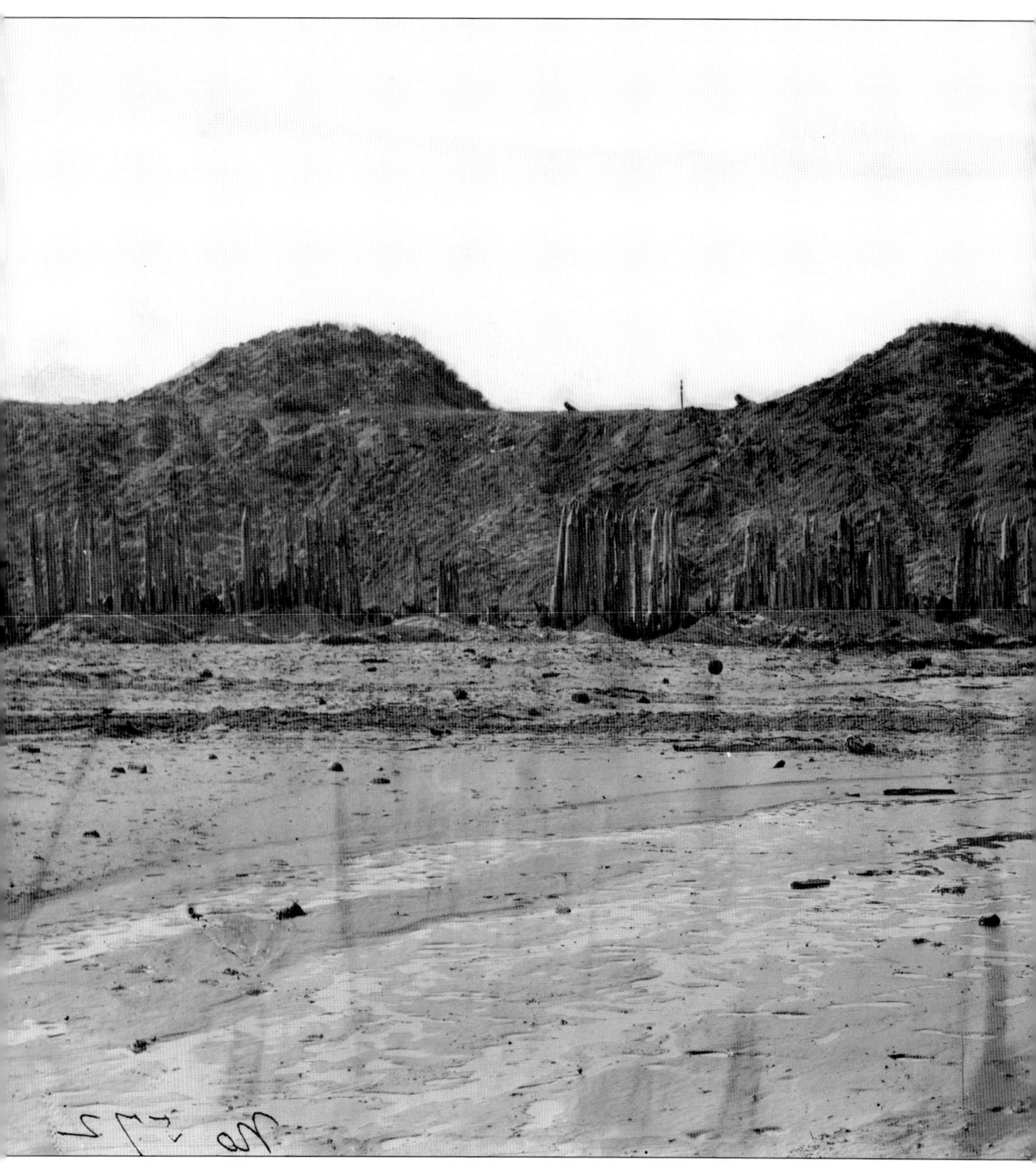

Timothy H. O'Sullivan took a set of panoramic photographs showing the land face of Fort

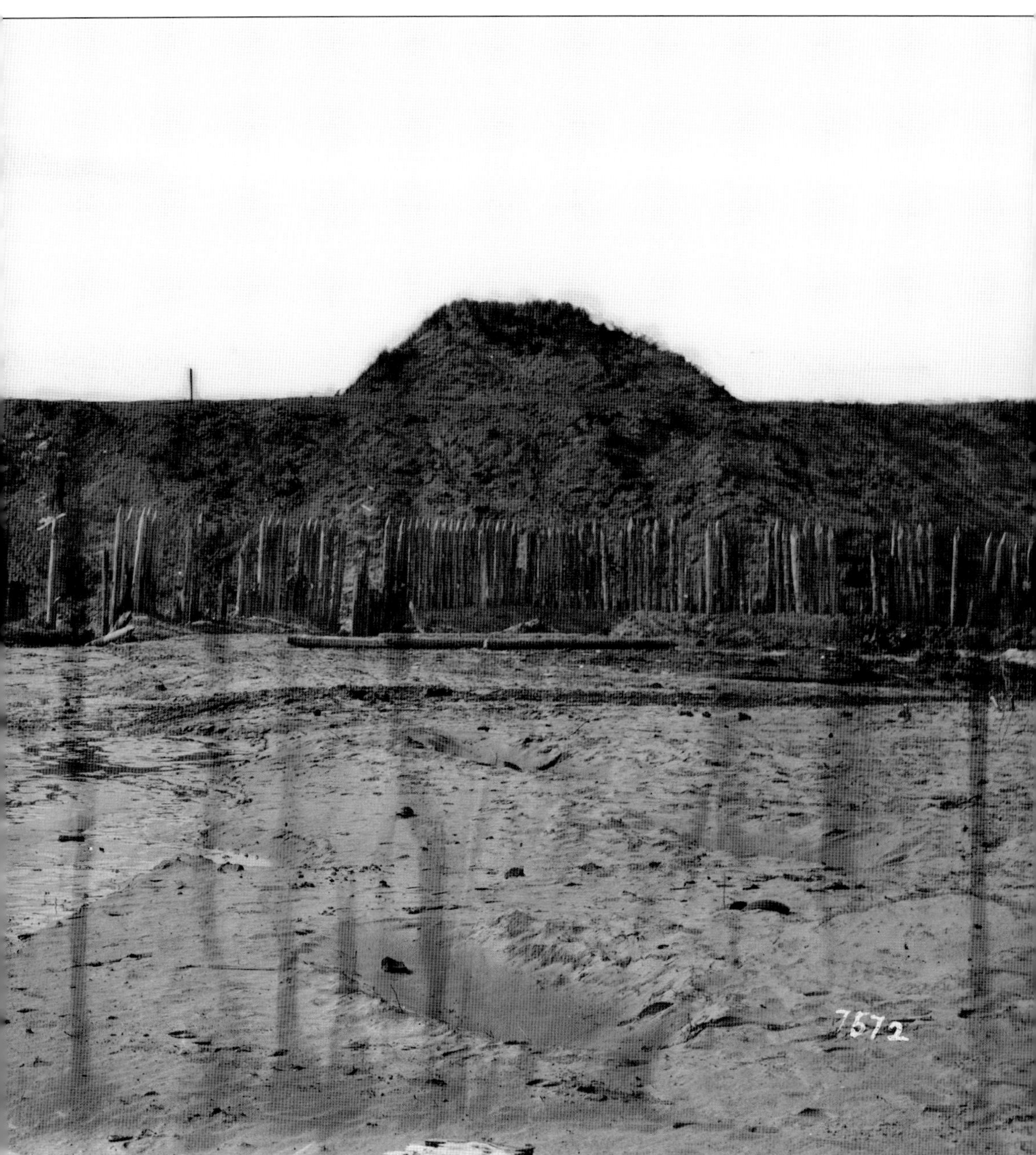

Fisher. (LOC.)

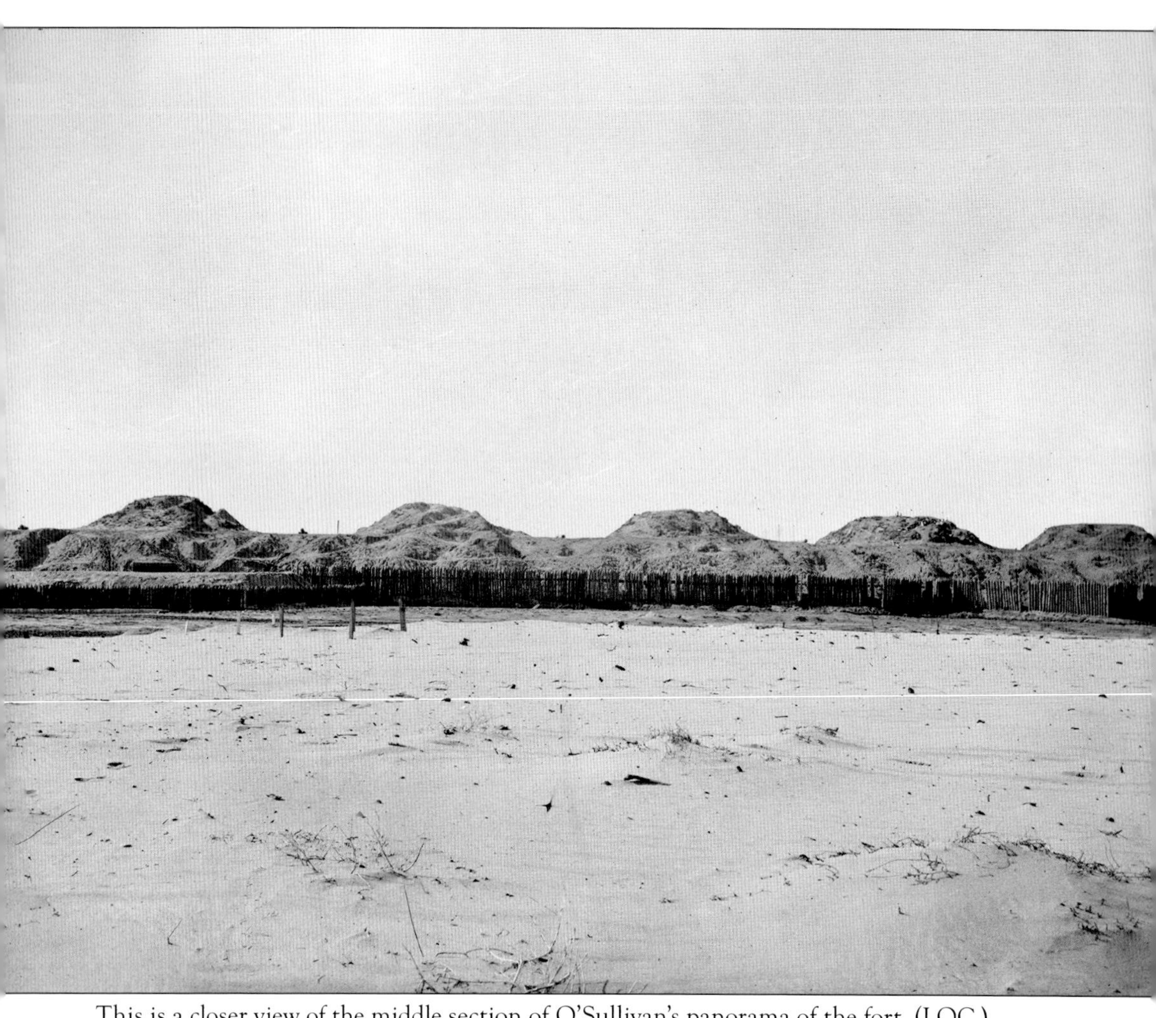

This is a closer view of the middle section of O'Sullivan's panorama of the fort. (LOC.)

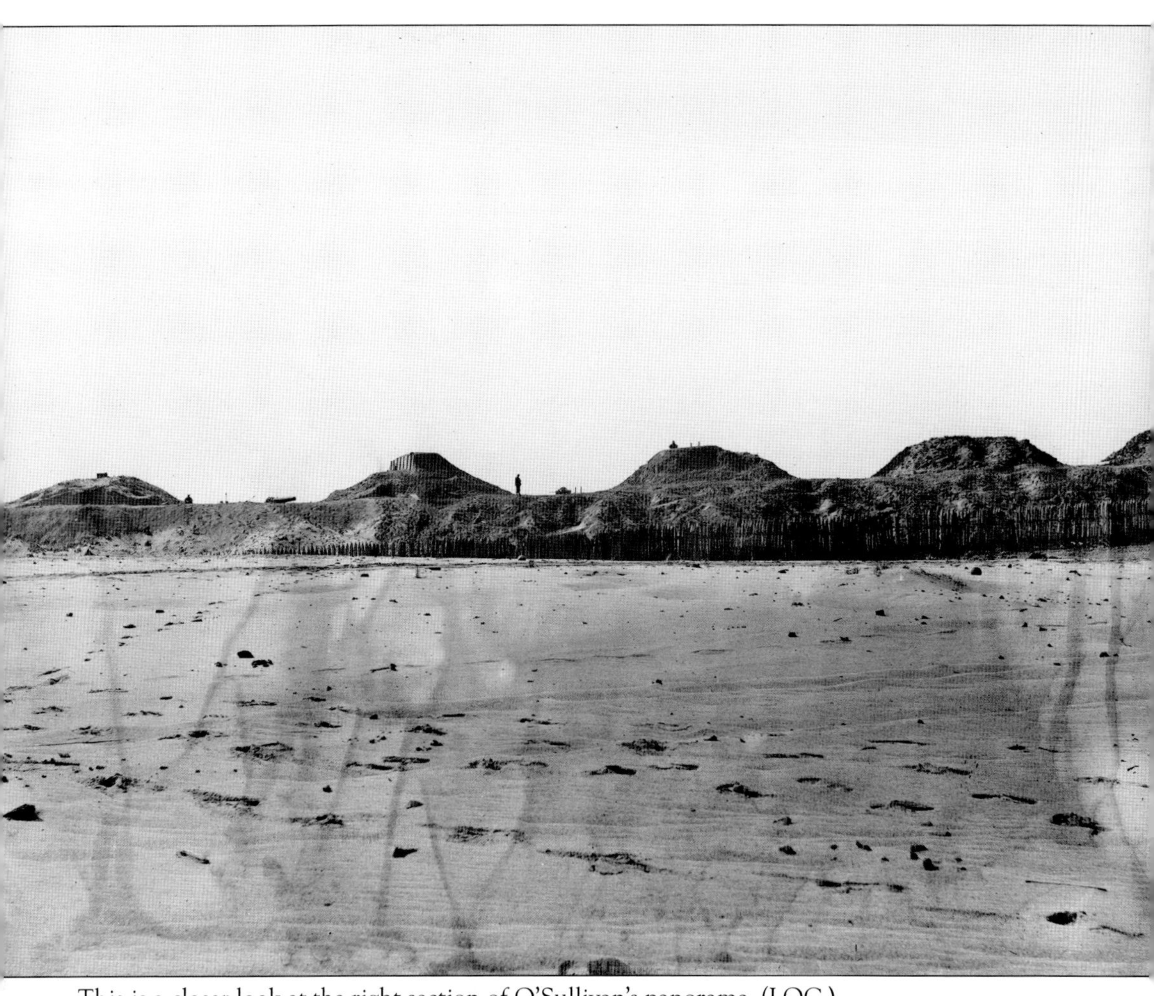

This is a closer look at the right section of O'Sullivan's panorama. (LOC.)

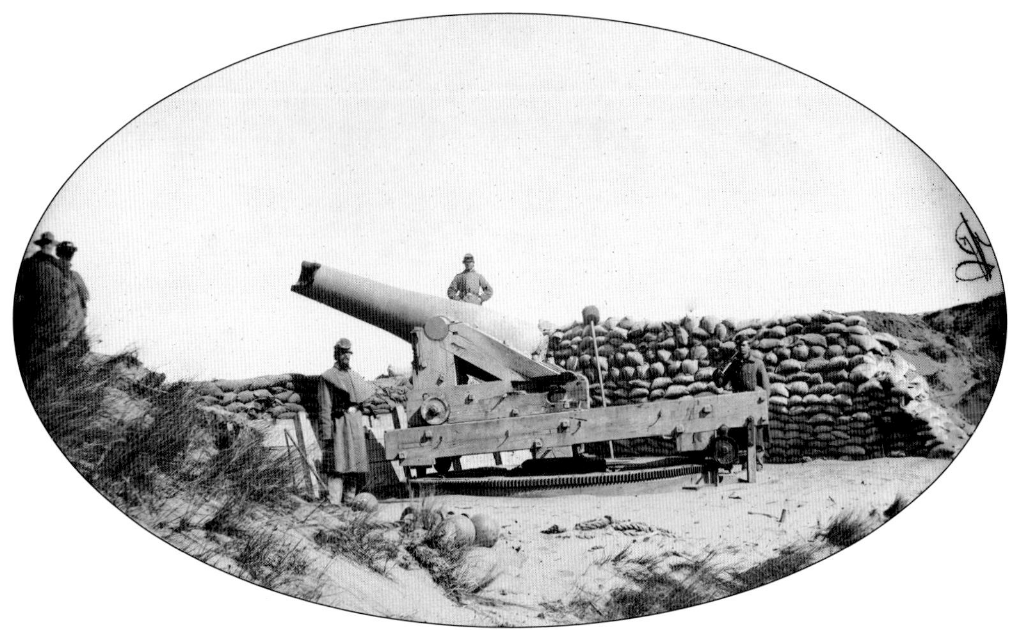

A 32-pound naval gun is pictured here with its muzzle blown away. Timothy H. O'Sullivan took this photograph. (LOC.)

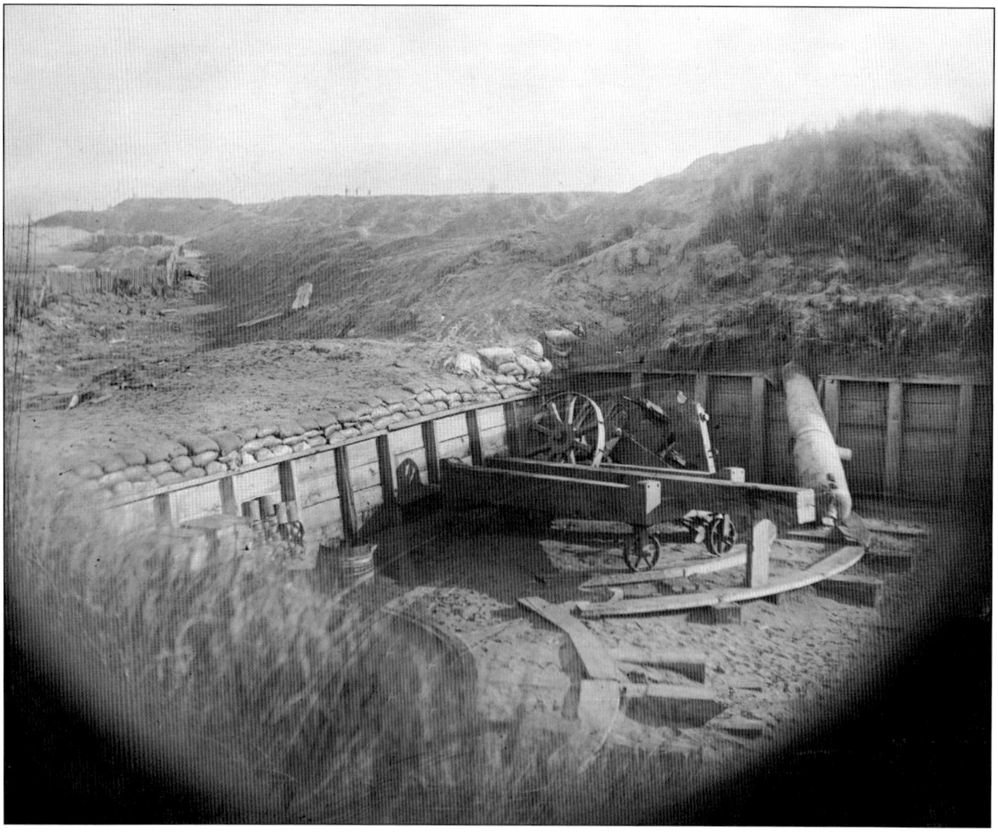

This shot by O'Sullivan shows guns blown from their carriages by Union fire. (LOC.)

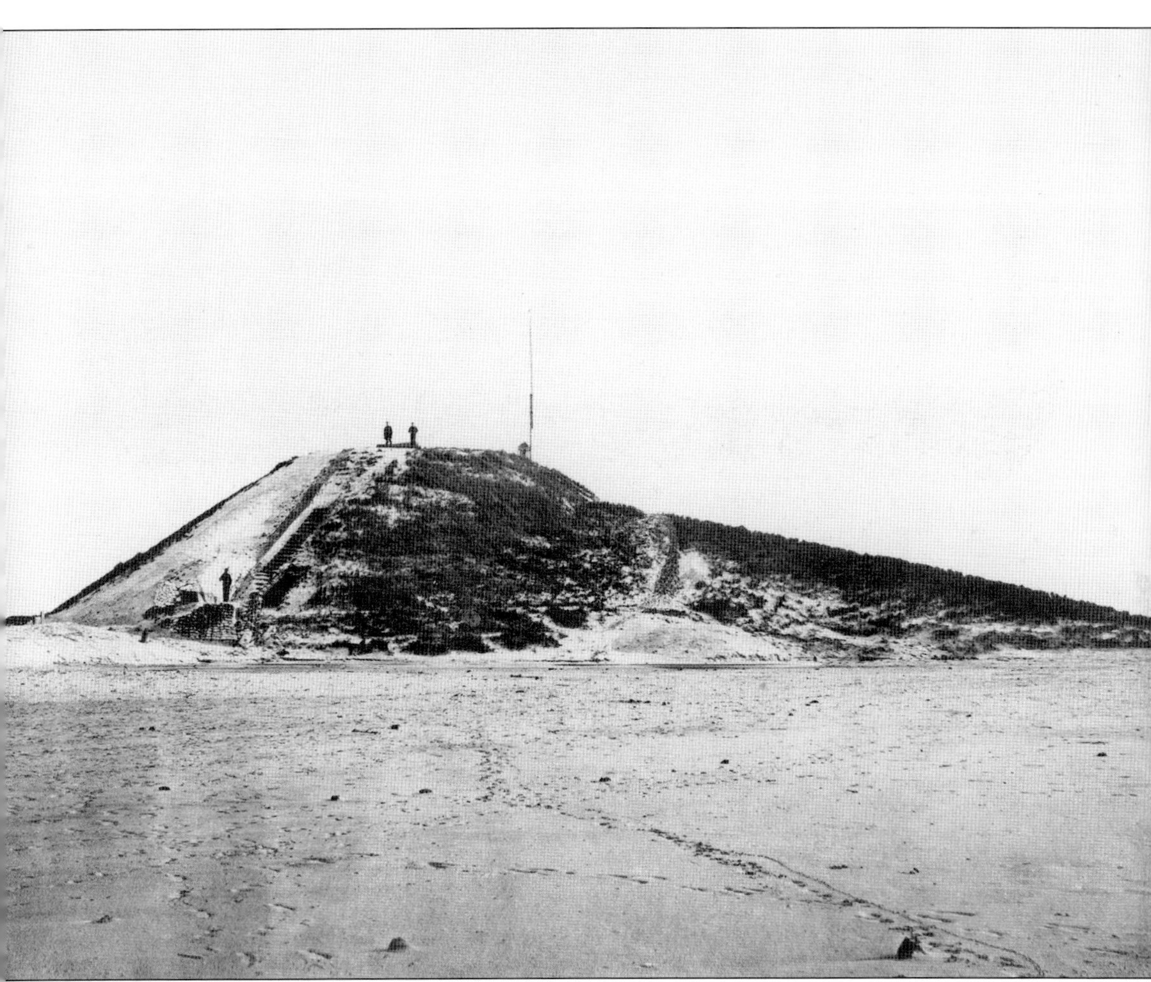

Although most people referred to it as the Mound Battery, its official designation was Battery Lamb. Named for the popular commander of the fort, Col. William Lamb, this was the tallest structure in the entire set of works, with some estimates placing it as high as 60 feet before it was pummelled during the battles. O'Sullivan took this photograph shortly after the fighting ended. Note iron and other detritus from the battle still lying about on the beach, while several men peer back at the photographer. (LOC.)

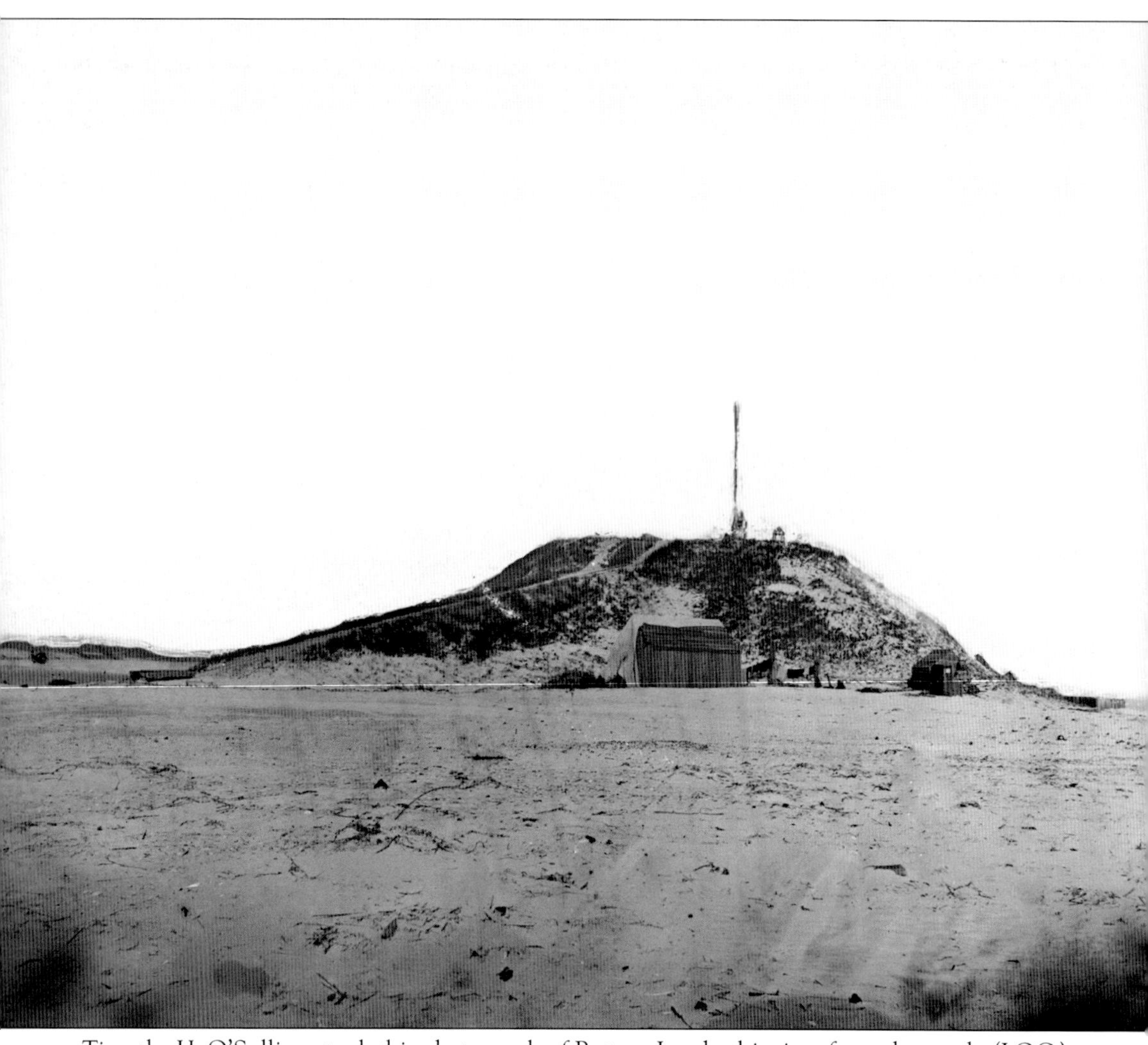

Timothy H. O'Sullivan took this photograph of Battery Lamb, this time from the south. (LOC.)

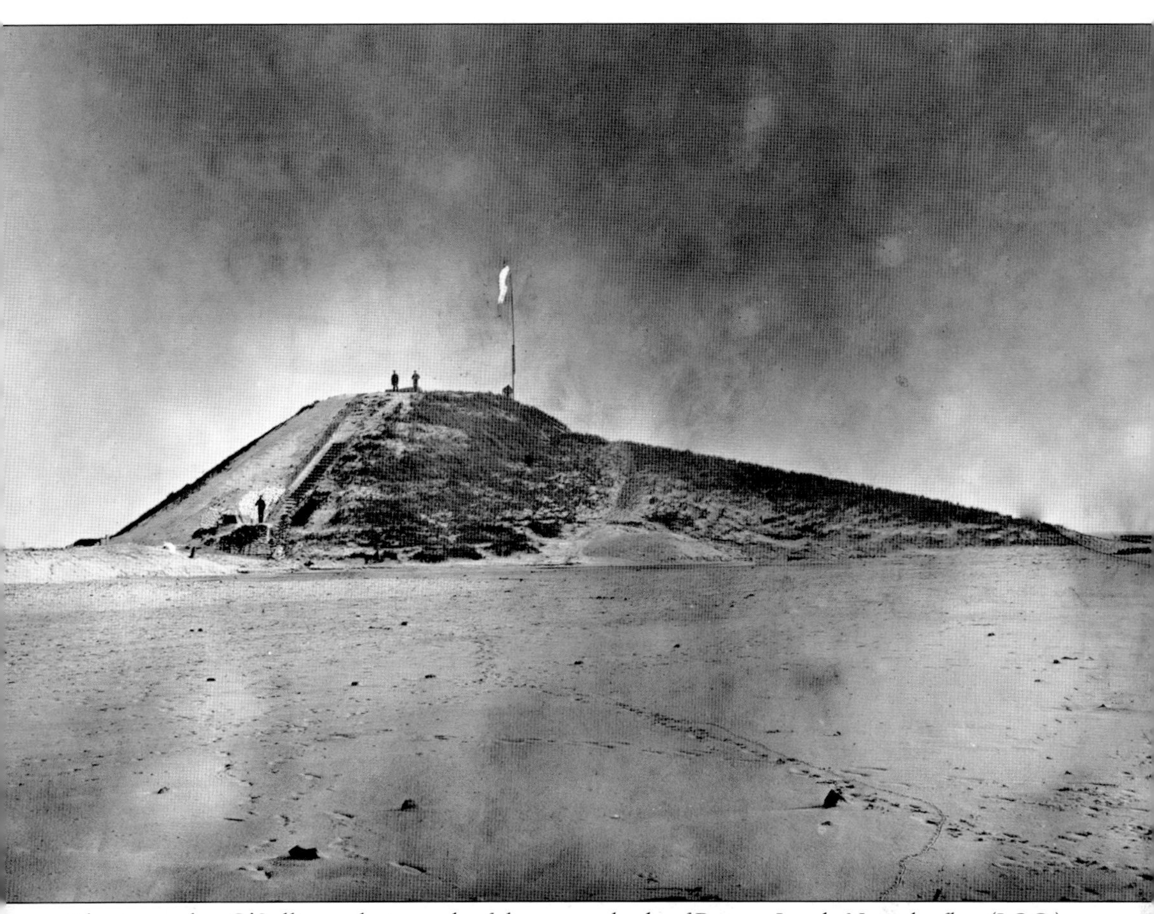

This is another O'Sullivan photograph of the seaward side of Battery Lamb. Note the flag. (LOC.)

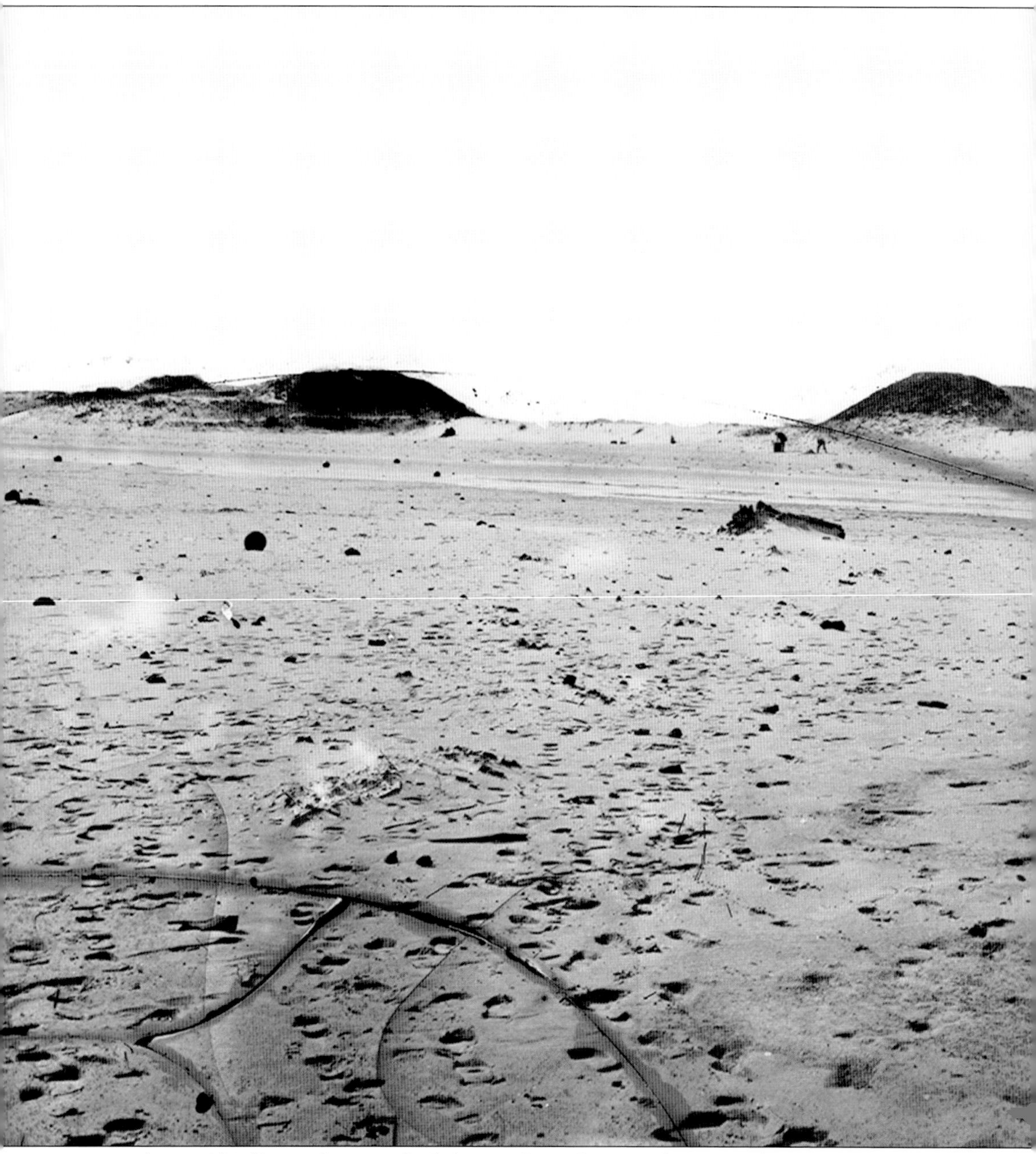

Timothy H. O'Sullivan photographed the sea face of Fort Fisher from the 10th traverse to the

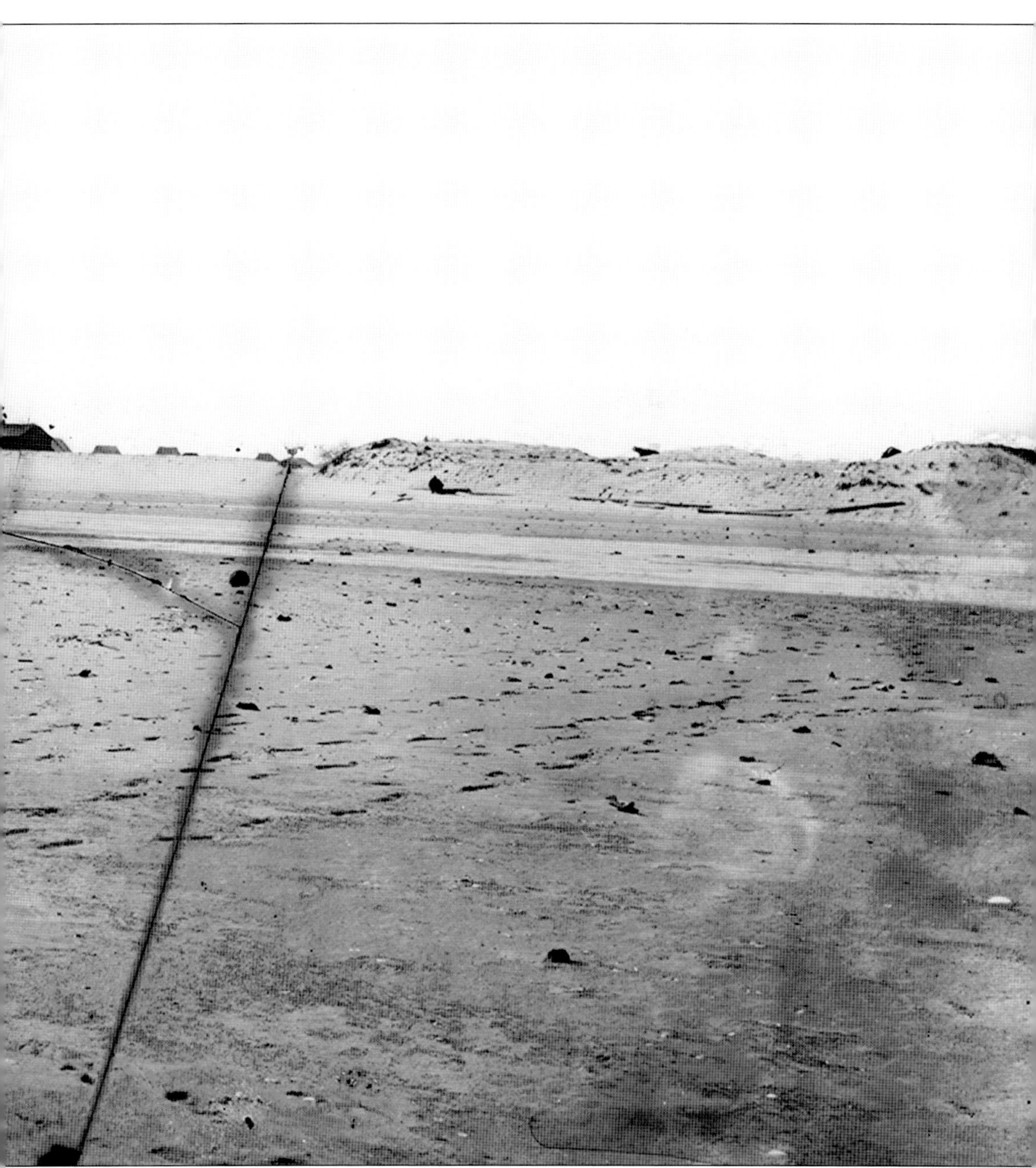

sea. (LOC.)

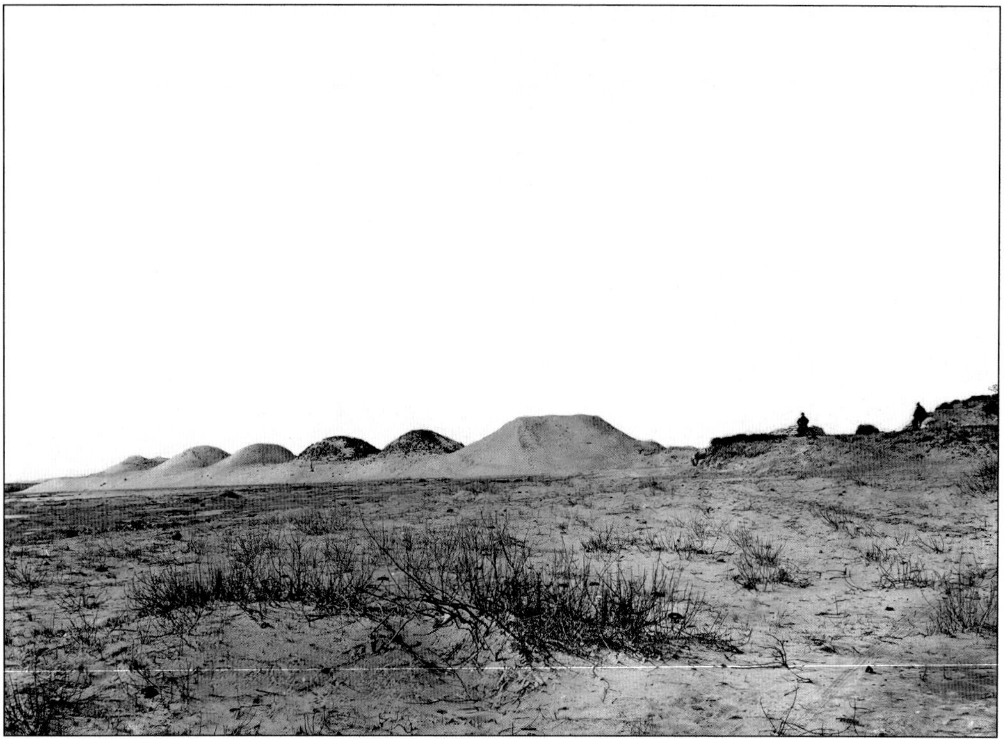

The first six traverses along the sea face are pictured here. (LOC.)

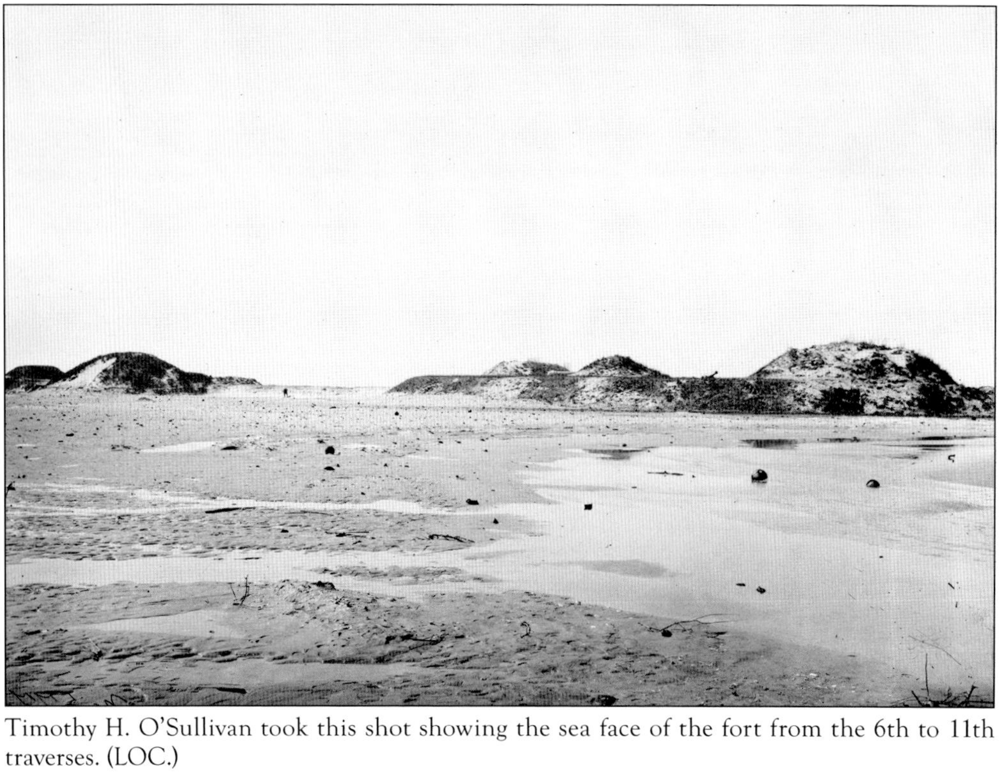

Timothy H. O'Sullivan took this shot showing the sea face of the fort from the 6th to 11th traverses. (LOC.)

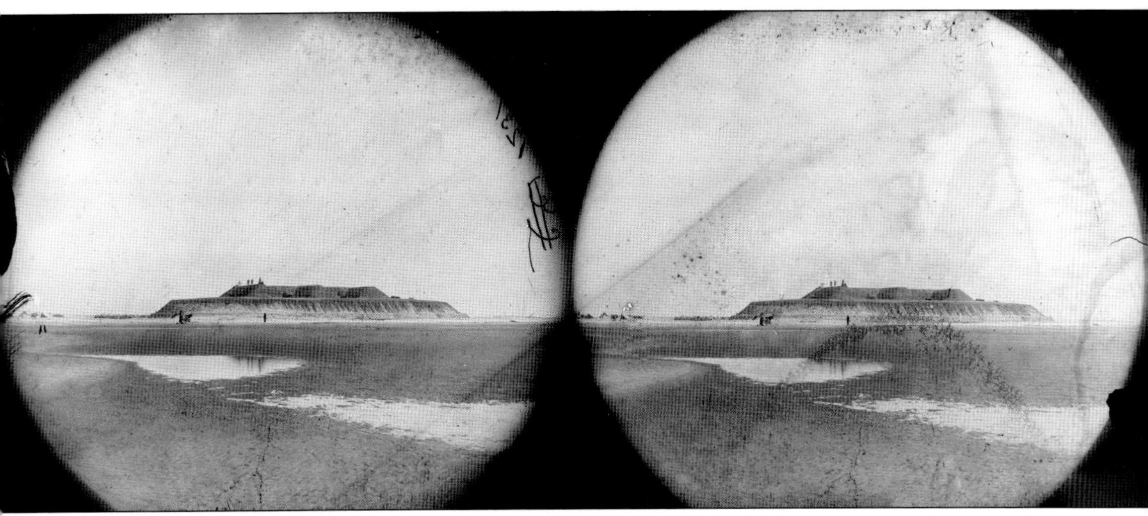

O'Sullivan made this stereograph of Battery Buchanan. (LOC.)

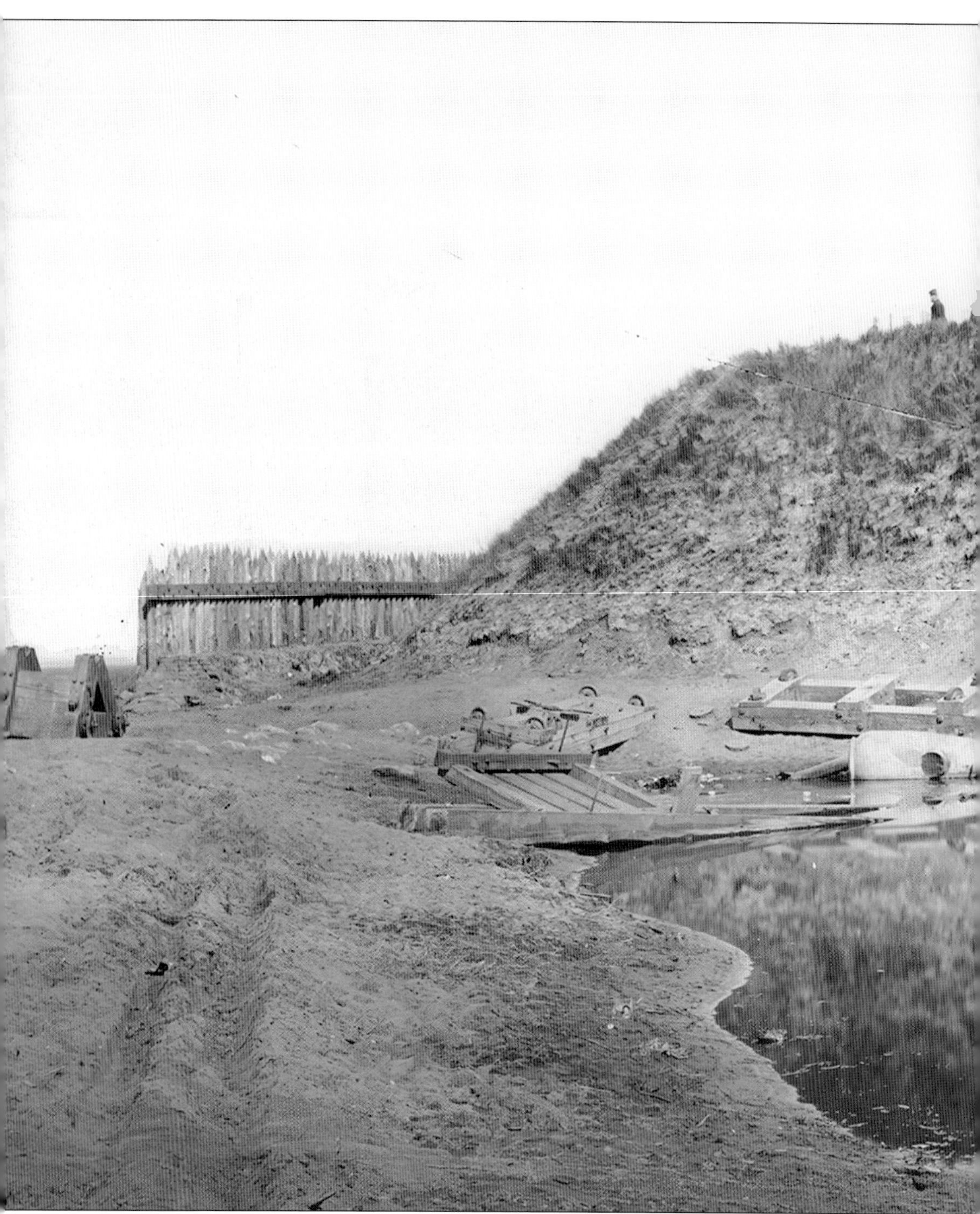

This Timothy H. O'Sullivan view shows the first traverse of the northwest end of the works and the entrance to the fort. This was the scene of much fierce fighting during the Second Battle of

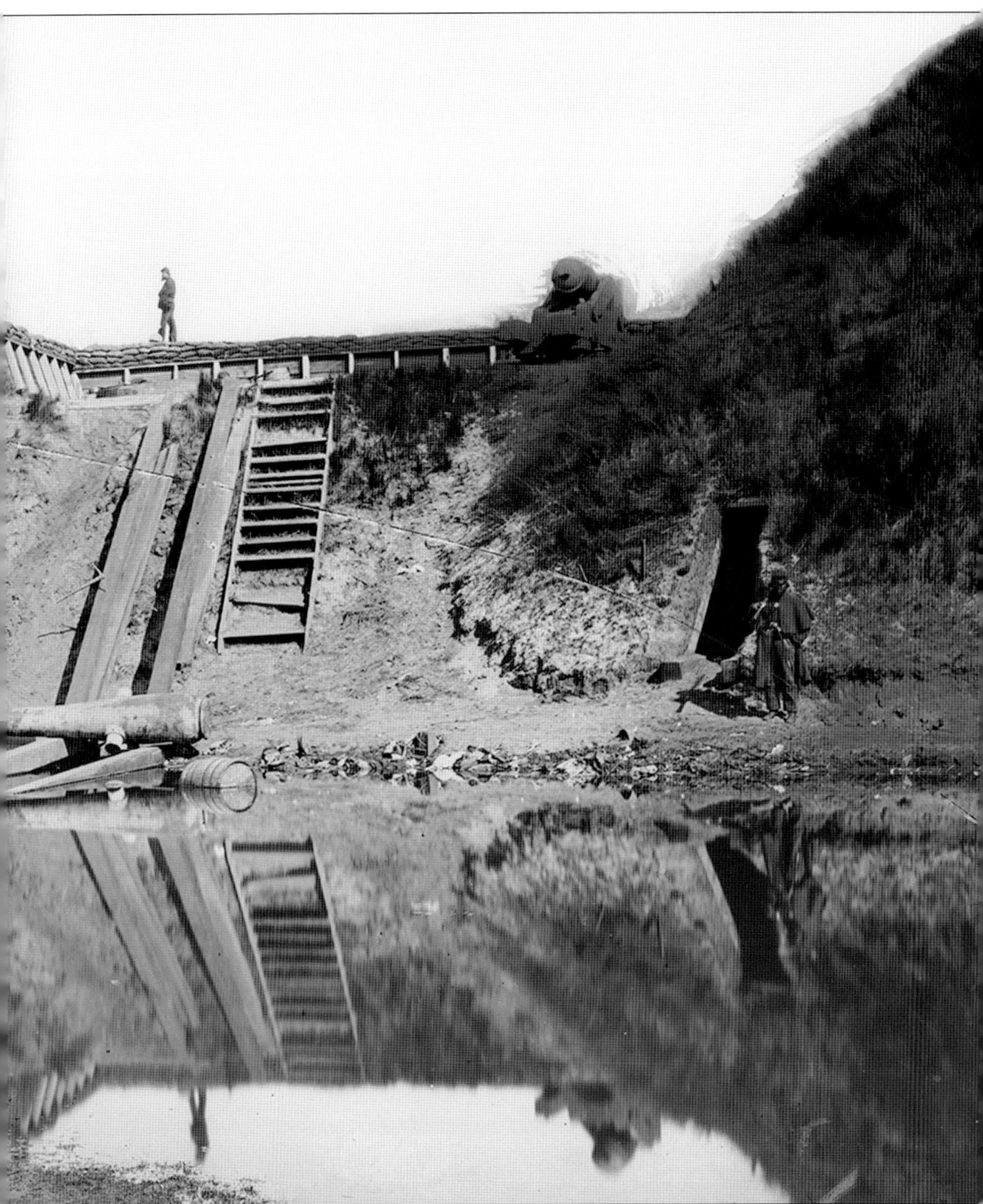

Fort Fisher and received the nickname "The Bloody Gate." (LOC.)

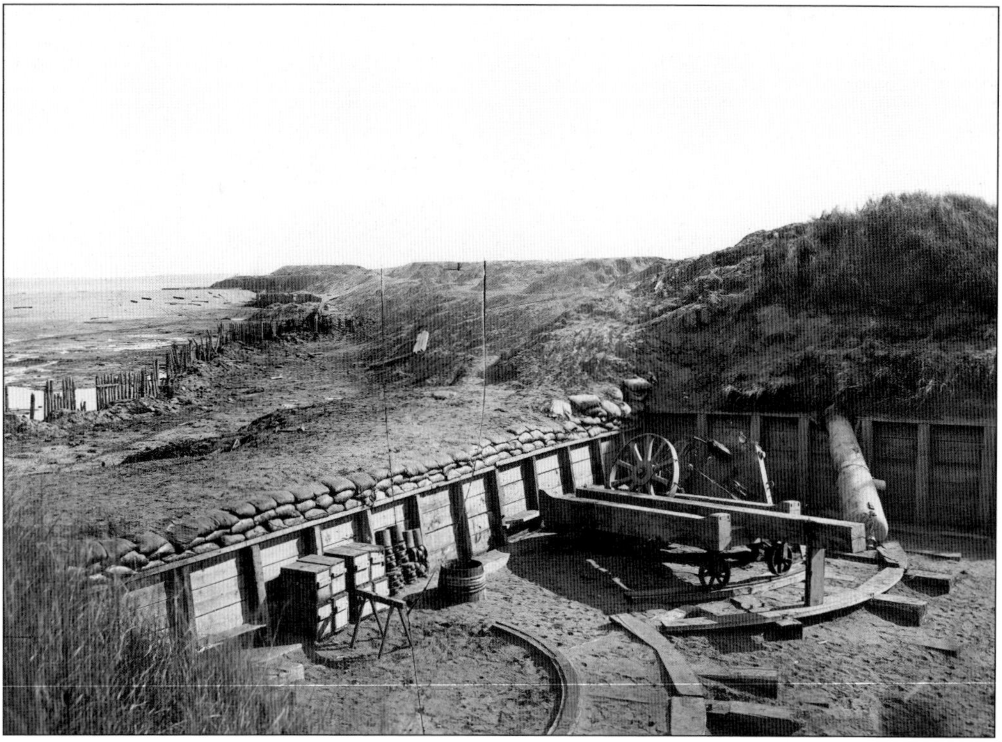

This view is showing the land face of the fort, with destroyed artillery pieces in the background. (LOC.)

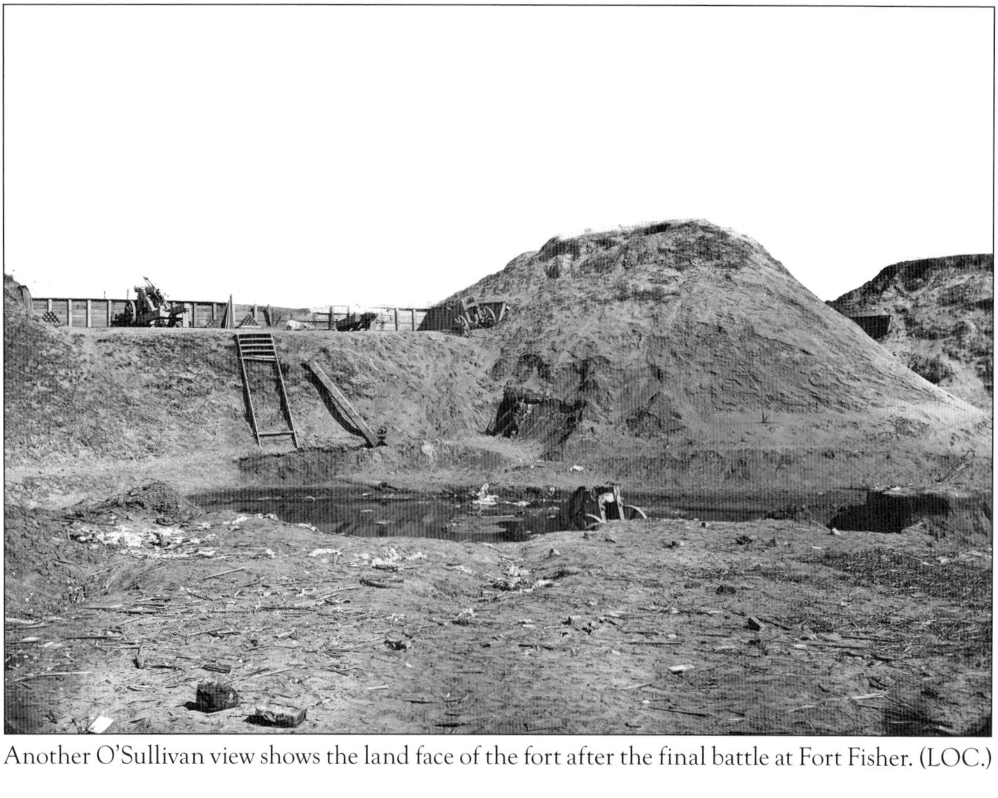

Another O'Sullivan view shows the land face of the fort after the final battle at Fort Fisher. (LOC.)

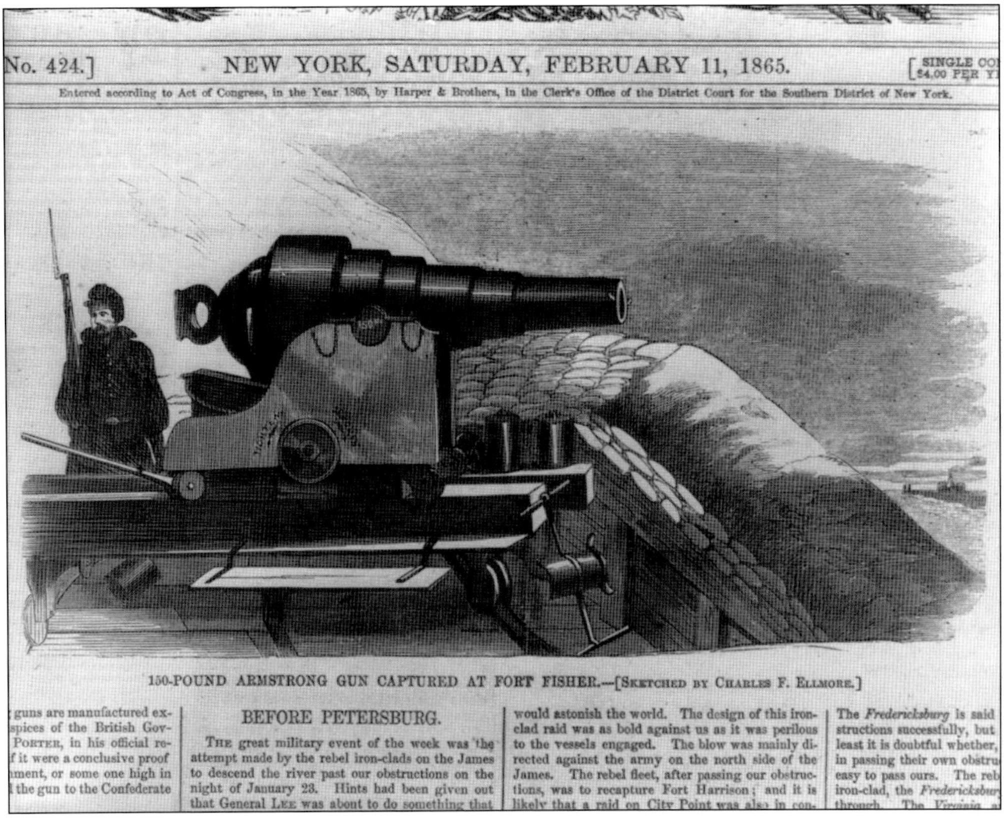

No. 424.] NEW YORK, SATURDAY, FEBRUARY 11, 1865. [SINGLE CO
$4.00 PER Y

Entered according to Act of Congress, in the Year 1865, by Harper & Brothers, in the Clerk's Office of the District Court for the Southern District of New York.

150-POUND ARMSTRONG GUN CAPTURED AT FORT FISHER.—[SKETCHED BY CHARLES F. ELLMORE.]

guns are manufactured ex-
spices of the British Gov-
PORTER, in his official re-
f it were a conclusive proof
ment, or some one high in
the gun to the Confederate

BEFORE PETERSBURG.

THE great military event of the week was the attempt made by the rebel iron-clads on the James to descend the river past our obstructions on the night of January 23. Hints had been given out that General LEE was about to do something that would astonish the world. The design of this iron-clad raid was as bold against us as it was perilous to the vessels engaged. The blow was mainly directed against the army on the north side of the James. The rebel fleet, after passing our obstructions, was to recapture Fort Harrison; and it is likely that a raid on City Point was also in con-

The *Fredericksburg* is said
structions successfully, but
least it is doubtful whether,
in passing their own obstru
easy to pass ours. The reb
iron-clad, the *Fredericksbur*
through. The *Virginia* a

This sketch by Charles Ellmore shows a Union solder beside the 160-pound Armstrong gun at Fort Fisher in February 1865. (LOC.)

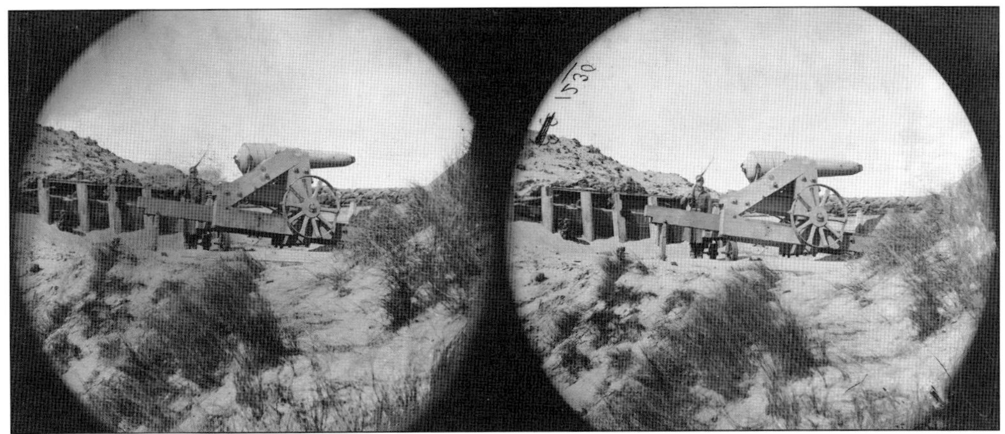

Timothy H. O'Sullivan took this stereoscopic image of a cannon with its barrel blown off. (LOC.)

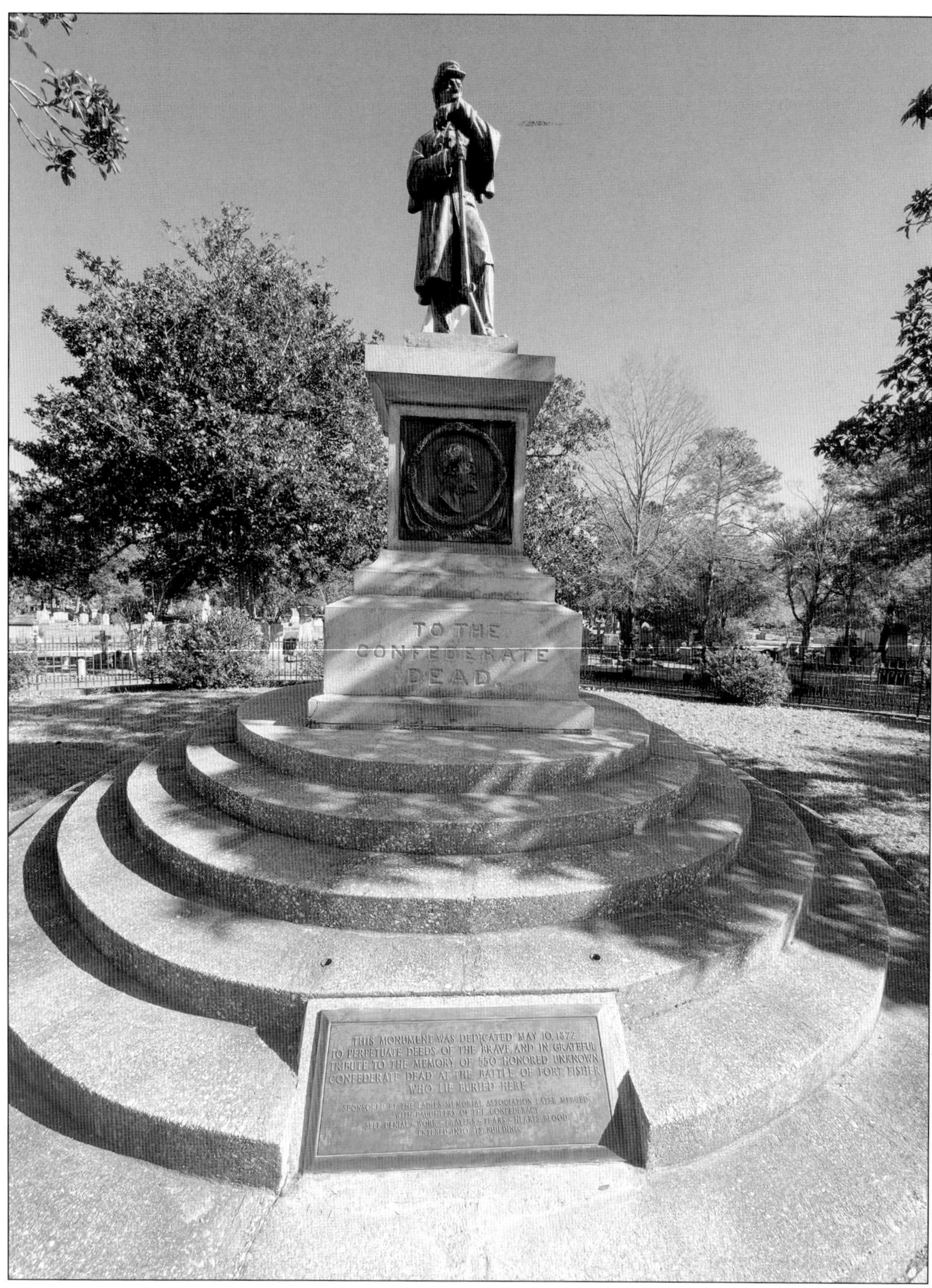

Confederates killed in action during the final battle were interred in a mass grave at Oakdale Cemetery in Wilmington. On May 10, 1872, this monument was dedicated to the fallen men from Fort Fisher.

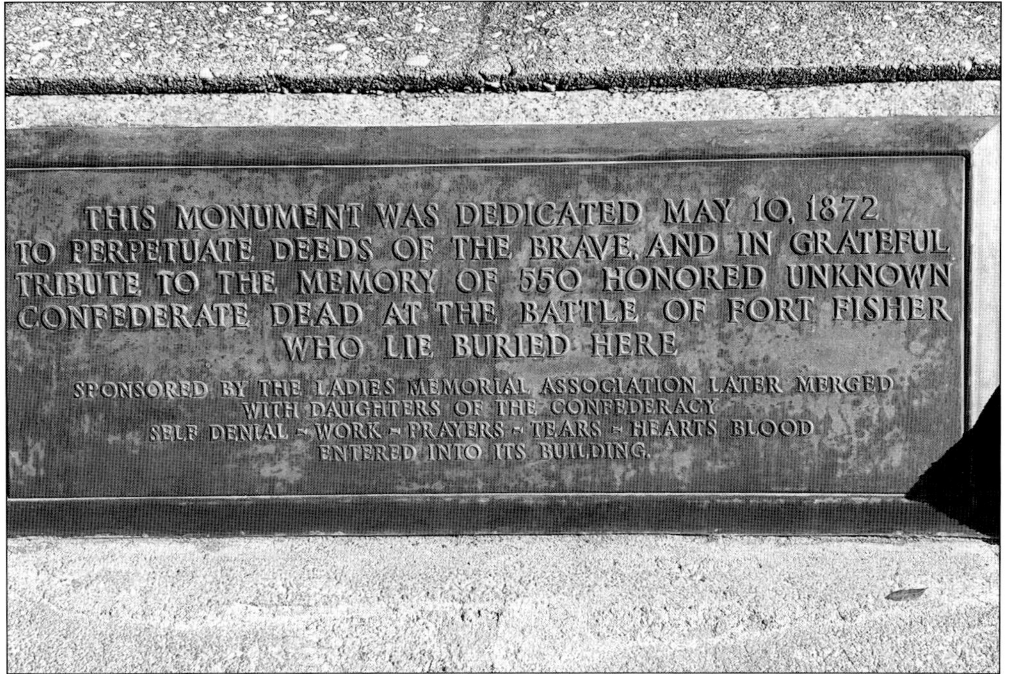

The plaque at the base of the monument tells that "550 Honored Unknown Confederate Dead" were killed during the Second Battle of Fort Fisher and are buried in a common grave underneath this mound.

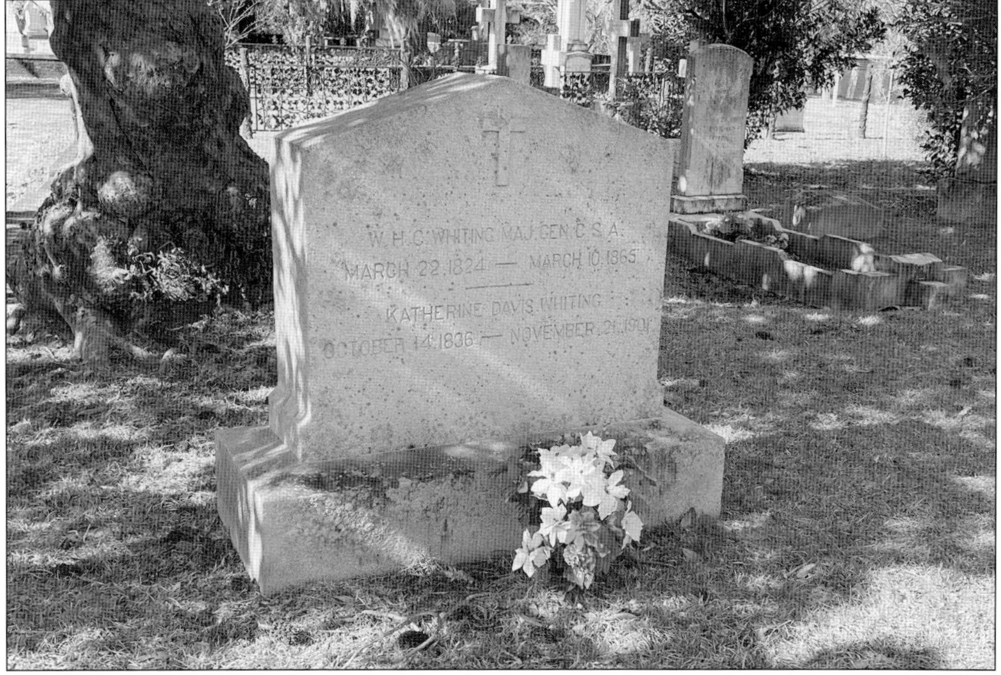

The remains of Gen. W.H.C. Whiting and his wife, Katherine Davis Whiting, rest in Oakdale Cemetery. Their headstone is near the burial mound for many of Whiting's men who were killed during the Second Battle of Fort Fisher.